JOHN F. KENNEDY

ON

EDUCATION

**SELECTED AND
EDITED BY
WILLIAM T. O'HARA**

With a foreword by
CONGRESSMAN JOHN BRADEMAS

1966
TEACHERS COLLEGE PRESS
COLUMBIA UNIVERSITY
NEW YORK

Designed by Felix Cooper

TO MY MOTHER

WHOSE MANY SACRIFICES MADE SO MUCH POSSIBLE

ACKNOWLEDGMENTS

My appreciation is extended to the following individuals for their assistance in making this work possible: Assistant United States Commissioner of Education Peter P. Muirhead; Dean Bert E. Hopkins of the University of Connecticut School of Law; Helen Miller of the Library of Congress; William F. Gaul, Counsel, Special Committee on Education, United States House of Representatives; Alicia Walker; Ronald G. Foster; Raymond C. Parrott; Caroline Cole; A. Wesley Barthelmes; Denise Ellich; Mrs. Adeline Krompegal of the University of Connecticut School of Law staff; and Mrs. Eileen Nixon, administrative assistant to Congressman R. N. Giaimo.

I also wish to thank Homer D. Babbidge, Jr., President of the University of Connecticut, for his encouragement as I embarked on this venture.

I am especially indebted to my secretary, Mrs. Rose Marie Bouchard, who worked so unselfishly during the preparation of the manuscript. Her dedication, willingness to work long hours, and general competence were an invaluable help.

Special thanks go to Monica Newland, a graduate of Saint Joseph College (Connecticut). A Peace Corpsman, Miss Newland, who embodies so many of the Kennedy ideals, has been particularly helpful with her constructive criticism.

To Congressman John Brademas, I extend sincere thanks for his willingness to contribute a foreword to this collection. It is most appropriate that his remarks appear here, for he was in the vanguard of those who advocated and supported the Kennedy education legislation.

"Education is the keystone in the arch of freedom and progress," President John F. Kennedy told Congress as he began his Special Message on Education of January 29, 1963. Kennedy went on to present the most sweeping program for federal help to education ever advocated by an American President.

Yet, as Arthur Schlesinger has recently reminded us, "Little disappointed the Kennedys more in domestic policy than their failure to make significant progress in federal aid to education." [1]

Schlesinger's judgment, while accurate, must be tempered. For less than three years after Kennedy's 1963 Message, nearly every education measure which he had then pressed Congress to enact had become law.

President Johnson's leadership, substantial margins in Congress committed to education, and widespread public support—all these factors helped produce the extraordinary record of education legislation of 1963–65: the Elementary and Secondary Education Act, the Higher Education Acts of 1963 and 1965, the Health Professions Educational Assistance Act, and major amendments to the Vocational Education and National Defense Education Acts, to cite only a few of the principal measures.

William O'Hara's book is a valuable documentation of the contribution of President Kennedy's leadership to the remarkable educational achievements of the 88th and 89th Congresses.

For despite the tragedy of the assassination and despite the hurdles which frustrated the passage of education bills during the three years of his Presidency, Kennedy, by his vigorous advocacy of increased federal support of education, helped make possible the later achievements.

By providing excerpts from Kennedy's public statements on education during his years as a Representative and Senator as well as during the 1960 campaign and the Presidential period, Mr. O'Hara has illumined a significant aspect of Kennedy's entire political career. These speeches and articles reveal Kennedy's continuing interest in education, in the broadest sense of the word. They reflect his profound concern with the quality of American life, his respect for in-

[1] *A Thousand Days: John F. Kennedy in the White House* (Boston: Houghton Mifflin Co., 1965), p. 662.

FOREWORD

telligence and ideas, his rapport with the academic community, and his preoccupation with the problems of young people.

Again and again Kennedy speaks of improving the dialogue between the politician and the scholar, of the responsibility of the young to prepare for leadership in a democracy, of the value of education not only as a national resource in the Cold War but as essential in enhancing the quality of the life of the individual.

The book moves from the Congressional years to the 1960 campaign and the Presidential years and concludes with a section on that most successful of all John F. Kennedy's appeals to American youth, the Peace Corps. The appendices will be useful to students of Kennedy's domestic policies. They list education bills he introduced while in Congress and those enacted into law during his Administration.

Mr. O'Hara, now Assistant Dean of the University of Connecticut School of Law, was, as Counsel to the Special Subcommittee on Education of the House Education and Labor Committee in 1962 and 1963, a direct participant in work on most of the education bills Congress considered during President Kennedy's Administration and is therefore well qualified to undertake this highly useful compilation.

Kennedy's interest in education as a public issue grew and matured over the years—from the Congressman's proposal to improve selection procedures for service academy appointments to the Senator's opposition to the loyalty oath requirement in the National Defense Education Act to the President's plea to Congress for federal aid to education over a broad spectrum. As a member of the two Congressional Committees with primary jurisdiction over education bills, the House Committee on Education and Labor and the Senate Labor and Public Welfare Committee, Kennedy was exceptionally well schooled in the politics of education by the time he came to the Presidency. As a legislator, he saw firsthand the major obstacles confronting advocates of education bills: the issues of civil rights, aid to church-related schools, and federal control.

All these issues are, in one way or other, still with us but all have, in at least one respect, been overcome: Congress is passing major education bills and the role of the federal government in support of American education has grown substantially in the last few years. Indeed, during my four terms in Congress, especially as a member of

Congressman Kennedy's old Committee, Education and Labor (and presently holder of his old seat as second-ranking member of the subcommittee which handles elementary and secondary school bills), I have myself witnessed this significant change.

Congress and the American people have been taking seriously President Kennedy's observation in his first Message to Congress on Education, on February 20, 1961, "The human mind is our fundamental resource." President Johnson has long shared this conviction and the nation is now investing more in this most valuable of all our resources. Mr. O'Hara's book traces the Kennedy commitment to that investment.

JOHN BRADEMAS, *Member of Congress*
Third District, State of Indiana

CONTENTS

JOHN F. KENNEDY
ON EDUCATION

INTRODUCTION

John Fitzgerald Kennedy was a President concerned with the youth of America. His messages to Congress on education and the attention he gave to his university and college speeches sparked renewed national interest in the educational goals of the United States. To a very great extent, a reciprocal concern came into being. The youth of the nation recognized the potential implicit in Kennedy's proposals and, to a greater degree than ever before, came to identify themselves with the President and his ambitions for America's education and young people.

The late President felt compelled to play the role of educator to the American people. He had planned to emphasize education as an important issue in the 1964 campaign. He spoke often of children as the greatest natural resource of a nation: a resource that had to be developed ceaselessly for the sake of the individual as well as the nation, in order to solve ultimately the problems of our nation and those of the world. He was not so naïve as to believe that education in and of itself would offer a panacea for our national or international problems; yet he did feel that there is no hope for the future without an effective system of producing the educated man and woman.

Two particular aspects of Kennedy's influence on education should be noted. First, the President had a unique rapport with students and scholars. From the very beginning of his administration, there was a clear line of communication to and from the academic community. When communicating, he did not limit the dialogue merely to education but covered every aspect of life in our times. In his speeches and statements he often indicated what ideas he wanted the students and teachers to consider, ponder, and act on. In this way he rendered direction to their thoughts that benefited the individual and the nation. Secondly, he epitomized the responsibility of a President to summarize the problems and issues confronting American education and at the same time provide a program to meet the problems and resolve the issues.

John Kennedy's interest in education was not born of the fact that he was President of the United States. Education had always been a source of concern to him; the concern was originally manifested in his early days in the House of Representatives. His interest matured while he was in the Senate and on the campaign trail seeking the

Presidency, reaching fruition during his two years and ten months in the White House.

To understand fully Kennedy's contribution to education, one should study the aspects of his life touching on education, including his early schooling, his own academic and literary accomplishments, and his attempts in public life to advance and improve education for all people.

Young Kennedy's formal education began at the Dexter School, a few blocks from his home in Brookline, Massachusetts. A few years later the family moved to Bronxville, New York, and Jack and his brother Joe entered the nearby Riverdale Country School as day students. At thirteen he enrolled at the Canterbury School, a prep school in New Milford, Connecticut, where he boarded. Although Canterbury employed a lay faculty, it was a Catholic school—the only Catholic school he ever attended.

Shortly before the Easter recess in 1931, Jack underwent an emergency appendectomy, which forced him to drop out of school. At his father's insistence, he did not return to Canterbury after his recuperation but joined Joe at the Choate School in Wallingford, Connecticut.[1]

Jack Kennedy, unlike his brother Joe, never achieved scholastic honors in his early years, although he always possessed considerable intellectual curiosity. His interest in history and the lives of great men was especially apparent during his years at Choate, when he read omnivorously. This enthusiasm was to serve him well throughout his public life.

At the suggestion of Joseph P. Kennedy, Sr., Joe, Jr., studied at the London School of Economics in 1933 under the famed and brilliant Fabian socialist Harold J. Laski. When John Kennedy graduated from Choate, sixty-fourth out of a class of one hundred twelve,[2] he also was urged to study under Laski. So in the summer of 1935, fresh out of prep school, John crossed the Atlantic to matriculate at the London School of Economics. This aspect of his education was abruptly halted, however, when he fell ill with jaundice and had to withdraw.

[1] Richard J. Whalen, *The Founding Father* (New York: New American Library, 1964), pp. 166–167.
[2] William H. A. Carr, *J.F.K.: A Complete Biography, 1917–1963* (New York: Lancer Books, 1964), p. 47.

Originally, John chose to attend Princeton University instead of Harvard, the alma mater of his father and brother. His illness during the summer of 1935 caused him to enter his freshman year several weeks late. His Princeton career was shortened considerably when he had a recurrence of jaundice at Christmastime and was compelled to leave school for the remainder of the year. The fall of 1936 found him a freshman at Harvard, having decided not to return to Princeton.

In his first two years, John Kennedy's work at Harvard was not outstanding. As a freshman, he took English, French, history, and economics. He achieved a C grade in all of his courses except economics, in which he earned a B. The second year was similar: four C's, one D, and one B.[3]

In his junior year, having decided to major in government, he concentrated on international relations, and his biographer, James MacGregor Burns, later wrote of this period:

Solid, sound, earnest, but not brilliant—this is how his professors of Government summed him up. "Kennedy is surprisingly able when he gets down to work," one of them noted. "His preparation may be spotty, but his general ability should bolster him up. A commendable fellow." [4]

After sophomore year, there was an obvious improvement in his grades. Some suggest the overall maturing so commonplace during a young man's college years; others trace it to his trip in the summer of 1937. While traveling through a politically uncertain Europe that summer, he wrote his father saying that he realized "the almost complete ignorance 95 percent of the people in the U.S. have about situations as a whole here." [5] He assured his father that "he had found a new incentive for studying harder." [6]

In the winter of 1939, John Kennedy received permission from Harvard to spend a term of his junior year in Europe. In those shaky times, he visited Poland, Latvia, Russia, Turkey, Palestine, and the

3 James MacGregor Burns, *John Kennedy: A Political Profile* (New York: Harcourt, Brace & World, 1959), p. 31.
4 *Ibid.,* p. 33.
5 *Ibid.,* p. 32.
6 Gerald Walker and Donald A. Allen, "Jack Kennedy at Harvard." *Coronet* (May, 1961), p. 90.

Balkans. After visiting each country he sent political reports to his father, who was then United States Ambassador to Great Britain.

After this unique experience Kennedy returned to Harvard to complete his senior year. He worked diligently, received B grades in his courses, and as a result became eligible for a degree with honors in political science. An honors degree at Harvard requires a thesis, and young Kennedy chose to write on "Apeasement at Munich." The thesis was judged by his faculty to be *magna cum laude* and he graduated in June, 1940, with honors in his major—government. The thesis had two arresting qualities:

One was Kennedy's emotional detachment from the crisis he described. The urgency in his paragraphs was purely intellectual. He criticized people for being too emotional over Munich. He was no alarmist, he insisted, as though being an alarmist in the spring of 1940 were a sin. The other arresting aspect was closely related to this—his emphasis on the point that men like Chamberlain and Stanley Baldwin were not mainly responsible for Munich, but, rather, that Munich was caused by deeper forces inherent in democracy and capitalism, by general apathy, concern with profits and security, pacifism, fear of regimentation, and so on. In this sense the thesis was mature and judicious in tone.[7]

After graduation Kennedy revised and extended the thesis, and it was published under the title *Why England Slept*. The book was an immediate success and sold over eighty thousand copies in the United States and England.[8]

Even in these early years, Kennedy perceived the importance to a democracy of producing qualified leaders. One of his conclusions in *Why England Slept* was that

Much of the cause of England's failure may be attributed to the leaders. The great advantage a democracy is presumed to have over a dictatorship is that ability and not brute force is the qualification for leadership. Therefore, if a democracy cannot produce able leaders, its chance for survival is slight.[9]

7 Burns, p. 40.
8 Whalen, p. 296.
9 John F. Kennedy, *Why England Slept* (New York: Wilfred Funk, 1940), p. 225.

As President, he never forgot this lesson. The underlying theme of many of his talks to young Americans was that they should continue their education. He believed strongly that education was the best possible means for preparing youth to assume the leadership of our democracy in the crucial years ahead.

Kennedy had planned to go to Yale Law School after graduating from Harvard. He changed his plans in the summer of 1940 and began graduate work in business administration that fall at Stanford University. The field of commerce came to seem too restricted for his interests, so he withdrew early in 1941, after one semester. During the following months he traveled and attempted to enlist in the service. The Army rejected him because of a back injury sustained in Harvard football practice. After several tries he was accepted by the Navy in September of 1941.

The tragedy at Pearl Harbor followed in December, and soon Kennedy, as commander of a PT boat, was shipped to the South Pacific. Young Kennedy's intellectual enthusiasm, developed in his junior and senior years at Harvard, had not waned after leaving Cambridge, for his naval colleagues reported his intense fascination with ideas and his avid reading. At the time his reading included such varied material as Franz Werfel's *The Forty Days of Musa Dagh,* John Buchan's *Pilgrim's Way,* and Tolstoy's *War and Peace.* A fellow Navy man recalls that "in the Solomons Lieutenant Kennedy's Tulagi tent became 'a world affairs forum, with the occupant as the moderator.' He would cross foils with anyone, on almost any topic." [10]

In 1945, John Kennedy came home a hero. He had been awarded the Purple Heart and the Navy and Marine Corps Medal for his bravery in the line of duty. Back in civilian life, he tried his hand at journalism and at one time considered a teaching career. He wrote a short paper entitled "Let's Try an Experiment in Peace," in which he proposed limiting postwar rearmament.[11] The paper drew no particular attention. He also compiled a tribute to his brother Joe, who was killed in action flying a mission over the English Channel. The

---

10 William Manchester, *Portrait of a President* (Boston: Little, Brown and Co., 1962), pp. 92–93.
11 Burns, p. 55.

book was entitled *As We Remember Joe*. It was published privately by the family and never distributed to the public.[12]

Years later Kennedy commented about his probable future after the war if Joe had lived. He said,

"I'm sure I would have gone to law school after the war. Beyond that, I can't say. I was at loose ends. I was interested in ideas, and I might have gone into journalism. The exchange of ideas that goes with teaching attracted me, but"—he shakes his head—"scholarship requires a special kind of discipline; it wouldn't be my strength." [13]

Some years later, while campaigning for the Senate in the college town of Amherst, Massachusetts, he took a different view of his qualifications for teaching. He commented on the University of Massachusetts to Larry O'Brien, "If it hadn't been for the death of my brother, I'd probably be teaching in some place like that." [14]

John F. Kennedy did not turn to journalism or to education, but to politics, and he was elected to the United States House of Representatives in November, 1946, as the Congressman from the Eleventh District of Massachusetts.

As a freshman in the Eightieth Congress, John Kennedy was appointed to the House Education and Labor Committee, which has primary jurisdiction over all general federal aid to education legislation. Historically the committee had been hostile to federal aid to education proposals. These first years were ones of observation and political self-education for John Kennedy.

In the Eighty-first Congress, which convened on January 3, 1949, Congressman Kennedy, serving his second term, was again appointed to the Education and Labor Committee. He served on the Federal Aid to Education Subcommittee, where he was the second Democrat in seniority. In 1949, he introduced a bill providing federal funds for buses, health services, and textbooks for private and parochial schools.[15] The public debate between Cardinal Spellman of New York and Eleanor Roosevelt over federal aid to parochial schools and other

---

12 Whalen, p. 56.
13 Manchester, p. 76.
14 *Ibid.*, pp. 76–77.
15 H.R. 5838, August 1, 1949.

factors made the passage of such legislation unlikely, if not impossible. As a result the measure never made any progress beyond the committee level and expired with the termination of the Eighty-first Congress on January 2, 1951.

In the Eighty-first Congress the Kennedy education bill had been overshadowed by S. 246, which provided, in general, for federal assistance to elementary and secondary schools. It was a critical time for the House committee because the House had failed to pass a federal aid to education bill in 1948 and 1949 after the Senate had done so. When the bill was before the committee, Congressman Kennedy expressed his support for the bill. During the committee's consideration of S. 246, Kennedy offered an amendment which provided that the federal government pay half the cost of bus service for private and parochial schools. The amendment, which broadened the bill passed in the Senate, was defeated by a vote of sixteen to nine in the committee. Kennedy's amendment aggravated the classic church-state controversy, which had stymied federal aid to education legislation so often in the past.

Although Kennedy essentially supported the legislation after the defeat of his amendment, he refused to vote S. 246 out of committee. His vote was crucial, for the final vote was thirteen to twelve against voting the bill out of the committee for floor action. Kennedy had always taken the position that fringe services such as bussing, school lunches, and police and fire protection were not of a religious nature and were therefore beyond the restrictions of the First Amendment.

It must be remembered that Kennedy's district was heavily Catholic. To justify his vote in favor of a bill solely aiding public elementary and secondary schools he had to show at least some benefit accruing to parochial schools. When his amendment failed, he had no recourse but to vote against the bill, which he thought prejudiced the parochial schools by excluding services in no way affiliated with the religious issue.

From the very beginning of his Congressional career, the young Congressman from Massachusetts paid special attention to his responsibility for appointing candidates to the United States Military and Naval academies. His concern was intensified in the summer of 1951. On August 3 of that year, the United States Military Academy announced that ninety cadets had been dismissed for violation of the West Point Honor Code. The investigation that followed indicated that the discharged cadets had been found guilty of cribbing. Of the ninety, thirty-seven had been football players, many of whom had been recruited for their football potential. The nation was shocked, and confidence in West Point was shaken severely. Secretary of the Army Frank Pace appointed a review board to investigate the cribbing scandal. The board consisted of Learned Hand, retired Judge of the Second United States Court of Appeals; Major General Robert M. Danford, former Commandant of West Point; and Lieutenant General Troy H. Middleton, President of Louisiana State University. After completing its investigation, the board submitted its report to Secretary Pace, supporting the dismissal of the ninety students.

Writing in the *New York Times Magazine* after the scandal, John Kennedy questioned the procedure of appointing students to the Military and Naval academies. His article encouraged his colleagues to take greater care in making their appointments. In addition, he recommended a study of the entire system by which members of Congress designate young men to attend West Point and Annapolis.

On August 20, 1951, John F. Kennedy introduced H.R. 5253. This was a bill to establish a commission for improving the method of selecting candidates for the United States Military and Naval academies. The measure was designed to create a twelve-member bipartisan committee to investigate and examine the methods and procedures used in the selection of candidates for the two academies. In addition, it would reexamine all laws relating to the appointment of such candidates, and the commission would survey and appraise the best means available for selecting men with leadership qualities.

After its introduction the bill was referred to the Secretary of Defense for a report. Three months later a report was received from the Department of the Army, containing no recommendations at that time. No further action was taken by the Congress, and the bill died a legislative death at the end of the Eighty-second Congress.

As early as 1948 Congressman Kennedy considered running for the Senate of the United States. Unfavorable political conditions in Massachusetts forced him to defer his participation in a race for a Senate seat until 1952. In that year, Senator Henry Cabot Lodge ran for reelection. After a vigorous campaign, Kennedy beat Lodge by a substantial margin despite an overwhelming Presidential vote for Eisenhower.

Upon taking his seat in January, 1953, Kennedy was appointed to the Senate Labor and Public Welfare Committee. This was considered a prestigious committee, for, like the House Education and Labor Committee, it was responsible for education legislation. Unlike the Education and Labor Committee, the Senate committee had been highly sympathetic in the past to federal aid to education legislation. At this time, unfortunately, the entire Congress was going through a period of decreased activity with regard to such legislation. A number of factors brought about this inactivity, among them the perennial impasse caused by the church-state question, the Korean war, and the passage of legislation providing aid to localities affected by defense and other federal government installations.[16] Known as "impacted areas" legislation, it recognized the responsibility of the federal government for the impact of its employees' children upon school construction needs and upon local education agencies.

In the summer of 1954, Senator Kennedy was confronted with a personal decision of the highest importance. His back, which had been injured initially while playing football at Harvard—the injury was aggravated when his PT boat was split in two by the Japanese destroyer *Amagiri* in the South Pacific—was causing crippling pain. On October 21, 1954, Senator Kennedy entered Manhattan's Hospital for Special Surgery, where doctors performed a double fusion of a spinal disc. His recuperation was lengthy, and it was not until December of that year that he was allowed to go to Palm Beach to continue his recovery.

As soon as he was able, he undertook to write a book about the political courage of noted American legislators. In 1956 this work, published under the title *Profiles in Courage,* became an immediate success, and in 1957 it was awarded the Pulitzer Prize for biography. Since its publication *Profiles in Courage* has been translated into a dozen languages, including Spanish, Arabic, Japanese, Turkish, Vietnamese, Telugu, and Indonesian. "No other honor has meant so much

16 P.L. 81–815 (64 Stat. 967) and P.L. 81–874 (64 Stat. 1100).

INTRODUCTION

to Kennedy as this recognition of intellectual and literary distinction," writes one biographer.[17]

In June of 1956, Harvard University, awarding Senator Kennedy an honorary degree, cited him thus: "Brave officer, able Senator, son of Harvard; loyal to party, he remains steadfast to principle." In his speech on this occasion, Kennedy made reference to the intellectual's important role in our society. He pointed out the need for the intellectual to understand the politician, and further supported his thesis by pointing out that political and intellectual freedom are indivisible.

Action on federal aid to education legislation had been sporadic in Congress since the failure of the House to report out the Senate bills in 1949–50. Political factors were primarily responsible for halting progress during the fifties. A Republican administration and a slim Democratic majority in the Congress made conditions unfavorable to decisive legislation. A second factor, which consistently created as much difficulty as the parochial school question, was conflict over segregation in the public schools.

In 1954 the Supreme Court decision in *Brown v Board of Education* [18] nullified the doctrine of "separate but equal" public education. The Court held that separate educational facilities were inherently unequal and that the plaintiffs, Negro students who were applying for admission to segregated schools, had been denied equal protection of the laws under the Fourteenth Amendment.

In both 1956 and 1957 Adam Clayton Powell, encouraged by the Supreme Court's decision of 1954, attached the Powell Amendment to the federal aid to education bills. In general, the Powell Amendment operated to withhold aid from segregated schools. The effect of the Powell Amendment was to split the support of the Democratic party and make passage of any federal aid to education bill impossible.

It was clear that the domestic issues of federal aid to private and parochial schools and the segregation question took federal aid legislation into a cul-de-sac. The situation seemed impossible until the fall of 1957, when Soviet scientists launched Sputnik. The astonished American people were shocked by the realization that the Soviet Union had taken giant strides in science and education. Sputnik acted as a

[17] Burns, p. 162.
[18] 347 U.S. 483 (1954).

10

catalyst and moved Congress to push aside domestic problems and meet an international challenge. Reacting to the challenge, Congress passed the National Defense Education Act in August of 1958. The measure had the full support of Senator Kennedy. In essence, the act provided loans to college students and financial aid for improving science, mathematics, and modern foreign language instruction. It included fellowship assistance and aid for guidance, counseling, and language development. In addition, this landmark legislation aided other areas and provided a long-needed impetus to American education.

In January of 1958 John Kennedy introduced legislation which provided federal assistance through the states to local communities to finance school construction.[19] The bill was directed towards eliminating the national shortage of classrooms by making grant payments to state educational agencies for school expansion. In addition, the bill also provided for the purchase of bonds issued by communities unable to obtain financing for their school construction. Finally, the bill also provided credit assistance to state school financing agencies to provide schools with assistance for classroom construction. The Labor and Public Welfare Committees did not act on this measure, and the bill met a legislative death when the Eighty-fifth Congress adjourned.

As NDEA was put into effect, a protest arose over the student loan-granting provisions of the Act. In order to obtain assistance under the loan provision, the applicant was required to sign a note attesting to his faith and allegiance to the United States. The provisions of the bill, Section 1001(f) required that:

No part of any funds appropriated or otherwise made available for expenditure under authority of this Act shall be used to make payments or loans to any individual unless such individual (1) has executed and filed with the Commissioner [of Education] an affidavit that he does not believe in, and is not a member of and does not support any organization that believes in or teaches, the overthrow of the United States Government by force or violence or by any illegal or unconstitutional methods, and (2) has taken and subscribed to an oath or affirmation in the following form: "I do solemnly swear (or affirm) that I will bear true faith and allegiance to the United

19 S. 3179.

States of America and will support and defend the Constitution and laws of the United States against all its enemies, foreign and domestic."

A number of colleges and universities refused to participate in the NDEA loan program as long as the disclaimer affidavit was compulsory. In addition, over fifty colleges, although accepting NDEA loan funds, protested against the affidavit.[20]

There had been no real discussion of the affidavit provision on the Senate floor before the bill was approved by the Senate. On January 29, 1959, John F. Kennedy, along with Senator Joseph Clark of Pennsylvania, submitted a bill, numbered S. 819, to repeal the provisions of NDEA requiring the non-Communist affidavit and loyalty oath. In supporting his bill on the floor of the Senate, Kennedy pointed out that the affidavit provision was "an insupportable invasion of educational autonomy, which has grave implications for the integrity of our educational system." Hearings were held on the bill during April and May of that same year, and the bill was favorably reported out of the Committee on June 29, 1959.[21] One month later the bill was brought to the floor of the Senate for a vote but was defeated on a 49–42 vote to recommit it.

The following January, at the beginning of the second session of the Eighty-sixth Congress, Senator Kennedy and Senator Clark, this time joined by Senator Jacob Javits of New York, introduced S. 2929. The measure differed from the earlier bill introduced by Kennedy and Clark in that it did not call for the abolishment of both the non-Communist affidavit and the loyalty oath. Instead it called for the repeal of the affidavit requirement and retained the oath of allegiance to the United States. Kennedy, in supporting the measure, pointed out that his objections to the affidavit of disbelief were based on several foundations. First, it was unnecessary. Since the standard loyalty oath of allegiance to the government, which was to be retained in the legislation, was sufficient, it was not necessary for a student to be required to swear that he was not disloyal as well as loyal to his country. Second, the affidavit was ineffective. Kennedy said that no convinced Com-

---

[20] Tom Kaser, "The Loyalty Oath, 1964–65." *Saturday Review* (November 21, 1964), p. 60.
[21] S. Rept. 454.

munist would ever hesitate to take either an oath or an affidavit if it was required of him. Third, the affidavit of disbelief defeated the purpose of the bill, and he pointed out that some of the finest institutions of higher education in the country had refused to accept funds because of the affidavit of disbelief. And, finally, said Senator Kennedy, the provision was discriminatory in nature. He pointed out that businessmen who receive government loans or contracts, farmers who receive government subsidies, veterans, and other recipients of government benefits are not required to file such a sworn statement.[22]

The bill was favorably reported out of Senate Committee (S. Rept. 1347) in the spring of 1960, went to the floor in June of that year, and was passed by the Senate with amendments. The bill was then sent to the House of Representatives, but no action was taken, and it died when the session came to an end in September of 1960.

John Kennedy as President did not forget his efforts to have the disclaimer affidavit deleted. Legislation was introduced in the first session of the Eighty-seventh Congress, and on October 16, 1962, the President signed P.L. 87-835 repealing the disclaimer affidavit provisions of the National Science Foundation Act of 1950 and the National Defense Education Act of 1958. John Kennedy worked for three years to insure that the oath taken by a recipient of NDEA loan funds would read as follows: "I do solemnly swear (or affirm) that I bear true faith and allegiance to the United States of America and will support and defend the Constitution and laws of the United States against all its enemies, foreign and domestic." [23]

On July 13, 1960, the delegates to the National Democratic Convention in Los Angeles declared their choice and nominated John F. Kennedy for President. The next day Lyndon B. Johnson accepted the candidate's offer to run for the Vice-Presidency. The convention ratified the choice, and the Democrats prepared for the campaign.

---

[22] *Congressional Record—Senate,* January 28, 1960, pp. 1378–1379.
[23] The provision made it a crime for any member of a Communist organization to apply for or use loan or fellowship funds provided by the National Science Foundation Act or the National Defense Education Act. In addition, anyone with a criminal record applying is required to make this fact known.

INTRODUCTION

In his acceptance speech, John Kennedy set the tempo for the forthcoming campaign with the words,

. . . The times are too grave, the challenge too urgent, the stakes too high to permit the customary passions of political debate. . . .

The problems are not all solved and the battles are not all won—and we stand today on the edge of a New Frontier—the frontier of the 1960's—a frontier of unknown opportunities and perils—a frontier of unfulfilled hopes and threats. . . .[24]

Significantly, an integral part of the "New Frontier" platform was concerned with American education. The Democrats had adopted a strong education plank at the convention in Los Angeles,[25] and the "New Frontier" stood firmly on this plank.

---

[24] Theodore H. White, *The Making of the President 1960* (New York: Atheneum Publishers, 1961), p. 177.

[25] Text of the education plank of the Democratic Party Platform adopted at the Democratic National Convention in Los Angeles, July 12, 1960:

America's young people are our greatest resources for the future. Each of them deserves the education which will best develop his potentialities.

We shall act at once to help in building the classrooms and employing the teachers that are essential if the right to a good education is to have genuine meaning for all the youth of America in the decade ahead.

As a national investment in our future we propose a program of loans and scholarship grants to assure that qualified young Americans will have full opportunity for higher education, at the institutions of their choice, regardless of the income of their parents.

The new Democratic administration will end eight years of official neglect of our educational system.

America's education faces a financial crisis. The tremendous increase in the number of children of school and college age has far outrun the available supply of educational facilities and qualified teachers. The classroom shortage alone is interfering with the education of ten million students.

America's teachers, parents, and school administrators have striven courageously to keep up with the increased challenge of education.

So have states and local communities. Education absorbs two-fifths of all their revenue. With limited resources, private educational institutions have shouldered their share of the burden.

Only the federal government is not doing its part. For eight years, measures for the relief of the educational crisis have been held up by the cynical maneuvers of the Republican Party in Congress and the White House.

When he launched his campaign, Senator Kennedy pointed to the need to develop our human resources, making special reference to federal aid to education and school construction.[26] Speaking on Labor Day at Cadillac Square in Detroit, Michigan, he told the American worker that "we can afford the best schools for our children and the best paid and the best trained teachers." [27]

As John Kennedy had predicted in his acceptance speech in Los Angeles, it was not an ordinary campaign. The weeks and months until November 8 were filled with electrifying tension, eloquent oratory, and unrivalled drama. The Republican nominee, Richard Nixon, and John Kennedy criss-crossed America in a campaign that will not soon be equalled. The television debates added an extra dimension in presenting the candidates to an unprecedented number of people.

Unlike many other Presidential campaigns, in this one education was a vivid issue. Both candidates paid particular attention to our educational needs and the necessity for federal assistance. Senator Kennedy constantly wove the theme of the need for better education into his campaign. He pointed out the need for 135,000 more teachers and 131,000 classrooms, as well as adequate salaries for teachers. He

---

We believe that America can meet its educational obligations only with generous federal financial support, within the traditional framework of local control. The assistance will take the form of federal grants to states for educational purposes they deem most pressing, including classroom construction and teachers' salaries. It will include aid for the construction of academic facilities as well as dormitories at colleges and universities.

We pledge further federal support for all phases of vocational education for youth and adults; for libraries and adult education; for realizing the potential of educational television; and for exchange of students and teachers with other nations.

As part of a broader concern for young people we recommend establishment of a Youth Conservation Corps to give underprivileged young people a rewarding experience in a healthful environment.

[26] "Special Labor Day message from Democratic Presidential Candidate John F. Kennedy, September 5, 1960." In *Freedom of Communications: Final Report of the Committee on Commerce, United States Senate, Prepared by its Subcommittee of the Subcommittee on Communications,* S. Rept. 994, Pt. 1, 87th Congress, 1st Session (Washington, D.C.: Government Printing Office, 1961), I, 109–110.

[27] "Speech of Senator John F. Kennedy, Cadillac Square, Detroit, Mich., September 5, 1960." *Ibid.,* p. 113.

urged that federal assistance be made available to the states to aid in the solution of these problems.

To resolve any doubts about federal control, he suggested that federal grants be made to the state and that the distribution of the funds become the duty of each individual state.

Repeatedly Kennedy expressed his concern that the Russians were producing twice as many scientists and engineers as the United States. The fact that 35 per cent of our brightest boys and girls who graduate from high school never go to college was a source of consternation to him. He was disturbed because the Negro child did not have the same educational opportunities as the white child. The lack of trained medical and dental personnel also caused him anxiety.

To these problems he pledged his immediate attention if elected. He wanted the nation to invest in better school systems, in vocational training programs, and in scholarship programs. He often stated that he wanted to be President of a country which would send more children to college and where children would not have to attend school on part-time shifts.

John Kennedy knew that by 1970 twice as many children would be applying for admission to college as in 1960. He anticipated that American universities and colleges would have to build more dormitories and classrooms to accommodate the influx of students than they had constructed in their entire history. He estimated that twenty new medical schools would have to be constructed to meet the national need for doctors in 1975.

The American people went to the polls on November 8, 1960, to elect the thirty-fifth President of the United States, and although the balloting was extremely close, John Kennedy awoke the next day to find himself President-elect of the United States.

The campaign had ended, Election Day had come and gone, and after a brief respite the future President set to work to assemble those men who would spearhead the new administration and the New Frontier. One of the first selections made by Kennedy was Abraham Ribicoff as Secretary of Health, Education, and Welfare. Ribicoff was Governor of the State of Connecticut and a valued lieutenant in the Kennedy push for the Presidency. As Secretary of Health, Education, and Welfare, Mr. Ribicoff had the United States Office of Education directly under his jurisdiction, and subsequently he played a large part in formulating the Kennedy program on education.

1961

Amidst sparkling snow and bitter cold, Senator John F. Kennedy became President John F. Kennedy on January 20, 1961. Ten days later he addressed a joint session of Congress and delivered his first State of the Union Message. In that speech he emphasized the educational needs of our nation. He pointed out that "federal grants for both higher and public school education can no longer be delayed." He emphasized the necessity for "basic research that lies at the root of all progress," and for the introduction of measures to expand opportunities for training medical personnel.[28]

On February 20, the President submitted his Special Message on Education to Congress. He asked for assistance to elementary and secondary public schools. Specifically he requested federal grants of 2.3 billion dollars over a three-year period to be used for the construction of elementary and secondary school classrooms and for teachers' salaries. In addition, he urged Congress to pass legislation authorizing loans for the construction of classrooms, laboratories, libraries, and related academic facilities. He also asked for the extension of the College Housing Loan Program for building dormitories. The message recommended a five-year scholarship program to be administered by the states. Finally he asked for a review and evaluation of the federal vocational education program.[29]

The President's message did not advocate funds for private and parochial schools. Protest was immediately forthcoming from Catholic education leaders. The age-old problem of federal aid to education was again brought to the fore. The President, in a press conference on March 8, expressed his views that grants to private and parochial primary and secondary schools were unconstitutional. He felt that there was room for debate about loans but expressed doubts about even their constitutionality. He placed colleges in a different category because of prior congressional willingness to make grants and loans to

[28] *Public Papers of the Presidents: John F. Kennedy,* 1961 (Washington, D.C.: Government Printing Office, 1962), p. 22.
[29] *Ibid.,* pp. 107–111.

non-public institutions of higher education. Kennedy also made the distinction that elementary and secondary school education was compulsory whereas higher education was not. As a result, the problems of constitutionality with regard to college aid were different and made possible a less restrictive interpretation.

The religious issue was not the only obstacle to a general school aid bill. In addition to those who opposed, in principle, federal aid to education and aid to private education, there were the proponents of no federal aid to areas maintaining racially segregated schools. At the beginning of the Eighty-seventh Congress, Adam Clayton Powell, Chairman of the House Education and Labor Committee, indicated that he would attach the "Powell Amendment" (no federal assistance to support segregated schools) to education legislation should he deem it necessary. In the past this had been the "kiss of death" for federal aid to education in the House of Representatives. Thus the specter of congressional defeat once again hung over a President's education program.

The elementary and secondary education bill was introduced and became S. 1021 in the Senate and H.R. 4970 in the House. It authorized a three-year program of 2.3 billion dollars. Funds were to be paid to the states for school construction and teachers' salaries as the states saw fit. The states were compelled to set aside 10 per cent of their grant to pay part of the costs of pilot demonstrations or experimental projects created to meet special school problems.

Hearings were held in March on S. 1021 before the Education Subcommittee of the Senate Labor and Public Welfare Committee. Throughout the hearings much of the testimony was related to the church-state issue. During the hearing Secretary Ribicoff was requested by Senator Wayne Morse to submit a legal brief on the constitutionality of federal aid to private schools.

In response to the Senator's request, the Department of Health, Education, and Welfare filed a brief which held that federal grants to primary and secondary sectarian schools for general educational purposes, construction of general school facilities, and increasing teachers' salaries were prohibited by the Constitution of the United States and the cases interpreting the First Amendment. The legal memorandum also pointed out that low-interest loans to private primary and secondary schools for general aid purposes would be unconstitutional because such loans would "provide measurable economic benefit to religious institutions." [30] The department's legal staff was unable to determine precisely whether programs rendering incidental benefits to sectarian schools were constitutional. The brief implied that when not directly connected with religion these would constitute no violation of the First Amendment.

With regard to higher education, the legal memorandum pointed out many historical and educational differences between compulsory elementary and secondary school education and voluntary college education. Hence the less restrictive approach to federal aid to higher education. Scholarships as well as a cost-of-education allowance were within constitutional bounds. Loans for construction of college academic facilities were ruled "less constitutionally vulnerable than grants" and therefore valid.[31] The Administration's proposals for higher education were thus found to be within constitutional limits. Finally, the brief suggested that if Congress wanted to test the constitutionality of federal aid to private schools, it could authorize a judicial review provision in the legislation.[32] The judicial review provision would be aimed at creating a case or controversy between the federal government and institutions seeking aid. The courts of the United States would then be able to review the matter and determine the constitutionality of federal aid to private schools.

The Senate Education Subcommittee accepted the brief and set to work on the Administration's bill. Later, on May 11, the full Labor and Public Welfare Committee voted the bill out for floor action. The bill, as amended in committee, authorized federal grants to the states for construction of public schools and raising public school teachers' salaries, but increased the authorization for a three-year period from $2.3 billion to $2.5 billion. The bill, as approved, continued aid to federally impacted areas. On May 25, by a 49–34 roll-call vote, the

---

[30] *Constitutionality of Federal Aid to Education in its Various Aspects.*
S. Doc. 29, 87th Congress, 1st Session, pp. 21, 22.
[31] *Ibid.,* p. 26.
[32] The Supreme Court has ruled that individual taxpayers and states are unable to invoke the power of the court to enjoin federal appropriations. *Massachusetts v Mellon,* 262 U.S. 447 (1923).

INTRODUCTION

Senate passed the School Assistance Act of 1961. The bill was amended during the debate to modify the Administration's proposal that 10 per cent of the funds be set aside for special educational projects, making these programs voluntary rather than mandatory.

The final vote came after eight days of debate, much of which centered on religious and civil rights issues. During the discussion a number of amendments were proposed that had direct bearing on segregation in the public schools. Senator Strom Thurmond of South Carolina submitted a proposal that prohibited withholding the bill's funds because of racial segregation. The measure was rejected by the Senate. Senator Prescott Bush of Connecticut presented an amendment that would make funds available only to states making progress toward ending segregation in public schools, but the Senate failed to adopt this. Senator Goldwater urged an amendment to provide loans for construction of private schools, and this also was rejected.

In the House, the General Education Subcommittee had conducted hearings on the general school aid bill (H.R. 4970) in March. The testimony was similar to that in the Senate. The Education and Labor Committee voted the bill out for floor action at the end of May. It contained provisions for a three-year program of close to $2.5 billion for public classroom construction and public school teachers' salaries. As did the Senate bill, it extended the "impacted" aid program. The bill was sent to the Rules Committee on June 20, where the committee voted to withhold action temporarily. On July 18, the Rules Committee voted to withhold all action on education legislation for the first session. In essence the Rules Committee vote killed the public school aid bill.

In August another attempt to pass a general school aid bill in the House failed. A version providing for a one-year program of public school construction without provisions for improving teachers' salaries was brought to the floor of the House under the Calendar Wednesday procedure—a method by which the chairmen of House legislative committees are permitted to call to the floor bills which have been approved by their committees but have not been cleared by the Rules Committee. The parliamentary device is aimed at avoiding the control of the Rules Committee. The strategy did not work, and the House refused to consider the bill by a 170–242 roll-call vote. In retrospect education legislation pending in the House had received a *coup de grâce* for 1961. Never in the history of federal aid to education had a measure been so overwhelmingly rejected.

Stymied, the House leadership decided to at least seek passage of legislation extending the National Defense Education Act and "impacted areas" legislation. In another effort to avoid the Rules Committee, the House, by using a procedure known as Suspension of the Rules, passed a measure extending the National Defense Education Act and "impacted" aid for two years. The suspension procedure requires a two-thirds vote for approval, and on September 6 the measure was passed by a 378–32 roll-call vote. The Senate, seeing that conditions were impossible in the House, agreed to the simple extension of both programs. Disappointed that the measure failed to encompass his earlier recommendations for NDEA and "impacted" aid legislation, President Kennedy signed the bill with "extreme reluctance" on October 3, 1961.[33]

Earlier in the session both House and Senate committees, pursuant to President Kennedy's recommendations, had voted out bills expanding and extending the highly successful National Defense Education legislation. As we have seen, the Rules Committee in the House refused to vote out any education bills. The Senate version was reported by the Labor and Public Welfare Committee but, in the light of House action, never went before the Senate for final action.

The college aid bills in both Houses of Congress were to meet a similar fate. Hearings were held on the Kennedy proposal to make federal loans to public and private colleges for construction of academic facilities and to provide college scholarships. The House version came out of the Education and Labor Committee providing grants and loans for construction of academic facilities. The Senate version included loan assistance for construction and aid for public junior colleges. Both House and Senate versions contained scholarship provisions. The refusal of the House Rules Committee to act on any education legislation dealt a death blow also to the higher education bill. Recognizing a hopeless situation, the Senate took no further action.

However, there was some light in the darkness. One outstanding

[33] *Public Papers of the Presidents,* 1961, p. 637.

accomplishment of the first session of the Eighty-seventh Congress was the enactment of the Juvenile Delinquency and Youth Offenses Control Act. Earlier President Kennedy had established a Presidential Committee on Juvenile Delinquency and Youth Crime.[34] Shortly thereafter Congresswoman Edith Green introduced the Administration's bill [35] in the House. The measure provided a five-year program of federal grants to state and local governments or public and non-profit private agencies to control juvenile delinquency and to provide traineeships for workers involved in juvenile delinquency work. A slightly different version had been introduced in the Senate.

The House Special Subcommittee on Education, under the chairmanship of Mrs. Green, conducted extensive hearings on juvenile delinquency. In August, the bill was reported out by the House Education and Labor Committee. The fellowship provisions formerly in the Administration bill had been deleted by the committee and the overall program shortened from five to three years. The measure passed the House on August 30, the Senate having voted its support of a similar bill at an earlier date. On September 22 the President signed the Juvenile Delinquency and Youth Offenses Control Act into law. It authorized $10 million annually for a three-year period to develop methods and techniques for the control and prevention of juvenile delinquency. On signing the legislation President Kennedy commented,

The resources provided under this program will help local communities in their efforts to stem the tide of juvenile delinquency and youthful offenses, and thus contribute to the preservation of human resources in this vital area of the life of our Nation.[36]

1962

The President's message on education was sent to the Congress on February 6. In his message, the President once again asked for legislation aiding elementary and secondary schools and institutions of higher education. He also asked for the enactment of legislation de-

[34] Executive Order 10940, May 11, 1961.
[35] H.R. 7178.
[36] *Public Papers of the Presidents,* 1961, p. 616.

signed to improve the quality of teaching in our schools and to provide special training for handicapped children as well as assistance for coping with adult illiteracy. In addition, he recommended an increase in the appropriation for the National Science Foundation to improve the teaching of science and mathematics in our schools. Other requests in the education message included programs to improve and expand medical and dental education, establish a Federal Advisory Council on the Arts, aid education for migrant workers and their children, and support educational television.

From the beginning, the Kennedy administration decided to press for action on the college aid bill. A good start had been made. Both the House and Senate had voted their approval of different versions of college aid bills early in the second session of the Eighty-seventh Congress. The scars of the 1961 battle over the general school aid bill were still fresh and too tender to attempt a major effort on behalf of elementary and secondary schools. In general the college aid bill, as passed in the House, provided grants and loans to both public and private institutions of higher education (including junior colleges and graduate schools) for the construction of academic facilities. The Senate version provided loans for construction aid to public junior colleges and scholarship aid to college students, but no grants. In February, there was an objection to a House-Senate Conference on the college bill. In May, the House Rules Committee voted to allow the bill to go to conference, after the House conferees agreed not to accept the Senate scholarship provision unless the whole House had an opportunity to vote on the matter.

During the conference period the grants-in-aid to private institutions of higher education were challenged by the Senate conferees. Representative Green held her ground and insisted that grants as well as loans were necessary for both public and private schools. She pointed out that most of the states placed prohibitions on public school borrowing; therefore grants were a necessity. Finally a compromise bill was worked out through the dedicated efforts of Mrs. Green and Senators Clark and Morse. The bill provided grants and loans to public and private colleges for classroom and library construction. Grants could be made only for buildings constructed for science, engineering, and libraries. Loans were available for the construction of any academic facility not intended for a religious or athletic purpose. The bill also provided grant assistance to public junior colleges and authorized funds for student loans. The loans were to be made through the colleges, and 20 per cent of each school's funds could be set aside for "exceptionally needy and promising students." These loans did not have to be repaid and were known as "nonreimbursable loans." All the conferees but Senators Hill of Alabama and Goldwater of Arizona, and Representative Carroll Kearns of Pennsylvania agreed to the compromise.

When the conference report was presented to the members of the House, it was rejected. Some felt that the conferees had violated their pledge concerning scholarships when they accepted the "nonreimbursable loans" aspect under the student loan provisions. Even more decisive was the church-state controversy, which intensified before the vote and substantially hampered efforts to obtain approval of the conference report. The House voted 214–186 to recommit it with instructions to delete the student assistance program appearing in the compromise bill. The vote dealt a fatal blow to the college bill for 1962. The failure in the House made any action futile in the Senate.

Of the remaining recommendations of the Kennedy administration for education in 1962, only two succeeded in becoming law. The first was the Educational Television Act. This provided a five-year program of grants to tax-supported educational agencies or to any non-profit agency, organized primarily to engage in or encourage educational television. The second was an increase in the annual appropriation for the National Science Foundation.

Late in the second session of the Eighty-seventh Congress, President Kennedy's long-time legislative ambition was realized when both Houses of Congress voted to eliminate the non-Communist disclaimer affidavit from the National Science Foundation Act of 1950 and the National Defense Education Act of 1958.

1963

Ironically, Congress gave its approval to the Kennedy education program after his assassination. What was refused during his lifetime was given freely after his death.

The somber and sorrowful weeks following the Dallas tragedy saw a series of events leading to the passage of education legislation that had been impossibly blocked in Congress. All but the most optimistic had abandoned hopes for the education program in the first session of the Eigthy-eighth Congress when the President left for his trip to Texas in November. The House and Senate conferees were hopelessly deadlocked over political factors concerning the higher education and vocational education bills. The extensive and rapid congressional action following November 22 led President Johnson to comment, "This session of the Congress will go down in history as the Education Congress of 1963."

To understand fully the accomplishments of the "Education Congress of 1963" it is necessary to look to January 29, when President Kennedy sent his education program to Congress, wrapped in new packaging. It was the most ambitious education program submitted by any President. In his Special Message to the Congress on Education in January, he specified three goals: improvement of the quality of education by stimulating interest in learning, by attracting and retaining better teachers, and by providing the best possible teaching materials and curricula; expansion of the nation's educational facilities to meet the needs of a growing population; and increased opportunities and incentives for all Americans to complete their education and to continue their self-improvement throughout life. To help formulate and spearhead the program, President Kennedy appointed Francis Keppel United States Commissioner of Education on December 10, 1962. Before his appointment, Keppel had served as the Dean of the Harvard University Graduate School of Education.

The failures of 1961 and 1962 convinced the Kennedy administration that a new approach for education legislation was mandatory. To gather the widest possible support for education, the President decided to submit an Omnibus Education Bill, combining all the administration's education programs into a single bill on the theory that the support of the various proponents of federal aid to education could be joined to pass the bill. In the past, the diverse education lobbies had pursued their own individual interests with little visible results. The President's strategy was to present a unified front which might alter the outcome of congressional action.

The President's bill provided for an extension and expansion of

INTRODUCTION

the National Defense Education Student Loan and Fellowship programs. It also amended NDEA to expand modern foreign language training and guidance and counseling programs. Federal assistance was provided for construction of college and graduate facilities, public community junior colleges, and college-level technical institutes. The Kennedy omnibus legislation contained aid for improving the training of teachers, including those working with handicapped children. Aid for college libraries, a part-time work program for college students, and an insurance program to guarantee commercial bank loans made to college students were all part of the Kennedy legislative proposal.

For elementary and secondary school education, the omnibus bill provided federal grants to public schools for teachers' salaries, for construction, and for strengthening science, mathematics, and foreign language instruction. The "impacted" aid programs were to be extended, vocational education was to be expanded and improved, and other programs were geared to aid still other aspects of education.[37]

The Congress did not greet President Kennedy's omnibus approach with enthusiasm. Many felt that this was not the way to pass education legislation in the House or Senate. Reluctantly, the Education and Labor Committee in the House commenced hearings on the omnibus bill (H.R. 3000). Even after the hearings had been concluded,

[37] Outline of the National Education Improvement Act of 1963: *Title I,* Expansion of Opportunities for Individuals in Higher Education: A) Student loans; B) Student loan insurance; C) Student work-study programs; D) Graduate fellowships. *Title II,* Expansion and Improvement of Higher Education: A) Higher education facilities; B) Public community college academic facilities; C) College level technical education; D) College and university libraries; E) Graduate schools; F) Modern foreign language training and research. *Title III,* Improvement of Educational Quality: A) Institutes for advanced study for teachers; B) Teacher preparation programs; C) Specialized training for teachers and related educational personnel; D) Educational research and demonstrations; E) State statistical services. *Title IV,* Strengthening Elementary and Secondary Education: A) Public elementary and secondary education; B) Science, mathematics, and modern foreign language instruction equipment; C) Guidance, counseling, and testing; D) Federal affected areas. *Title V,* Expansion and Improvement of Vocational and Special Education: A) Vocational education; B) Education of handicapped children. *Title VI,* Expansion of Continuing Education: A) General university extension education; B) Adult basic education; C) Public community libraries.

considerable doubt remained whether the House members would stay with the bill.

The matter was at a standstill when Adam Clayton Powell, chairman of the House Education and Labor Committee, announced in May that his committee would divide the bill into four categories: elementary and secondary school education; college education; vocational-adult education and extension of NDEA programs; and "impacted" aid legislation.

The Senate approached the matter somewhat differently. Hearings on the omnibus bill (S. 580) were delayed until the spring, and the Senate Subcommittee on Education continued its deliberation on the bill well after it was decided to drop the one-unit approach. It was not until September that the Labor and Public Welfare Committee of the Senate reported out separate education bills.

In addition to the omnibus education bill, President Kennedy also submitted proposals for improving medical education and the creation of a National Service Corps. The National Service Corps, modeled after the Peace Corps, would be established to meet problems of the states in the areas of poverty, education, and other domestic need. A Youth Conservation Corps was also proposed by the President to provide training and work for young men between the ages of sixteen and twenty-one.

The college bill in the House was the first to be ready for floor action after the Kennedy package was broken up and was passed by the House on August 14. Earlier action would have been possible had the White House not made a decision to seek passage of the Health Professions Educational Assistance Act. On April 24, the House passed a bill providing funds to improve medical and dental training; the Senate did the same on September 12. The Act which President Kennedy signed into law on September 24 as P.L. 88-129 provided a three-year program of matching federal grants for the construction of teaching facilities for training medical, dental, and related personnel. In addition, the legislation authorized funds for a loan program to help medical and dental students meet their school expenses.

The House bill on higher education, sponsored by Edith Green, added grants to President Kennedy's loan recommendations for college aid. In essence a three-year program of grants and loans for the construction of academic facilities in public and private institutions of higher education would be established. The bill also provided aid to graduate schools as well as to public junior colleges and college-level technical institutes.

The inclusion of a judicial review provision was contemplated but excluded in committee and never became part of the House version. It should be noted that none of the funds made available by the bill were to be used for a religious purpose.

However, the Senate bill for higher education passed on October 21 did include a judicial review provision, but provided that grants could only be made for the construction of science, engineering, and library facilities. The Senate version also made specific grant assistance available to public junior colleges. The House had set aside a certain percentage (22 per cent) of the general grant funds for public and private junior colleges and technical schools.

When the House and Senate conferees met in early November to resolve their differences on the college bill, the success of the higher education bill became inextricably involved with disputes that had arisen over the vocational education bill. Senate conferees refused to sanction the conference report on the college bill until the differences on the vocational education bill had been resolved.

To understand the situation entirely, the legislative history of the vocational education bill must be examined. In his Education Message of 1963, President Kennedy had requested for the first time new and improved vocational education programs. His Civil Rights Message of June, 1963, added impetus to the need for better vocational education.[38] The House Education and Labor Committee reported its vocational education bill in June and the entire House acted favorably on the legislation on August 6. The Senate committee, Labor and Public Welfare, completed its work on the vocational education bill early in October, and the Senate voted its approval of the bill on October 8. The Senate action added two additional titles which extended the National Defense Education Act and "impacted areas" aid programs. In the vocational education title of the bill, the inclusion of an allotment formula for making grants to the states caused considerable

[38] *Public Papers of the Presidents,* 1963, pp. 468–471, 483–494.

controversy in conference. The House wished to make distribution dependent on population. The Senate wished to consider per capita income in addition to population. Neither side would yield and the final approval of the higher education bill was held up in the Senate until differences over the vocational education bill could be resolved.

These differences seemed to be insignificant in the aftermath of Dallas. In addition, President Lyndon B. Johnson was extremely effective in bringing the House-Senate conferees to an agreeable compromise, and the final approval of the higher education and vocational education bills was soon forthcoming. The legislation was ready for Presidential action on December 16, 1963. President Johnson signed the Higher Education Facilities Act into law on that day, and it became Public Law 88-204. On December 18, the Vocational Education Act became P.L. 88-210.

As signed into law, the Higher Education Facilities Act contained no judicial review provision and the categorical approach of the Senate had been adopted but expanded. In addition to grants for science, engineering, and library facilities, it allowed grants for facilities designed for mathematics and modern foreign languages. Finally, the program was to be a five-year program but authorizations were made only for three years and totaled approximately $1.2 billion.

The question raised by the distribution formula in the Vocational Education Act was resolved by accepting the Senate version and using per capita income and population as the basis for distribution. The compromise included a stipulation that no state would receive more than one and a half times as much as any other. Differences in the amounts to be authorized for the vocational education grants and National Defense student loans were also compromised. As the Vocational Education Act was signed into law, it provided matching grants to the states to expand and improve vocational education programs. Assistance would be rendered to high school students, high school dropouts, and handicapped children. Funds were made available for construction of area vocational schools, teacher training, residential vocational schools and vocational work-study programs. Existing federal vocational education programs were expanded under the Act. The measure also amended the National Defense Education Act, extending its operation to June 30, 1965, and likewise extended the "impacted areas" aid programs until June 30, 1965.

The education program passed during 1963 was the first major education program enacted by the Congress since the passage of the National Defense Education Act in 1958. Not since World War II had the Congress acted to pass significant education legislation unaffiliated with national defense. It was truly a milestone and a tribute to John F. Kennedy. His perseverance in the face of severe setbacks to his education program in 1961 and 1962; his unique understanding of youth and education and their problems; and his decision to give education top priority in the "New Frontier"—all placed education among the ranks of the highest accomplishments of the Kennedy administration.

Few of the late President's proposals contained in his omnibus bill remained to be acted upon at the end of the Eighty-eighth Congress. Surely his tragic and untimely death played a part in making the President's education program a reality. Also, President Johnson's deft political management and excellent relationship with Congress helped immeasurably to forge the deadlocked education bills into law after the President's assassination. Yet the education legislation enacted in 1963 and 1964 definitely bears the Kennedy mark. College and medical school aid, vocational education, NDEA, "impacted areas" aid, and a training program for teachers of the handicapped became law in 1963. Aid for adult education, library services, teacher improvement, and college work-study programs was provided in 1964. Primary and secondary school aid, university extension education, and the federally insured student loan program alone were not acted upon by Congress during 1963–64.

It is impossible at this time to assess John F. Kennedy's total contribution to American education. It is safe to assume that the broad dimensions of his ideas will affect the role of the President of the United States as an educator. He placed a major emphasis on education and its improvement—a memorable legacy to this generation, and to all future generations.

He intended to address those of every generation at the Trade Mart in Dallas, Texas, on November 22, 1963. Fate did not afford him the opportunity, but we do have his words. The "silent speech" of that day read in part:

In a world of complex and continuing problems, in a world full of frustrations and irritations, America's leadership must be guided by the lights of learning and reason. . . .

Only an America which has fully educated its citizens is fully capable of tackling the complex problems and perceiving the hidden dangers of the world in which we live. . . .[39]

[39] *Ibid.*, pp. 890–894.

ONE

THE CONGRESSIONAL
YEARS 1947-1960

Subsequent to the 1951 dismissal of ninety cadets from West Point for Honor Code violations, John F. Kennedy criticized the selection of candidates for the service academies. In a *New York Times Magazine* article, he questioned the methods used by some congressmen to make West Point and Annapolis appointments, at the same time outlining his own method. He deplored the attrition rate of cadets and midshipmen during their course of study and after they were commissioned and urged the improvement of selection by considering dedication and good officer material as well as academic proficiency.

Pursuant to his recommendations to improve academy appointments, Representative Kennedy introduced H.R. 5253 on August 20, 1951. The bill was to establish a commission to review and investigate the method of selecting candidates for the military and naval academies. It was never acted upon by Congress.

The recent disclosure that ninety West Point cadets have been involved in "cribbing" on examinations has shocked the nation. While this unfortunate scandal is a cause for concern it serves to call attention to the graver issue of the selection methods used in choosing our future military and naval leaders. Young men are finding their way into the service academies by political favoritism, inadequate screening, and misplaced emphasis on qualities that are of little importance in military leaders.

Public attention has focused on the number of football players involved in the scandal at West Point. It is quite apparent that the first impulse toward moral breakdown came when these young men were approached by academy officials and athletic scouts who offered them appointments to West Point. It is, of course, imperative that immediate steps be taken to stop such professional recruiting of athletes. But there is more to it than that; special preference for football players is only one of numerous faults in the entire system of selecting entrants for West Point and Annapolis.

"How Should Cadets Be Picked—The West Point Scandal Calls Attention to the Weakness of an Outmoded System for Making Service-School Appointments." *The New York Times Magazine,* August 19, 1951, pp. 16, 44–45. © 1951 by the New York Times Company. Reprinted by permission.

SERVICE ACADEMIES

Our present system, developed to insure the supremacy of the civilian over the military, makes the majority of appointments to West Point and Annapolis a personal prerogative of Senators and Representatives. That system is far from a success, especially when our safety may hinge on our ability to draw into the service academies young men who are best fitted to meet the vast responsibilities that will later be placed upon them in our armed forces.

The broad facts as I have gathered them after some months of study with the assistance of Army and Navy officials, who recognized the deficiencies of the present system, disclose a situation so serious that we cannot afford to ignore it. These facts will show that the service academies are unfilled; that the best men are not being attracted to them; and that an undesirably high number of graduates, upon whom the Government has spent large sums of money, fail to stay with the armed services.

Congressmen are not required by law to use any particular standard in making their appointments. In response to an inquiry I find that while half of them employ some type of competitive test, mostly the so-called civil service designating examination, the marks made by the candidates are not usually considered to be the controlling factor. Congressmen frequently make their choice on grounds of "first come, first served," or on grounds of political obligation, or perhaps because of reasons of friendship.

The weakness in our present system of selection can be pointed up by the results that the Coast Guard has obtained through its system of recruiting its students by open competition. As contrasted with West Point and Annapolis, it has eight or nine times as many applicants as vacancies—men who in many cases might have gone to the other academies but who felt they did not have the political influence to get an appointment. Moreover, statistics from the Educational Testing Service, an affiliate of the College Entrance Examination Board, reveal that in 1945, 1946 and 1947 (years in which this agency prepared examinations for both the Coast Guard Academy and the Naval Academy) the Coast Guard candidates achieved a higher score than the Annapolis candidates.

Further evidence of the deficiencies of our present system of selection was provided by the study made for the War Department in 1944 by Major Oscar K. Buros, Jr. Comparing the records of cadets who were appointed by Congressmen with those appointed in special categories as a result of a competitive examination, it was found that over a ten year period the cadets who were not Congressional appointees performed academically, year after year, better than Congressional appointees.

The present system of Congressional appointments is, in addition to being unfair, obviously not producing the best men for the service academies. Evidence of this is to be found in the "attrition studies" made of the classes of 1915, 1925 and 1935 at both West Point and Annapolis.

"Undesirable attrition" is the term employed in these studies to represent those men who have been accepted for admission who later became lost to the armed services for reasons of lack of suitable temperament, want of proficiency, or absence of emotional stability. The figures on undesirable attrition are truly startling. . . .

Of particular interest in this time of emergency are statistics on attrition in the academies at the end of World War II. From 1945 to 1947 there were 306 resignations from undergraduates from Annapolis and 380 from West Point. Among the graduates of the academies the attrition is even more noteworthy. About 30 per cent of the Annapolis Academy graduates of Classes 1943–1946 have resigned their Navy commissions, and it is reasonable to estimate that the country has today less than 50 per cent of all men entering the Naval Academy from 1940 to 1943.

The resignation figures of the Military Academy were a great deal less but it is evident that in troubled years too great a percentage of young men consider the academies as a place of refuge rather than as the foundation of a life's career in the service of their country.

The entrance tests for appointees to the Academies compound in many cases the original errors made in Congressional selection, although recently they have been substantially improved by being administered by the Educational Testing Service, with its experience in the field of giving college entrance examinations.

One deficiency that seems to characterize them is that they fail to equalize the opportunities of all candidates to meet the academic requirements for admission. The candidate who has private tutoring or who has attended a preparatory school with instruction oriented toward entering one of the academies will, as a rule, achieve higher marks on the entrance examinations of the academy than will a candidate who has equal or greater native intelligence and academic aptitude but who has the benefit only of a high-school education.

According to a survey made of the class of 1942, 97.3 per cent of the 298 members of the class who qualified by passing the regular entrance examination had preparation supplementary to their high school courses. That survey substantially confirms four previous studies which have shown that more than 95 per cent of the candidates who passed the regular examination had extra instruction in addition to their regular high school work. This has led to the development of "cram schools" and this trend has handicapped the boy without funds.

A second deficiency that seems to characterize these tests is that in doing the job they purport to do they do it very imperfectly. Some 15 to 20 per cent of the young men entering Annapolis and West Point, despite having passed these tests, fail to graduate because of academic deficiencies—a percentage that represents pure educational waste and that is substantially higher than that which characterizes other comparable institutions.

Furthermore, the entrance requirements of the academies consist of mental and physical qualifications and make little attempt usually to determine a candidate's personality, character and leadership potential, but rather rely on the judgment of the members of Congress, who themselves have no effective means, beyond personal knowledge, of determining the presence of these attributes. . . .

The obvious method of improving the quality of men applying for entrance to Annapolis and West Point is to pursue some such method of recruitment and selection as that practiced by the Coast Guard Academy. I doubt today whether this is a practical method. Our goal must be to develop as effective a system as possible within the framework of Congressional responsibility for the selection of applicants. But there are ways, however, for immense improvements in the framework of the existing system—ways which I have attempted since 1947 to adapt to the selection of candidates from the Eleventh Massachusetts District for the service academies.

Each year I have announced that open examinations would be

held for the appointments that I was entitled to make to the two academies. All applicants are subjected to a physical examination based on standards applied by the Army and Navy, an obvious necessity, as between 12 per cent and 30 per cent of those appointed by their Congressmen fail to pass the physical examination given at the academies.

Those who are physically acceptable are then given aptitude and achievement tests, especially developed by the training division of the Civil Service Commission, which measure their ability to learn and their proficiency in academic subjects. Their scholastic records in high school and preparatory school are carefully compiled and evaluated.

Objective reference questionnaires devised to bring out all the relevant data relating to the candidate's character and personality are sent to former teachers, supervisors, and others who have personally observed the candidate over a period of time. These questionnaires are drawn in such fashion that it is difficult to give any candidate high marks. This was done to get a more accurate report on an individual than the usual letter of recommendation provides.

The candidates are finally interviewed by a selection board composed of three members, consisting of a clergyman who formerly was an Army combat chaplain, a psychologist and doctor of medicine at Harvard University, and a former Army doctor with long experience in conducting interviews while in the service. The selection board, after these interviews, finally evaluates the competitive rank of each candidate and notifies, by wire, the candidates it has selected for appointment.

Some system such as this, obviously much improved, can easily be made available to all Congressmen. The Civil Service Commission, or the College Entrance Examination Board, or some similar organization, could undoubtedly devise better and more comprehensive tests which could be made available to any Congressman who might want to employ them. Local citizens of responsibility and experience could be prevailed upon to conduct the necessary personal interviews, and thus real merit would become the basis for appointment.

The cost for the introduction and operation of such a system would be negligible. It would not be compulsory, but a simple request by a Congressman would set the entire system in operation.

In addition, the admission tests given by the academies themselves must be improved because they fail sufficiently to emphasize the qualities which, in addition to academic proficiency, make for good officers.

We all know that although two individuals may have identical intelligence levels and mechanical aptitudes, one may succeed at a given job and the other fail because of the difference in personality, attitude, and motivation. This field of character evaluation is developing rapidly. Industry and other educational institutions are availing themselves of its already demonstrated results to pretest both executives and promising college material.

What scientific advancement in this field has proven is that, although tests and evaluations of character traits are not too accurate as applied to the individual, they are highly dependable in analyzing the average characteristics of a group as a whole. In other words, while one cannot be sure of selecting a particular future leader, one can pick a group of several hundred from which future leaders can be developed with far greater frequency than from an unselected group of the same size.

During the war the psychologists and the educators achieved marked success with these techniques at the Coast Guard Academy. In evaluating reserve officer cadets they were able to predict, with an error of two to four cases, how many individuals out of a class of 200 to 300 reserve officer cadets would actually receive commissions. The same general sort of techniques were applied by the Army and Navy air arms in selecting candidates to become pilots, bombardiers and navigators, with startling success in reducing to almost negligible proportions the number who would eventually fail to qualify.

I believe that it is essential that some system similar to the one that I have discussed be placed into operation as quickly as possible. Common justice requires that all boys in this country of ours have an equal opportunity to attend a service academy, and the needs of the country require that the best boys be chosen.

We dare not continue to pick the men who may direct another war with new weapons and new techniques by methods developed almost a century ago and shown to be wanting. There is no better place to begin than with the improvement of the process of selecting candidates for the two academies, for it is from these that the generals and admirals of tomorrow will be made. The Congress, I am certain, given the facts, would recognize its responsibilities to do a better job. To do so it must provide itself with the tools that are needed. They can easily be created, and at a negligible cost. And since the world rumbles of war and unfortunately is not likely to be soon at peace, the Congress dare no longer delay the discharge of its responsibilities as wisely and as best it may.

VOCATIONAL EDUCATION

Speaking to a vocational high school graduating class, Congressman Kennedy reminded the graduates of the vital role that technically trained workers play in our national defense. In addition, he urged them to take an active interest in the affairs of local, state, and national government after graduation. The speech, in June of 1952, marked the opening in western Massachusetts of Kennedy's bid for a Senate seat.

I am deeply honored to participate in this graduation exercise. You young people who are graduating today carry the burden of a unique responsibility. You carry the responsibility that all students must bear to those who have taught them. Your teachers have high hopes for you and confidence in you. They will be satisfied and feel well repaid if you live as responsible citizens, devoted to the ideals which have made this country of ours great.

I do not need to tell you what sort of world we live in today. There are two basic systems of government which are engaged in mortal combat in ideas, in the production of the machines and materials of war, and on the battlefield itself—in the hills, the rice paddies and the muddy roads of Korea.

That is why the young person who is skilled and trained in the use of his hands is more important to our nation today than ever before in our long history. The production of machine tools, for example, has the highest priority in our defense planning. You will be building those tools and running them, and in doing so you will be helping in the defense of your country, your homes and the ideals of free peoples everywhere.

As the voters and leaders of the future you will play a decisive part in the solution of our problems. A recent survey has shown that four in every eight workers in the country are manual workers, with one in every eight a skilled craftsman. This great concentration of voting power in the hands of manual workers means that you as a group will have an important impact on the policies of your government.

From the typescript of an address at the Holyoke Trade High School, Holyoke, Massachusetts, June, 1952.

It goes without saying that with this power goes a like responsibility. It is of this responsibility that I would like to talk briefly with you tonight.

Wherever you may go, after your graduation here today, you are critically needed. The problems that require your help are many. You must join in attempting to find solutions to these problems. To do this, we must all—as citizens—become increasingly aware of our obligation to participate in the processes of our government. . . .

The times require leadership which will stand against the soft winds of indifference and easy popularity and personal gain. They require leadership which is disinterested, responsible, and dedicated. They require the kind of leadership which you can furnish. . . .

I do not mean by that that you should all embark on careers in the executive or legislative branch of our national government. But all are obligated to participate in, to contribute to the national life at all levels.

In your community, in your state and in your national government, widespread opportunities are before you.

Those among you who, because of temperament or other reasons, would not aspire to public office, can certainly be of help to responsible candidates in your own home town. Remember too, that your national government does not require the services of administrators and lawyers alone. You who possess technical abilities and training can make use of your talents to contribute materially to efficient and worthwhile government.

That is certainly the major challenge that any graduate this year must face.

High on the wall of the House of Representatives in Washington so that everyone can see, are written words that should be our guide. They are from a speech by a distinguished senator from our native state of Massachusetts—Daniel Webster: "Let us develop the resources of our land, call forth its powers, build up its institutions, and promote all its great interests and see whether we also in our day and generation may not perform something worthy to be remembered."

MEDICAL EDUCATION

Senator Kennedy spoke at an observance of the opening of the Albert Einstein College of Medicine of Yeshiva University on October 17, 1955. After commending the objectives of the medical school, he viewed the tremendous strides that had been made in medical science.

He pointed out that if such progress were to continue, greater attention must be given to medical education. Of considerable concern to him was the failure to increase the number of medical colleges and doctors in proportion to our growing population. He urged immediate attention to meet the needs for more medical personnel.

As a representative and senator, Kennedy introduced several bills to provide aid to both medical students and medical schools; such legislation was enacted during his presidential administration. See pp. 95, 137–138, 230–231, 246–247.

. . . No medical school serves a purely local function. Its student body comes from all parts of the country and from every racial and religious group. Its faculty has been recruited from leading universities, medical schools and hospital centers in different parts of the country. Its graduates will go on to serve far flung communities, in all branches of medicine. Some will become general practitioners—who are still the back-bone of American medicine; some will become specialists; some will become teachers who in turn, will train other students for medical careers. Many will go into research and contribute their talents and skills towards the conquest of disease and the prolonging of human life.

The benefits of medical research transcend the boundaries of time and geography. The discoveries of the past have been the stepping stones to present day medical research just as the discoveries of our day will serve as the pathway to great new discoveries in the future. . . .

From an advance copy of an address at a dinner in honor of the Hon. James J. Lyons, President of the Borough of the Bronx, and marking the opening of the Albert Einstein College of Medicine of Yeshiva University, October 17, 1955.

. . . the expansion of educational facilities to train physicians and research scientists has number one priority.

The nation's facilities for medical education have lagged far behind our achievements in the field of medicine. There are fewer medical schools in the country today than there were 50 years ago. The number of doctors graduated each year is only slightly higher than the number graduated 50 years ago, although our population has almost doubled.

Several years ago, the President's Commission on the Health Needs of the Nation reported a serious and growing shortage of doctors, and predicted that by 1960 the nation would be at least 30,000 physicians short unless facilities for medical education are expanded. The report stated that the basic barrier to increasing the number of physicians is the limited capacity of our medical schools.

The number of doctors graduated is about equal to the number who die or retire each year. American hospitals have 12,000 interneships available and only 6,000 [internes] to fill them. There are 19,000 residencies open and only 12,000 doctors available. Of the nearly 17,000 qualified students who apply to medical schools each year, approximately 7,000 can be accepted. The proportion of young people who are admitted to medical schools has remained almost constant for the past 20 years, while the proportion who receive a college education has more than quadrupled and the proportion entering engineering has increased sixfold.

. . . I am sure we are all equally aware of the deep significance of the cause for which we are gathered here tonight. . . .

. . . The health of our people is our nation's most precious resource. It touches every American family and every American home. Your participation in this program is, therefore, an investment in the health and welfare of your families, your neighbors and your community. We can all take pride in what you have achieved and in the promise of what lies ahead.

THE POLITICIAN AND THE SCHOLAR

Harvard awarded John Kennedy an honorary Doctor of Laws degree on June 14, 1956. Delivering the commencement address on that occasion, the Senator spoke of the relationship of the intellectual to the politician, and the friction that exists between the two. He asked a cessation of hostility between the two camps and based his appeal on what the politician and the intellectual share in American life. Historically the first American politicians were great writers and scholars. Both have always operated in a common framework of liberty; they stand or fall simultaneously, and each will gain immeasurably by cooperating with the other.

. . . it is regrettable that the gap between the intellectual and the politician seems to be growing. Instead of synthesis, clash and discord now characterize the relations between the two groups much of the time. Authors, scholars, and intellectuals can praise every aspect of American society but the political. My desk is flooded with books, articles, and pamphlets criticizing Congress. But, rarely, if ever, have I seen any intellectual bestow praise on either the political profession or any political body for its accomplishments, its ability, or its integrity—much less for its intelligence. To many universities and scholars we reap nothing but censure, investigators and perpetrators of what has been called the swinish cult of anti-intellectualism. . . .

But in fairness, the way of the intellectual is not altogether serene; in fact, so great has become popular suspicion that a recent survey of American intellectuals by a national magazine elicited from one of our foremost literary figures the guarded response, "I ain't no intellectual."

Both sides in this battle, it seems to me, are motivated by largely unfounded feelings of distrust. The politician, whose authority rests upon the mandate of the popular will, is resentful of the scholar who can, with dexterity, slip from position to position without dragging the anchor of public opinion. It was this skill that caused Lord Melbourne to say of the youthful historian Macauley that he wished he was as sure of anything as Macauley was of everything. The in-

Congressional Record—Senate, June 22, 1956, pp. 10800–10801.

tellectual, on the other hand, finds it difficult to accept the differences between the laboratory and the legislature. In the former, the goal is truth, pure and simple, without regard to changing currents of public opinion; in the latter, compromises and majorities and procedural customs and rights affect the ultimate decision as to what is right or just or good. And even when they realize this difference, most intellectuals consider their chief functions that of the critic—and politicians are sensitive to critics (possibly because we have so many of them). . . .

It seems to me that the time has come for intellectuals and politicians alike to put aside those horrible weapons of modern internecine warfare, the barbed thrust, the acid pen, and, most sinister of all, the rhetorical blast. Let us not emphasize all on which we differ but all we have in common. Let us consider not what we fear separately but what we share together.

First, I would ask both groups to recall that the American politician of today and the American intellectual of today are descended from a common ancestry. Our Nation's first great politicians were also among the Nation's first great writers and scholars. The founders of the American Constitution were also the founders of American scholarship. The works of Jefferson, Madison, Hamilton, Franklin, Paine, and John Adams—to name but a few—influenced the literature of the world as well as its geography. Books were their tools, not their enemies. Locke, Milton, Sydney, Montesquieu, Coke, and Bolingbroke were among those widely read in political circles and frequently quoted in political pamphlets. Our political leaders traded in the free commerce of ideas with lasting results both here and abroad.

In those golden years, our political leaders moved from one field to another with amazing versatility and vitality. Jefferson and Franklin still throw long shadows over many fields of learning. . . .

This link between the American scholar and the American politician remained for more than a century. Just one hundred years ago in the presidential campaign of 1856, the Republicans sent three brilliant orators around the campaign circuit: William Cullen Bryant, Henry Wadsworth Longfellow, and Ralph Waldo Emerson. Those were the carefree days when the eggheads were all Republicans. . . .

THE POLITICIAN AND THE SCHOLAR

Secondly, I would remind both groups that the American politician and the American intellectual operate within a common framework—a framework we call liberty. Freedom of expression is not divisible into political expression and intellectual expression. The lock on the door of the legislature, the Parliament, or the assembly hall—by order of the King, the Commissar, or the Fuehrer—has historically been followed or preceded by a lock on the door of the university, the library, or the print shop. And if the first blow for freedom in any subjugated land is struck by a political leader, the second is struck by a book, a newspaper, or a pamphlet.

Unfortunately, in more recent times, politicians and intellectuals have quarreled bitterly, too bitterly in some cases, over how each group has met the modern challenge to freedom both at home and abroad. Politicians have questioned the discernment with which intellectuals have reacted to the siren call of the extreme left; and intellectuals have tended to accuse politicians of not always being aware, especially here at home, of the toxic effects of freedom restrained.

While differences in judgment where freedom is endangered are perhaps inevitable, there should, nevertheless, be more basic agreement on fundamentals. In this field we should be natural allies, working more closely together for the common cause against the common enemy.

Third and finally, I would stress the great potential gain for both groups resulting from increased political cooperation.

The American intellectual and scholar today must decide, as Goethe put it, whether he is to be an anvil or a hammer. Today, for many, the stage of the anvil, at least in its formal phases, is complete. The question he faces is whether he is to be a hammer—whether he is to give to the world in which he was reared and educated the broadest possible benefits of his learning. As one who is familiar with the political world, I can testify that we need it.

For example: The password for all legislation, promoted by either party, is progress. But how do we tell what is progress and what is retreat? Those of us who may be too close to the issue, or too politically or emotionally involved in it, look for the objective word of the scholar. Indeed, the operation of our political life is such that we may not even be debating the real issues.

In foreign affairs, for example, the parties dispute over which is best fitted to implement the long-accepted policies of collective security and Soviet containment. But perhaps these policies are no longer adequate, perhaps these goals are no longer meaningful; the debate goes on nevertheless, for neither party is in a position to undertake the reappraisal necessary, particularly if the solutions presented are more complex to, and less popular with, the electorate.

Or take our agricultural program, for another example. Republicans and Democrats debate long over whether flexible or rigid price supports should be in effect. But this may not be the real issue at all —and in fact I am convinced that it is not, that neither program offers any long-range solution to our many real farm problems. The scholars and the universities might reexamine this whole area and come up with some real answers—the political parties and their conventions rarely will.

Other examples could be given indefinitely: where do we draw the line between free trade and protection; when does taxation become prohibitive; what is the most effective use we can make of our present nuclear potential? The intellectuals who can draw upon their rational disinterested approach and their fund of learning to help reshape our political life can make a tremendous contribution to their society while gaining new respect for their own group.

I do not say that our political and public life should be turned over to experts who ignore public opinion. . . .

But, I would urge that our political parties and our universities recognize the need for greater cooperation and understanding between politicians and intellectuals. We do not need scholars or politicians like Lord John Russell, of whom Queen Victoria remarked, he would be a better man if he knew a third subject—but he was interested in nothing but the constitution of 1688 and himself. What we need are men who can ride easily over broad fields of knowledge and recognize the mutual dependence of our two worlds. . . .

THE EDUCATION OF AN AMERICAN POLITICIAN

In a speech to the annual convention of the American Association of School Administrators and National School Boards Association in February of 1957, Kennedy stressed what "the world of politics needs from the world of education." He expressed concern over the reputation politicians enjoy in this world. And, as in his Harvard speech of the preceding June, he emphasized the vital role education must play in the governmental process.

As President, he showed something of what the world of politics can do with the world of education, in his legislative program as well as in his appointment of educators to work in his administration. It might, indeed, be said that both he and his appointees knew something about poetry.

. . . My announced topic for this evening was "The Education of an American Politician." It was a title which frankly I thought might stimulate some interest—for the simple reason that most Americans, including educators, are not accustomed to thinking of us politicians as educated men. We may be experienced, or cynical, or skillful, or shrewd or even fluent—but no more education is required for this kind of success than that provided by smoke-filled rooms and back-stage deals. Even those of you who are required to be elected at the polls to your post as school superintendent or school board member do not, I dare say, like to regard yourselves as politicians. You may consider yourself public servants or leaders of your community—but never politicians.

It is disheartening to me, and I think alarming for our Republic, to realize how poorly the political profession is regarded in America. Mothers may still want their favorite sons to grow up to be President but, according to a famous Gallup poll of some years ago, they do not want them to become politicians in the process. . . .

Unfortunately, this disdain for the political profession is not only shared but intensified by the educational profession. . . .

This disdain for the political profession in our schools and communities did not matter quite as much in the days when active

Congressional Record—Senate, February 21, 1957, pp. 2385–2387.

participation in the political affairs of the Nation was limited to a select few. But today, the implications of national policy necessarily make politicians of all of us. Today, every citizen, regardless of his interest in politics, holds office; every one of us is in a position of responsibility; and, in the final analysis, the kind of Government we get depends upon how we fulfill those responsibilities. We, the people, are the boss, and we will get the kind of political leadership, be it good or bad, that we demand and deserve.

Consider, for example, the changes in our Nation's role in world affairs which make it impossible to prevent the man in the street from influencing, or being influenced by, our foreign policy. In the past, public interest in and knowledge of American international commitments have reached their peak only in time of war, when extraordinary demands were made upon our manpower and material resources. Even then, war touched only indirectly the lives of many Americans. But the next world war, unlike any other, will sear the lives of every American, and bring for the first time massive death and destruction within our own borders.

Moreover, what has in the past been normal in peacetime is no more relevant to a discussion of the public's participation in politics today than it is to an analysis of current budgets or airpower requirements; for this is a peace which resembles none previously experienced. Frequent hostilities, uneasy truces, military alliances, a worldwide struggle for the minds of men and a furious armaments race characterize the war upon which we have placed the curious epithet "cold"—a struggle which will continue in our generation to maintain the same excessive wartime demands upon our lives and pocketbooks and maintain the same heightened public interest.

Thus the American politician of whom I speak today, and with whose education I am concerned, is in effect potentially each and every American citizen. His opinions, his votes, and his efforts define the limits of our policy, provide its guideposts, and authorize its implementation. In Lincoln's words, that man on the street, the average citizen, the educated voter, "makes statutes possible or impossible to execute." . . .

. . . What kind of training is necessary to prepare young Americans for a more active and enlightened role in the political affairs of their Nation? Permit me to offer a few suggestions from my vantage point in the political arena.

First, I would emphasize that we need not an overconcentration upon civic and political affairs, but the development of a broad range of talents. . . . We need . . . men with the education of Thomas Jefferson, described by a contemporary as "A gentleman of 32, who could calculate an eclipse, survey an estate, tie an artery, plan an edifice, try a cause, break a horse, dance a minuet, and play the violin." We need men like Daniel Webster, who could throw thunderbolts at Hayne on the Senate floor and then stroll a few steps down the corridor and dominate the Supreme Court as the foremost lawyer of his time; like John Quincy Adams, who, after being summarily dismissed from the Senate for a notable display of independence, could become Boylston professor [of] rhetoric and oratory at Harvard and then become a great Secretary of State. (Those were the happy days when Harvard professors had no difficulty getting Senate confirmation.) . . .

Secondly, I would emphasize that we need scholarship fitted for practical action, for something more than merely discussing political issues and deploring their solutions with learned phrases, intellectual achievements fitted for more than the delights of abstract discourse. . . .

Third, I would emphasize the importance, in teaching students about public affairs, of avoiding the confusion of political idealism with political fantasy or rigidity. We need idealism in our public life; we need young men and women who will stand for the right regardless of their personal ambitions or welfare. But let us not permit them to carry that idealism to the point of fantasy—to the point where any compromise or concession is regarded as immoral. . . .

Fourth, I would emphasize the importance, in teaching students about public affairs, of avoiding the confusion of national patriotism with national mythology. Instillation of a sense of patriotism, of national pride, of awareness of gratitude for the liberties and opportunities that are ours as Americans—these are precepts which, of course, it is hoped every student shall grasp. But at the same time let us recognize the necessity of clearing away these false axioms and myths which, however comforting to our sense of security or appealing to our sense of patriotism, impair a realistic view of our Nation's role in the world. I refer to those myths, among others, that are based upon the untouchability of national sovereignty; the existence of inherently good, bad, or backward nations; the emphasis of governmental economy over national security; or the impairment of an aggressor's power by refusing him our diplomatic recognition.

Many Americans persist in the myth that the scientific skill of the United States cannot be duplicated in any other country; that the democratic way of life, inasmuch as it is the best way, will inevitably be the victor in any struggle with an alien power; that the United States can never lose a war, or that its shores can never be attacked. Many still hold to the belief that our allies owe homage and gratitude to the United States and to all of its views at all times. There are those who believe the United States can still halt aggression by the arrival of a few American gunboats and marines. There are those who oppose assistance to or cooperation with our allies, those who reject bargaining or diplomatic pressure as a method of dealing with international disputes. Education for citizenship, for increased participation in American political life, must dispel these myths, if it is to avoid the description once furnished by Lord Bryce of a political education "sufficient to enable them to think they know something about the great problems of politics, but insufficient to show them how little they know."

Fifth and finally, I would emphasize that this kind of education requires quality as well as quantity. . . . Better trained, better paid teachers, using better techniques and textbooks, are necessary if we are to improve still further the education of our citizens for the responsibilities of citizenship. . . .

Of one thing we can be sure—the graduates of our schools and of our universities will be expected to play an increasingly important role in American political affairs. The effort and expenditure by which society has made their education possible have not been undertaken merely to give them an economic advantage in the life struggle. They are expected to offer leadership and guidance for all. It was Prince Bismarck who said that one-third of the students of German universities broke down from overwork; another third broke down from dissipation; but the other third ruled Germany. . . .

THE EDUCATION OF AN AMERICAN POLITICIAN

Those who are to be among the rulers of our land, in the sense that all thinking citizens must of necessity become political leaders, will not lack problems to which their education can be applied—increasing farm foreclosures, for example, in the midst of national prosperity—record small business failures at a time of record profits, pockets of chronic unemployment and sweat-shop wages amidst the wonders of automation, the care of the chronically and mentally ill, monopoly, race relations, taxation, international trade and, above all, the knotty complex problems of war and peace, of untangling the strife-ridden Middle East, of preventing man's eventual destruction of mankind. If those whom you send to solve these problems are truly educated politicians, . . . if they can ride easily over broad fields of knowledge, . . . then there is no limit to the contribution they can make to the society which gave them that education. . . .

I have . . . stressed to you tonight the assistance which the world of politics needs from the world of education; and to that end I ask your thoughtful attention to the task of uniting our two worlds still further.

"Don't teach my boy poetry," an English mother recently wrote the provost of Harrow. "Don't teach my boy poetry; he is going to stand for Parliament." Well, perhaps she was right, but if more politicians knew poetry, and more poets knew politics, I am convinced the world would be a little better place to live on this 19th of February, 1957.

On the tenth anniversary of the United States National Student Association's founding, Senator Kennedy sent a message of greeting to the young men and women of the organization—a confederation of student governments of colleges and universities throughout the country. Kennedy recognized that the membership of NSA is deeply concerned with the great issues of our times and that as an organization it is politically and socially active.

The association has not only done much to stimulate the student community's interest in national and international affairs, but has provided a valued and time-tested institutional framework by means of which students throughout the country can make their valuable contribution to the life of the nation. From the ranks of those who have been active in the association has come a most outstanding group of young men and women who are already shouldering major responsibilities in journalism, law, politics and the sciences. The nation is indebted to the National Student Association for its contribution to our national life. My sincere hope is that you will continue to meet the challenges of our times in the same forthright and courageous spirit as you have during the past ten years.

American Student—Profile and Promise (Philadelphia: United States National Student Association, [1957]), p. 16.

EDUCATION AND THE COLD WAR

Speaking at the Maryland State Teachers' Association convention on October 10, 1957, Kennedy compared the Senate to a classroom. In his opinion, the future of the United States depends far more on the work done in the classroom than on that done by the Senate. He noted that the needs of the Cold War demand knowledge as never before and that the Soviet Union produces more engineers and scientists than the United States and Western Europe together. He concluded that the survival of the free world depends in large part on the success of the teaching profession in the next thirty years.

I am deeply honored that you have asked me to meet with you today on this occasion of such importance to the future of your profession, your State and your nation. I come to you today as a refugee from a very exclusive public school known as the United States Senate. There the course of instruction is often difficult, the recesses all too rare and the recitation so lengthy that the entire class is frequently kept after school. There are, moreover, two major difficulties to this school on Capitol Hill: first, it is not always possible to tell the teachers from the students; and, secondly, while many mothers are clamoring to have their children admitted to the school, no student ever wants to graduate. . . .

But however important a role the Senate may play in our national life, I think I can say without resorting to exaggeration that I feel privileged to be here today before one of the most influential gatherings in the country. Your influence is not in bombs or wealth or national fame; nor is it dependent upon political parties, pressure groups or sheer force of numbers. But the fact remains that you and your associates in the teaching profession will in the long run have more to say about the future of this country and the world than any of these—not on the battlefield, not in the council room, but in the classroom. We the people of America have entrusted into your hands the future leaders of this nation, the most powerful nation on earth—

The Maryland Teacher (November, 1957), pp. 15, 35.

and the way in which you fulfill this trust, in guidance and direction which you give to America's youth, will have a more profound effect on our national future than perhaps any decision we may make in the Senate.

All of you are familiar with the motto credited to Francis Bacon, but actually traceable back to ancient scriptures, that reads: "Knowledge is power—Nam et ipsa scientia potestas est." No doubt that slogan has appeared on many a school or teachers' college bulletin board. But now this truism is truer than ever before, a statement that sums up volumes of prose about the cold war. Which nation has the scientific personnel and know-how to develop the first so-called "clean" atomic bomb for tactical use—the first earth satellite—the first intercontinental ballistic missile? How long will the West retain its lead in productivity and living standards—to what extent can it export to its less wealthy friends the capital, the technical assistance, the skills and other knowledge they need? The answers to these questions over the long run are in your hands. We no longer complacently believe that the educational and scientific capabilities of this country cannot be duplicated elsewhere. We recognize that the race for advantage in the Cold War is not only a competition of armaments, production, ideology, propaganda and diplomacy but a race of education and research as well.

The advantages which will enable the United States to win the race, however, whether they take the form of better proximity fuses or the new hybrid seed corns, which recently won us friends behind the Iron Curtain, will not instantly spring up in the hour they are required. There is a lag of from five to ten years between the results of fundamental research and the practical application of those results; before that research takes place, several years of training and experience are required; and even before that, the mind of the future scientist must be properly molded and stimulated by his elementary and secondary school teacher.

Recent Soviet advancements—including the first earth satellite, an intercontinental ballistic missile, a new hydrogen explosion and others —all point up how critical this race has become. The Soviet Union already has available for this work more engineers and scientists than we presently have in any capacity in this country, and very nearly as

EDUCATION AND THE COLD WAR

many as this country and Western Europe combined. In recent years, the output of new engineers and scientists in the U.S.S.R. has surpassed that of the total United States and Western Europe graduating classes in these fields—their current enrollment of such students in institutions of higher education exceeds our own—and we are already falling far short of even our current needs. Their lead may become even more serious, and in the most critical areas of technical knowledge within the next decade, according to Allen Dulles of the CIA, "unless we quickly take new measures to increase our facilities for scientific education."

It is apparent, too that this lead is not merely one of numbers, but of quality as well. A special study concluded by the Joint Atomic Energy Committee of the Congress concluded that "the training given Soviet engineers and scientists is of a high order and compares favorably with the best in the United States and Europe."

The same study pointed up the responsibility of our public school systems in this area. The teaching of physical sciences and mathematics in our secondary schools has declined; about half of those with talent in these fields who graduate from high school are either unable or uninterested in going to college; and of the half who enter college, scarcely 40% graduate. The task of reversing these disturbing trends is in large measure up to our public schools and their teachers.

In short, our position in the world and our hopes for survival ten, twenty or thirty years from now depend in large measure upon the kind of education which you in the teaching profession are able to offer your pupils today.

But we need something more than a nation of scientists and technicians—something more than an arsenal of super-weapons and ingenious inventions. We must have men and women capable of leading the "free world," of making the hard and unpopular decisions necessary to preserve world peace and national security. In our concern over the education of more scientists and engineers for the future America, we dare not neglect its politicians. . . .

Under our form of government, we must put our ultimate faith in ordinary men, not machines or experts. In the words of Thomas Jefferson: "If we think them not enlightened enough to exercise their control with a wholesome discretion, [then] the remedy is not to take it from them—but to inform their discretion by education."

"To inform their discretion by education"—that is your task, and the task of every teacher in every city and village in America. The students of today who may discourage you, harass you, and hopefully sometimes cheer you include the leaders and diplomats of tomorrow. . . .

ASSISTANCE FOR SCHOOL CONSTRUCTION

> Introducing a bill providing assistance to public schools for classroom construction, Senator Kennedy spoke of the serious national shortage of classrooms. The bill, S. 3179, was introduced on January 28, 1958. It provided grant assistance to the states, federal financing of bond issues, and federal credit assistance to state agencies established for school financing.
>
> The Senate never acted on S. 3179.

Mr. President, I am introducing today a bill to authorize Federal assistance to the States and local communities in the financing of public-school construction. . . .

This bill . . . emphasizes the traditional concept of State and local responsibility, strongly forbids any Federal control, requires maximum effort on the part of the States and local school districts and recognizes that the emergency role of the Federal Government is a temporary one. It provides for a minimum program designed to give assistance to those areas in most critical need of help, through matching grants totaling $300 million a year for 5 years, allocated according to the size of each State's school-age population, and supplemented by Federal purchase of school bonds and loans to State school-financing agencies. The $300 million figure is a rockbottom minimum, which is set that low only on the assumption that other pending measures will make additional funds available to our hard-pressed schools.

Three hundred million dollars is, quite obviously, the minimum figure. I believe it should be more. But I am introducing the bill as reported by the House, in the hope that in our concentration today on scholarships, which I do not really think represent the primary need in education, we will not lose sight of the necessity for developing facilities on the public school and college levels, which I believe in the next 10 years will be the major crisis facing education.

John Fitzgerald Kennedy—A Compendium of Speeches, Statements, and Remarks Delivered During His Service in the Congress of the United States, 88th Congress, 2nd Session, Senate Document No. 79, pp. 575–577.

ASSISTANCE FOR SCHOOL CONSTRUCTION

. . . Official Office of Education figures, which most experts deem to be on the conservative side, showed our Nation's schools to be short 140,400 classrooms now—that another 44,000 will be needed next year to take care of still higher enrollments—and that another 14,000 to 20,000 are needed each year to replace outmoded and obsolete buildings, firetraps, and health hazards. School enrollment having already increased some 50 per cent in the last decade, it is significant to note that the largest increase this year was concentrated in the elementary schools, a warning to the Nation that this need must be met for many years to come. Already nearly a million boys and girls are being deprived by the classroom shortage of full-time schooling, and hundreds of thousands more held back in classes of unwieldy size.

In October, the advent of the space age awakened all Americans to the critical importance of improving our educational system from the bottom up. And at year's end, the difficult fiscal position of the State and local authorities—who are spending at the rate of nearly $3 billion a year constructing some 70,800 classrooms without eliminating the shortage—made it clear that the Federal Government, with its far greater as well as more effective means of raising public revenues, could not avoid its responsibility to meet this nationwide problem. . . .

CAN THE PROBLEM BE DEFERRED?

The President, who together with other administration spokesmen thoroughly documented 1 year ago the urgent need for Federal action on the growing classroom shortage, has decided this year to abandon the school construction program. It is, he asserts, merely being deferred in favor of a new postsputnik emphasis on educating scientists.

But how can the solution to a critical problem which increases in magnitude each year be deferred, as though the overflow children could stay at home until their case comes up for consideration again? The school population 1 year from now will be even greater; more old schools will be condemned, obsolete, or rendered unusable; and State and local authorities will be even more hard pressed to finance additional classrooms. Congress cannot ignore or forget the classroom shortage by deferring action on it. We can only worsen it.

ASSISTANCE FOR SCHOOL CONSTRUCTION

MORE SCHOLARSHIPS OR MORE CLASSROOMS?

The administration's program and other new proposals in the field of education are intended to increase the production of American scientists to offset the Russian lead in this area. I welcome these proposals and share their objective. But scientifically inclined students do not spring up overnight to apply for special college scholarships or even to receive improved high school instruction. Additional aptitude tests may identify more such students but they will not produce them. The real shaping of the scientific mind, as Dr. Teller and others have emphasized, begins on the grade school and junior high school level—before the student is 12 years old, according to Dr. Teller. Yet this is the very kind of careful, thorough instruction that suffers most in an overcrowded classroom too jammed to permit any individual assistance. It is necessarily neglected in schools operating on a part-time shift that permits no extra effort for talented pupils. It is the kind of instruction that is not usually available to students collected in outmoded, unequipped, or dangerous classrooms. It is not enough merely to increase through scholarships and fellowships the number of poorly trained high school graduates who go on to our already overcrowded colleges. We shall not measurably improve the production of scientists at the college level, in short, unless we begin at the bottom instead of the top.

Moreover, even in the high schools, the improved teaching of science and mathematics expected to result from the new administration proposals will not fulfill its goals without additional classroom construction. Of what avail are new techniques and better materials in a classroom too crowded to enable concentration, too unsafe to permit various experiments, too unsightly to attract good teachers? We shall compete with the Russians in science education at the graduate level only when we solve the classroom shortage at every public school level.

Finally, are we concerned only with the production of scientists, mathematicians, engineers, and foreign-language specialists? Recognizing our serious handicaps in those areas, are we not in equally urgent need of improving the education of all Americans—the diplomats and politicians who must make the hard decisions of the cold war, the judges and educators and writers who must carry on the American way in its hour of greatest challenge, the citizens of every occupation and status who will decide, in the last analysis, whether we stand or fall as a nation? More and better educated scientists cannot alone save the United States today. All American education is in crisis. This bill is aimed at attacking that crisis at its roots. Let us hope it is not already too late. . . .

RESPONSIBILITY FOR EDUCATION

In an article written for the *NEA Journal* in 1958, Kennedy questioned the capability of our educational system to meet effectively the demands of our role in the modern world. He proposed federal, state, and local cooperation to bolster flagging efforts to improve education, urging federal assistance with control remaining at the local level. In addition, he advocated better and more classrooms and improved standards for attracting and retaining the most effective teachers. He cited the tremendous need for all to share in advancing education, thus guaranteeing the nation's security and future.

Crucial questions confront America today: Will we provide world leadership or display fatal weakness? Will we succeed or fail in the struggle for survival during the years to come?

The answers, I sincerely believe, depend on whether our educational system is capable of meeting the challenge of today or whether a shortage of teachers, classrooms, and money—with a consequent lack of high-quality education—will prove in the long run to be the undoing of our nation.

That public education is in a state of crisis today is well known. There is less agreement on the cause and the cure. I only hope that those who recognize the urgent need of improving public education in this country will not exhaust their efforts in looking for a scapegoat but will join in attacking the problem at its very roots.

The responsibility for ending this crisis, in my opinion, must be shared at three levels—federal, state, and local.

First, the federal government, which has far greater, as well as more effective, means for raising public revenues, has an unavoidable responsibility to enact promptly a bold and imaginative program of federal assistance to the states and to local school districts for the construction of public schools, leaving all direction of academic content and standards, of course, in local hands.

Our teachers cannot be expected to fulfill their critical respon-

"The Fate of the Nation." *NEA Journal*, XLVII (January, 1958), pp. 10–11.

sibilities when nearly a million boys and girls are deprived by the classroom shortage of full-time schooling, and when hundreds of thousands more are held back in unwieldy classes of 40 or more. We need this year additional classrooms to meet the requirements of several million more pupils than we presently have adequate room for in our elementary and secondary schools.

The valiant efforts of state and local authorities, which spent over $2.5 billion in school construction during the last school year, must be supplemented by federal action to meet this nation-wide crisis.

But more and better classrooms are not enough. More and better teachers are also needed—better trained, better paid, better utilized. Here the state and local authorities share responsibility.

Our state governments must provide teachers colleges that attract the best students and provide the best education. Some states still have too many teachers colleges, which are, as a result, too small, too poorly financed and staffed, and too ill equipped in terms of physical plant, libraries, laboratories, and other facilities.

Authorities on the state level could also take steps to improve teacher certification, re-examining outmoded statutory requirements, maintaining and gradually elevating minimum standards, and providing for those who become certificated a sense of accomplishment and prestige comparable to that felt by candidates admitted to the legal and medical professions.

Finally, a large measure of responsibility for improving the quality of teaching in our schools rests with local school boards and school administrators.

Not as a United States Senator, but as an interested citizen, I would respectfully suggest that present methods for recruiting teachers be improved in order to attract the best students, to select the best graduates, and to compete in the labor market with the expertly developed recruitment methods of American business.

Although the figure is too staggering to comprehend fully, the fact is that our schools must recruit in the next three years alone almost three quarters of a million new teachers—more than our entire school system contained not too long ago.

Once teachers are recruited and hired, more can be done to improve the methods of teacher promotion. We must find better means for providing better rewards for our better teachers, we must make actual use of probationary periods to retain only those with satisfactory performance records, and we must demonstrate concretely to young beginners in the field that real opportunities for advancement await those whose contribution is of the highest caliber.

More can be done, also, in terms of better teacher utilization—by removing burdensome administrative details and paper work that might better be done by electronic computers or by parent volunteers.

And perhaps most important, school boards, school patrons, and all of our citizens must cooperate in the effort to achieve better teachers' salaries. No profession of such importance in the United States today is so poorly paid. No other occupational group in the country is asked to do so much for so little.

No amount of new classrooms, television, training, and recruitment techniques can attract and retain good teachers as long as their salaries are beneath the responsibility and dignity of their position. We pay the average railway conductor nearly twice as much as we pay the teacher who conducts our elementary classes. Plumbers, plasterers, and steamfitters are paid more for improving our homes than we pay teachers for improving our children.

Help from the federal level for more and better classrooms; help from the state level for better teachers colleges and better teacher certification; help from the local level for better salaries and for better recruitment, promotion, and utilization of teachers—those are the goals toward which must move all who recognize that upon education rests the fate of the nation. . . .

"Knowledge is power." . . . It is also light. In the dark and despairing days ahead, our youth shall need all the light the teaching profession can bring to bear upon the future.

In his book, *One Man's America,* Alistair Cooke tells a story which illustrates my point. On May 19, 1780, as he describes it, in Hartford, Connecticut, the skies at noon turned from blue to gray "and by mid-afternoon had blackened over so densely that, in that religious age, men fell on their knees and begged a final blessing before the end came.

"The Connecticut House of Representatives was in session. And as some men fell down [in the darkened chamber] and others clamored for an immediate adjournment, the Speaker of the House, one Colonel

Davenport, came to his feet. And he silenced the din with these words: 'The Day of Judgment is either approaching or it is not. If it is not, there is no cause for adjournment. If it is, I choose to be found doing my duty. I wish, therefore, that candles may be brought.' "

Today, all of us who hope for future peace and security must look to the teachers of America as we ask that "candles may be brought" to light the way ahead.

FEDERAL FUNDS FOR PRIVATE SCHOOLS

American politics before 1960 had never accepted a Catholic in the nation's highest political office. As the 1960 campaign approached, the issue was hotly debated. Kennedy, as a Catholic and as a front-running candidate, made his position known on several occasions. In a *Look* article, he said, "Whatever one's religion in his private life may be, for the officeholder, nothing takes precedence over his oath to uphold the Constitution and all its parts—including the First Amendment and the strict separation of church and state." He then went on to comment on federal funds for private schools.

The First Amendment to the Constitution is an infinitely wise one. There can be no question of Federal funds being used for support of parochial or private schools. It's unconstitutional under the First Amendment as interpreted by the Supreme Court. I'm opposed to the Federal Government's extending support to sustain any church or its schools. As for such fringe matters as buses, lunches and other services, the issue is primarily social and economic and not religious. Each case must be judged on its merits within the law as interpreted by the courts.

"Democratic Forecast: A Catholic in 1960." *Look*, XXIII (March 3, 1959), 17.

THE EDUCATIONAL DEVELOPMENT OF AFRICA

Speaking at Wesleyan University, Lincoln, Nebraska (while chairman of the Senate Foreign Relations Subcommittee on Africa), Kennedy emphasized the importance of education to the development of the newly independent African states. He had often predicted—and would continue to do so—that without a sound and open educational system the United States could never fully realize its potential; here, he suggested that the African nations must recognize the same importance of education in their growth. He felt that Americans have a definite responsibility to help and that indifference would lead to African disenchantment with independence that could have severe repercussions for both Africans and Americans.

Regardless of what Africa has been in truth or in myth, she will be that no longer. Call it nationalism, call it anticolonialism, call it what you will, Africa is going through a revolution.

Africans want a higher standard of living. Seventy-five per cent of the population now lives by subsistence agriculture. They want opportunity to manage and benefit directly from the resources in, on, and under their land. They want to govern their own affairs believing that political freedom is the precondition to economic and social development. Most of all, they want education—for education is in their eyes the backbone to gaining and maintaining the political institutions they want. Education is the means to personal and national prestige. Education is, in truth, the only way to genuine African independence and progress.

I believe that most Americans are sympathetic to these desires of the African people. After all, it was in our schools that some of the most renowned African leaders learned about the dignity and equality of men, and saw in practice the virtues of representative government, widespread education, and economic opportunity. These are the ideas and ideals that have caused a revolution—a largely bloodless revolution, but no less far reaching for that.

The Strategy of Peace, edited by Allan Nevins (New York: Harper & Row, 1960), pp. 130–132. The speech was delivered on October 13, 1959.

THE EDUCATIONAL DEVELOPMENT OF AFRICA

But having been the catalyst to many of these changes, do we see the implications to ourselves? We cannot simply sit by and watch on the sidelines. There are no sidelines. Under the laws of physics, in order to maintain the same relative position to a moving body, one cannot stand still. As others change, so must we, if we wish to maintain our relative political or economic position.

The African peoples believe that the science, technology, and education available in the modern world can overcome their struggle for existence. They believe that their poverty, squalor, ignorance, and disease can be conquered. This is their quest and their faith. To us the challenge is not one of preserving our wealth and our civilization—it is one of extension. Actually, they are the same challenge. To preserve, we must extend. And if the scientific, technical, and educational benefits of the West cannot be extended to all the world, our status will be preserved only with great difficulty—for the balance of power is shifting, shifting into the hands of the two-thirds of the world's people who want to share what the one-third has already taken for granted. Within 10 years, for example, African nations alone may control 25 per cent of all U.N. votes.

To thus extend ourselves will require a political decision. But such a decision will take economic and educational forms. For what Africa needs and wants first is education, to know how to develop the resources and run the industries and administer the government; and second, capital, for without the initial capital—to develop the resources and spur the trade—they will never generate sufficient capital themselves to provide for expanding services and development. An initial injection of capital, personnel to train others, and scholarship opportunities is necessary to start this spiral on its way.

As chairman of the Senate Foreign Relations Subcommittee on Africa, I have proposed that we in the United States establish an Educational Development Fund for Africa, and that, in cooperation with many nations, there should be established a multinational Economic Development Fund for Africa. These, or better proposals to accomplish the same purposes, must be carried through while the initiative for constructive and peaceful action is still open to us.

If African progress falters because of lack of capital and education, if these new states and emerging peoples turn bitter in their taste of independence, then the reason will be that the Western powers, by indifference or lack of imagination, have failed to see that it is their own future that is also at stake. As economist Barbara Ward stated it, "The profoundest matter at stake in Africa is the quality and capacity of Western society itself." Will we accept this challenge—or will it be that some future historian will say of us, as of previous civilizations, that "where there is no vision the people perish"?

COLLEGE LOYALTY OATHS

Opposing the loyalty oath provision of the National Defense Education Act, Kennedy pointed out that loyalty cannot be legislated: Communists will not hesitate to take the oath if it will advance their cause; many loyal individuals will refuse to take it on the basis of principle. The Senator was concerned for the overall success of NDEA should the oath not be repealed. In addition, he expressed anxiety about the effect the oath requirement would have on those who refused to sign, and the danger it would have of legislating orthodoxy in our colleges and universities.

As President, Kennedy achieved his ambition to have modified the oath and disclaimer provisions of the NDEA. See pp. 151–152.

In 1776, Benjamin Franklin—fully aware of the risk—decided to entrust secret plans of the American Revolution to a French agent. He believed the man's word of honor that even British torture would never wring these facts from him. What more could he ask? "He would have given me his oath for it," Franklin reported to the Continental Congress, "if I laid stress upon oaths. But I have never regarded them otherwise than as the last recourse of liars."

Franklin knew that many an American agent had hypocritically taken the new British oath of allegiance. On the other hand, he knew that little could be expected from those colonists with Tory sympathies who had been compelled by their crusading neighbors to take oaths supporting the Revolution.

Unfortunately the American nation born in that year of divided loyalties has rarely heeded Ben Franklin's sage advice. In times of crisis to the state—times of war, insurrection or suspected subversion—both Federal and state governments have repeatedly sought some swift, convenient and reassuring means of publicly identifying and compelling citizen loyalty. Elaborate loyalty oaths and affidavits—going far beyond the simple pledge of allegiance or the oath to uphold and defend the Constitution—have inevitably been the answer.

"Let's Get Rid of College Loyalty Oaths!" *Coronet* (April, 1960), pp. 89–94. Reprinted by permission of Esquire, Inc. © 1960 By Esquire, Inc.

But there is no evidence that they have ever contributed substantially to the security of the nation.

Yet overzealous patriots keep trying to legislate loyalty. The latest example of this is the case of the National Defense Education Act of 1958, which contains a welcome program for student loans.

Many bright students, whose talents this nation needs to develop in competing with the Soviets, require financial assistance to continue their studies. But today, if those needy students attend Harvard, Yale, Mills, Grinnell, Sarah Lawrence, Oberlin, Swarthmore and a dozen or so other schools—including some of our best science laboratories—they *cannot* obtain a Federal loan.

These colleges and universities are refusing to participate in the loan program. They need the money—they know their students need the money—but they refuse to administer one of the bill's strangest provisions: a section which requires every student, teacher, scientist or other scholar applying for a loan to not only sign the customary oath of allegiance, but also to sign a vague, sweeping affidavit declaring that he does not *believe in* or support any organization which *believes in* or teaches the overthrow of the Government by illegal methods.

How can our universities police this affidavit they find so distasteful and humiliating? How can they investigate what organizations their students might "believe in," and what those organizations believe? If a student does not belong to a subversive organization, might not his beliefs still be contrary to the affidavit? Which methods of overthrowing the Government are illegal and which are not?

No one can quarrel with the principle that all Americans should be loyal citizens and should be willing to swear allegiance to our country. But this is quite different from a doctrine which singles out students—and only those students who need to borrow money to continue their education—as a group which must sign a rather vague affidavit as to their *beliefs* as well as their *acts*.

Congress appeared, on the one hand, in this Act to recognize that our students and teachers were one of our greatest assets in the cold war, our hope for the future—but then, in the same Act, to single them out for scorn and suspicion in a demonstration of no confidence. An *affirmative* oath of allegiance may be understandable—but the *negative* disclaimer is at variance with the declared purposes of the Act. It adds a needless barrier to many prospective students. More and more of our leading colleges and universities are refusing to participate in the loan program because of it.

The president of Wisconsin State College calls it "unnecessary and distasteful." Father Michael J. Walsh, the president of Boston College, says it "represents a lack of confidence in the youth of the country." Mills College in California would not accept these funds because this section "invades the privacy and questions the integrity of individual belief." President Nathan M. Pusey of Harvard called it "vague in intent, useless in effect, inappropriate in context and insulting to the very group the Congress seeks to encourage." Oberlin College in Ohio declined all loans under the program because, its president stated, "it cannot compromise its historical devotion to freedom of expression and belief."

In introducing a bill to repeal this provision last year, I called it "a futile gesture to the memory of an earlier age." Between the end of World War II and the end of the Korean War, a rising tide of fear and suspicion engulfed many Americans. The detection of Communist agents and the erection of new standards of loyalty and security were no longer left to responsible authorities. Neighbors, fellow workers, faculty members, Federal employees, friends—anyone might turn out to be "Red" (or said to be by someone). Easy answers and convenient scapegoats were sought—and provided—in a troubled time when the answers (How did the Russians get the bomb? Why did we lose China?) were not easy.

But one easy answer was the oath. Those who took it were loyal; those who refused were not. What could be simpler? And so countless hundreds of new oaths sprang up, administered by Federal, state and local bodies; oaths for school teachers, oaths for notary publics, oaths for professors, students and scientists and, in one state, a loyalty oath for professional wrestlers.

Finally, the furor died down—the atmosphere changed. Senator Joseph R. McCarthy of Wisconsin departed from the scene and the American people turned their attention from oaths of loyalty to the more positive tasks necessary for strengthening our national security.

But in the summer of 1958, one relic of this earlier era crept into the National Defense Education Act.

The historical background of this kind of special oath is not confined to the recent era of hate and suspicion.

The first soldier in Washington's army to hang for treason—in a plot to capture the Continental Congress—had sworn to two special oaths of loyalty.

During the Civil War when Congress extended special oath-taking to itself, the only result was the resignation of a loyal but indignant Senator from Delaware, James A. Bayard. Another reluctant oathtaker, a civil servant in the Census Bureau whom a Congressional Committee had cited for disloyal feelings, enlisted in the Union Army and lost his sight at Gettysburg; while another Federal employee, when apprehended for disloyal conduct and asked about his oath, replied: "I could take 500,000 such oaths, as they amount to nothing."

In the post World War I era, New York's famous Lusk Laws included oaths among other special tests of teacher loyalty. But after only two years they were repealed, dismissed teachers were reinstated and Governor Al Smith called the laws "repugnant to the fundamentals of American democracy."

Nearly 2,000,000 W.P.A. workers were required to swear their loyalty in the unsettled days prior to World War II, before they could pick up their tools and rakes. After the war, when the Taft-Hartley Act required special non-Communist affidavits from union leaders, Harry Bridges took the oath—but John L. Lewis, a fighting anti-Communist, would not. Among the Federally employed scientists working on secret weapons projects who took a special oath was David Greenglass, convicted atomic spy.

This is hardly historical justification for the imposition of a special oath on student loan applicants today. And the history of special oaths in other lands should also have taught us a lesson. The student affidavit of disbelief is directly descended from the hated test oaths imposed centuries ago by successive contenders for the British crown. Under Charles II, for example, no one could teach at a university or school without taking an Anglican oath—and also an oath that the earlier oath imposed by Oliver Cromwell was unlawful! Article VI of our own Constitution reflected the fear of religious test oaths which had driven many to these shores.

In the 1930s our universities benefited from Italian professors fleeing Mussolini's requirement that all faculty members take a special oath stating that their teaching would be aimed at instilling devotion "to the Fascist regime."

The tragic fact is—as the history of loyalty oaths demonstrates—that the affidavit will not keep Communists or other subversives out of the student loan program. Card-carrying members of the Communist party will have no hesitancy about perjuring themselves in the affidavit. I am proud as a United States Senator to reaffirm my own pledge to uphold the Constitution and Flag. But I regard a special affidavit as to a person's beliefs—imposed on average citizens who have no special position of trust—as a wholly meaningless, impractical weapon against real subversives. This is particularly so when they are singled out because they cannot afford the tuition their classmates can afford.

The only students who are adversely affected by this discriminatory provision are honest, non-Communist students—including:

(a) students who attend universities that refuse to participate in this program;

(b) students who feel they cannot execute the oath and affidavit for reasons of religion or conscience;

(c) students who resent the requirement or consider it an unnecessary limitation on their academic freedom;

(d) students who are overapprehensive in their interpretation of the affidavit or unnecessarily fearful of some official's interpretation.

It is all very well to ask: "Why not sign, if you're not guilty?" Most students will sign. Most universities will participate. Those who reject loans may be dismissed by some as overconscientious or as eccentrics, non-conformists and chronic dissenters. But I thought the purpose of this Act was to attract into scientific and other vital pursuits the best talents of the country, the most inquiring minds, the most thoughtful students. How can we if we exclude the overconscientious, the eccentrics, the non-conformists and the chronic dissenters? What is the purpose of a provision that in operation could result in some Communists getting loans and some non-Communists dropping out of school—in some talented, needy students being included but some equally talented, equally needy—and equally loyal—students being left out?

There is a very real danger that this unnecessary, futile gesture toward the memory of an earlier age will defeat the purposes of the National Defense Education Act. Unlike the Soviets, we cannot take steps to keep our brightest minds *in* scientific careers—but we might take steps that keep them *out.*

Early in the last session of Congress, I introduced and conducted hearings upon a bill to repeal this provision. But after two days of Senate debate—sometimes bitter, often confused—the bill was recommitted, dead for the session.

Another attempt to eliminate the affidavit will be made this year— this time emphasizing that it is the vague, sweeping, negative affidavit that is most objectionable and discriminatory. That may satisfy those who opposed us last year, who could not understand why the customary affirmative pledge of allegiance should not be taken by all students as a positive act of rededication.

But it will not satisfy those who want the negative affidavit retained, who insist that only subversives would oppose signing it, who criticize institutions refusing to participate, on the grounds they are denying aid to needy students merely to demonstrate abstract theories of academic freedom—and those who shrug off non-participants with the reply that there are other colleges and students eager to get the money. This is a minor issue, they say, raised by a few "eggheads" and unrealistic professors.

But if this affidavit remains on the statute books, we will have cause for concern. *First:* I will be concerned about the chances for success of the entire National Defense Education program, with some of our leading science-trained institutions and best-known colleges refusing to participate. These colleges need the additional source of scholarship money—all colleges do, as enrollments and costs increase faster than available funds. But they also know that once they accept this precedent of Federal dictation as to the beliefs of their scholarship or loan applicants, a tradition of American education will have been shattered.

These colleges, training future atomic scientists in their laboratories, do not want to protect Communists—but they know that any

COLLEGE LOYALTY OATHS

Communist will gladly take any number of oaths. They cannot understand why a prosperous freshman is assumed to be loyal, but—if his financial needs become more pressing so that a Federal loan is required —he suddenly becomes suspect in his sophomore year. And why is a less talented student, ineligible for a Federal loan, permitted in the laboratory without question—while a more talented student is denied entry unless he executes a vague affidavit which he may not accept or even understand.

To waste desperately needed educational funds trying to administer this kind of provision is the height of folly.

Secondly: I would be concerned about those students who did sign the affidavit. We want their minds to be free and flexible, searching out new ideas and trying out new principles. But a young student who has sworn—under penalty of a Federal indictment for perjury— as to what he privately believes (and what he thinks some organization he believes in believes) is likely to be rather cautious about changing his beliefs or joining new organizations. Other students may feel that Federal inquiry into their beliefs is so unrealistic as to be meaningless —and, in their minds, oaths of allegiance as well as sworn affidavits will be dangerously cheapened.

Perhaps a few perjurers will be caught under this requirement. But we already have enough anti-Communist, anti-sedition and anti-espionage statutes to catch these few students, if any, without damaging—in the minds of millions of other students—their respect for free inquiry and free government.

If William Penn or Benjamin Franklin or Henry Thoreau attended college in America today, I doubt that they would sign this affidavit, despite their great loyalty to this country. And our effort to develop the best minds of the country needs all the Penns and Franklins and Thoreaus we can attract.

Finally: I would be concerned, if we cannot eliminate this provision, about the U.S.A. Never before have we tried to legislate orthodoxy in our colleges, sought to put students in jeopardy for their private beliefs or assumed a scholar is disloyal until he swears to the contrary.

Surely this is not the way to "catch up" with the new Russian excellence in education, science and research—by imitating their objective of teaching students *what* to think instead of *how* to think. What kind of security is it that assumes all is well because thousands of affidavits are signed: do we really believe that loyalty can be reduced to an automatic formula, coerced and compelled instead of inspired?

I think it high time that we recalled the words of Mr. Justice Hugo L. Black: "Loyalty to the United States can never be secured by the endless proliferation of loyalty oaths. Loyalty must arise spontaneously from the hearts of people who love their country and respect their government."

TWO

THE CAMPAIGN 1960

"THE KEY TO OUR FUTURE"

While campaigning for the Presidency, Kennedy summarized a four-point program to meet the education crisis in the United States: an extensive construction program for public schools and colleges; an increase in teachers' salaries; a scholarship program; and an expansion of basic research in the government, universities, and private laboratories.

. . . In a time when education is the key to our future—in a time when science, languages, and a whole host of other studies are essential to our prestige and our security—this Nation is short 50,000 teachers. This Nation is short 132,000 classrooms. This Nation requires hundreds of thousands of students to go to school on a part-time, swing-shift basis. And this Nation has found no way to enable more than 150,000 of our brightest students to go on to college when their families are not able to afford it.

When we neglect education, we neglect the Nation. It is difficult to realize that roughly one out of every five young men fails to pass the Selective Service mental test. It is difficult to realize that some 50 per cent of our high school and college graduates, in a recent survey, could not identify the Bill of Rights—and only one out of three could list one advantage of our economic system over that of the Soviet Union.

It is time to realize that we are faced with New Frontiers in education. The old system of financing schools primarily from property taxes is no longer sufficient. The old attitudes toward teachers and teachers' colleges, diminishing the quality of that honored profession, can no longer prevail. The old philosophy of leaving the financing of

"Remarks made by Senator John F. Kennedy in Eugene, Ore., Courthouse Square, September 7, 1960 (Advance release text)." In *Freedom of Communications: Final Report of the Committee on Commerce, United States Senate, Prepared by its Subcommittee of the Subcommittee on Communications, Pursuant to S. Res. 305, 86th Congress* (hereafter cited as *Freedom of Communications*), *Part I: The Speeches, Remarks, Press Conferences, and Statements of Senator John F. Kennedy, August 1 through November 7, 1960.* S. Rept. 994, Pt. 1, 87th Congress, 1st Session (Washington, D.C.: Government Printing Office, 1961), pp. 996–998.

"THE KEY TO OUR FUTURE"

public school education to State and local taxpayers, and the financing of college education principally to parents, is no longer sufficient.

It is time for action in public education—not for Federal control —not for Federal replacement of local effort—but for emergency Federal action to help halt the decline in American education.

First. We must launch a massive construction program for both our public schools and our colleges—to make up our present shortage, and to prepare for the coming wave of new students.

A recent Government survey found that one school building in five was a potential firetrap. Another one in five was a borderline case. We urgently need Federal grants to aid State construction programs.

On the college level, our need for new buildings in the next 10 years will equal all the structures built on all U.S. campuses since the American Revolution. By a system of loans and matching grants, not only dormitory facilities, but also classrooms, libraries, and laboratories must be provided.

Second. Federal aid to education should include funds for [teachers'] salaries. . . .

Third. We must create a sizable and effective scholarship program. And the place to begin is to restore the Federal-State college scholarship program that was dropped from the National Defense Education Act. That would assist at least 20,000 of our best high school students to go on to a college education they could not otherwise afford —and we as a Nation cannot afford any other policy.

Fourth. We must expand our support of basic research—in the Government—in the universities—in private laboratories. For only in this way can we push back the New Frontier of knowledge. We have enough gimmicks and gadgets for the present—now we need new concepts of man and matter for the future.

The Democratic candidate's appearance before the Greater Houston Ministerial Association was one of the high points of the 1960 campaign. Fears of Vatican influence and qualms about the Catholic faith in general had worked to exclude many Roman Catholics from running for the Presidency. The Democratic Party had tried but failed to destroy the political taboo in 1928; the Republican Party had never challenged the unwritten law. The Democrats were ready for another try in 1960 when they nominated John Kennedy. From the outset of the campaign, Kennedy realized that the religious issue must be confronted directly and frankly. Before the Ministerial Association his approach was one of complete candor. He made it clear that, if elected, his religious convictions would never conflict with his Presidential obligations and responsibilities; that should there be a conflict he would resign from the Presidency.

. . . I believe in an America where the separation of church and state is absolute—where no Catholic prelate would tell the President (should he be Catholic) how to act, and no Protestant minister would tell his parishioners for whom to vote—where no church or church school is granted any public funds or political preference. . . .

"Speech of Senator John F. Kennedy, Greater Houston Ministerial Association, Rice Hotel, Houston, Texas, Monday Evening, September 12, 1960." *Freedom of Communications*, I, 208.

EDUCATION FOR AFRICAN FREEDOM

Speaking about the large number of African leaders gathered for the opening of the 1960 General Assembly of the United Nations, Kennedy addressed himself to the failure of United States policy to respond to the desperate needs of African education. He proposed a program that involved creating an educational partnership between the African nations and the United States tailored to meet African needs and priorities; gaining the cooperation of American universities, colleges, churches, and foundations to assist the educational progress of Africa; and establishing a permanent and independent educational system in Africa.

In consultation with the African leaders, we must undertake now a comprehensive program mobilizing all our resources for a full attack on Africa's desperate need for education at all levels. . . .

If Africa's need is to be met without further loss of valuable time, the State Department must be instructed to inform the African leaders now assembling in New York of this undertaking and invite them to join in presenting to us a statement of their most pressing needs and overall requirements. . . .

Equally important there must be full cooperation with the United Nations in mobilizing the resources of all countries who are ready to assist. . . .

Senator Kennedy listed the following points as indicative of the urgency of the situation:

1. Although the crisis of African education which is now upon us has been clearly visible for many years, U.S. Government programs for educational exchange have not responded to the need. According to the best available data there were studying in the United States during the past academic year less than 1500 African students (excluding the U.A.R.), and of these only 200 were receiving United States Government aid.

2. In some of the most critical countries, where United States educational exchange programs have been subordinated to European

"Statement of Senator Kennedy on 'Education for African Freedom,' Washington, D.C., September 21, 1960." *Freedom of Communications,* I, 312–314. Summaries in original publication, here italicized.

colonial policies, our efforts have been virtually nonexistent. For example, from all of French, Belgian, and Portuguese tropical Africa, an area containing roughly 75 million people—about half the population of tropical Africa—there were in this country last year only 8 students, all of them under private auspices. At the same time, there were several hundred students from these same areas in Soviet bloc universities.

3. The appalling nature of this neglect is underlined by the fact that when the Congo achieved independence it had only a handful of college graduates, and virtually none trained in the skills necessary for self-government. Furthermore, not one of the few Congolese college graduates was educated in the United States.

4. By contrast, the Soviet Union, its satellites, and Communist China are making Africa a major target for educational and propaganda activities. Soviet bloc educational exchange programs for Africa are doubling almost every year. Their greatest success is in precisely the areas where we have done the least. In addition to existing programs, the Soviet Union is now opening a new university in Moscow, solely to serve students from the underdeveloped areas, with red-carpet treatment and all expenses paid, and with a planned capacity of 3000 to 4000 students. . . .

[*Senator Kennedy continued*]

To be successful we must meet these conditions:

1. This must be a partnership undertaking tailored to African needs and priorities, not a unilateral American plan based on the insistence that "America knows best."

2. It must be a plan which makes coordinated use of all American resources. Although, by the very magnitude of the effort, the major part of the financial burden must necessarily fall on the Government, the program cannot succeed unless it is undertaken in the true spirit of partnership between Government and private groups such as universities, church groups, and foundations with their valuable assets of experience and background.

3. This program must look to the establishment on a permanent basis of an educational system in Africa, for Africans, and sustained by Africans. It cannot be confined to educational exchange programs, although these are important, and it cannot consist of a few isolated show-place projects. . . .

QUESTIONS AND ANSWERS

John Kennedy responded to a group of questions posed by the *New York Herald Tribune* on issues in education: aid to private schools, school segregation, the merits of an advisory council on education, expansion of federal loan programs to college students (the existing program being part of NDEA), and tax deductions for college tuition.

Q. If Federal aid is to be granted, shall it go only to public schools, or to private and parochial schools, too? Should such aid be withheld from States which have not integrated their classrooms in compliance with the United States Supreme Court decision of 1954?

A. Federal aid should go only to public schools. The principle of church-State separation precludes aid to parochial schools, and private schools enjoy the abundant resources of private enterprises.

The Supreme Court's school decision, which I support and which we all must recognize as the law of the land, must be implemented in Federal district courts. The pace of desegregation was to vary from community to community so no sweeping statewide rule would be in order. But I would assume that any Federal aid program should be administered so as not to conflict with the law of the land. The Supreme Court has made it clear that the prohibition against racial discrimination by States and cities applies also to all the activities of the Federal Government. The executive branch must consider itself and all of its programs in line with this constitutional rule of equal treatment. In addition, in order to facilitate the process of desegregation, I favor and have sponsored legislation providing technical and financial assistance to districts facing special problems of transition.

Q. Should there be a National Council or Presidential Advisory Commission on Education, composed of leading educators and laymen, to help raise school standards, or should such matters be attacked locally?

A. This is one case where as many cooks as possible would improve, rather than spoil, the broth. The problem of raising school

New York Herald Tribune, September 25, 1960.

standards has such broad and critical implications for our national survival that we ought to have all the people we can giving it their intelligence, and indeed prayerful consideration, whether in State, local or national groups.

Educational councils or commissions on every level can be tremendously worthwhile in pointing up what has not been done and what cries out to be done. . . .

Q. Should existing college and graduate Federal loan programs be expanded?

A. Definitely the existing college and graduate Federal loan program should be expanded. It has been estimated that in the decade of the 1960's there will be a 100-per cent increase in the number of our college students. Many, as today, will need to borrow to pursue their higher education, and loans should be readily available to them. We certainly cannot afford to skimp in this vital area when the Russians are spending two-and-a-half times as much of their national income on education as the United States is doing.

Q. Should the Federal Government offer a tax deduction to college students and their parents to help them in meeting rapidly rising tuition fees?

A. The size of the Government's revenues over the next decade is going to be a crucial matter for the country as a whole, and rather than take the tax-deduction route of easing the financial strain on the student and his family, I would hope that other aid measures . . . would suffice.

THE FIRST DEBATE

During the first Kennedy-Nixon television debate, on September 26, 1960, Kennedy made several references to education.

This is a great country, but I think it could be a greater country, and this is a powerful country but I think it could be a more powerful country. . . .

I saw cases in West Virginia, here in the United States, where children took home part of their school lunch in order to feed their families, because I don't think we are meeting our obligations toward these Americans.

I'm not satisfied when the Soviet Union is turning out twice as many scientists and engineers as we are.

I'm not satisfied when many of our teachers are inadequately paid or when our children go to school [on] part-time shifts. I think we should have an educational system second to none. . . .

. . . I support Federal aid to education and Federal aid for teachers' salaries. I think that's a good investment. I think we're going to have to do it. And I think to heap the burden further on the property tax, which is already strained in many of our communities, will . . . insure, in my opinion, that many of our children will not be adequately educated and many of our teachers not adequately compensated. . . .

I don't want the Federal Government paying teachers' salaries directly; but if the money will go to the States and the States can then determine whether it shall go for school construction or for teachers' salaries, in my opinion you protect the local authority over the school board and the school committees. . . .

"John F. Kennedy's Opening Statement in the First Television-Radio Debate, Chicago, Ill., September 26, 1960." *Freedom of Communications*, III: *The Joint Appearances of Senator John F. Kennedy and Vice President Richard M. Nixon and Other 1960 Campaign Presentations*, 74, 83, 85, 86, 88, 90.

". . . EVERY POSSIBLE OPPORTUNITY"

The student newspaper of Proviso West High School, Hillside, Illinois, requested a message from both Presidential candidates in observance of American Education Week. In his letter, Senator Kennedy urged the students to take every opportunity to advance their education, for the effective leadership of our nation depends on the informed citizen who is capable of solving the complex problems of our society.

. . . Take advantage of every possible opportunity to increase your knowledge of the world in which you live, and of the ideas which have contributed to the development of our civilization as it now exists. For you will soon be discovering that you can take a direct hand in many ways in shaping and influencing the sort of world we live in.

This is particularly true of our own country. While it is correct that in a democracy the citizen is paramount, it is the informed citizen on whom we must increasingly depend for guidance and leadership.

Whether or not your formal schooling ends with high school graduation—and if at all possible it should not end then—your education must continue for the rest of your life. We need to develop to the fullest the talents of every citizen; for ours is a complex society requiring many specialized skills.

But specialization in a particular field is not enough; you must learn a great deal about a great many other things, too. Above all, you must learn how to track down the facts you need in order to reach informed opinions on the issues which confront you as a citizen.

Furthermore, if you are able to express those opinions clearly and persuasively, and if you can also contribute new and useful ideas to your fellow citizens, you will certainly find a place in the vanguard of leadership in our society—and that is where I expect many of you will eventually be.

"Candidates Reply to Profile; State Educational Stands." *Freedom of Communications*, IV: *The 15-Minute Radio and Television Network Newscasts for the Period September 23 through November 7, 1960*, 579–580. Written from Washington, D. C., October 3, 1960.

THE CRISIS IN EDUCATION

In a statement prepared for the National Education Association, at the Association's request, Kennedy linked efforts toward peace and economic growth to progress in education. He cited overcrowded classrooms and underpaid and overworked teachers as evidence of the deficiencies in our educational system. He stated that state and local support for schools is insufficient and that federal aid is necessary to meet the mounting cost of teaching our children. He pointed out that any program of federal school aid must in no way disturb academic freedom or local control of education.

We face a crisis in education. The exploding school population is bursting open inadequate classrooms. Our competition with the Soviets depends in part on the science training in our high schools. Our stature abroad—the legend of the "Ugly American"—is affected by how many language teachers are available in the lower grades. The wisdom of our legislators—holding in their hands the power of war or peace—is dependent upon the wisdom and the education of Americans in every remote corner of the Nation.

Moreover, advances in technology require a more highly skilled working force. History has shown that increases in productivity account for two-thirds of our economic growth. The rise in productivity comes from improvements in the skills of the labor force, improvements in technology, and better organization of production. In these areas, education is vital and its advancement will increase our rate of growth.

Local school boards listen to urgent appeals from scientists, admirals, and orators about improving the quality of our education, giving more time to gifted students and instituting more specialized courses at all levels. But they see children struggling—frequently on a half-day shift basis—to get proper attention in an overcrowded or makeshift classroom, with teachers who are underpaid, overworked, and, too often, untrained.

The expenditures per pupil in the 10 poorest States are less than half the expenditures made in the 10 richest States. The resulting dif-

NEA Journal, L (October, 1960), 10–11.

ferences in the quality of education received in the various States make the need for remedial action painfully evident.

These conditions cannot get better without substantial assistance from the Federal Government. In 4 years, 4.3 million more children will be clamoring for admission to our schools. By 1969, high school enrollment will increase at least 40 per cent.

We are devoting less than $1 out of every $30 to our educational system. State and local governments cannot keep up with fast-riding construction demands. They are already spending six times as much for education as they did 20 years ago. Meanwhile, the Federal Government has failed to do its share.

The Federal Government did well by education in the Northwest Territory Ordinances of 1785 and 1787. It did well again in the Morrill Act, more often called the Land Grant College Act, of 1862. But it has not done so well in the deepening education crisis of the past 7 years.

Because the administration's proposal merely to guarantee school bonds was grossly inadequate, I cosponsored Senate bills for Federal support to public schools for classroom construction and teachers' salaries as each State may determine its needs. This is the only effective way the Federal Government can help and also insure local control. And only effective Federal support will meet the crisis. . . .

The issue is not one of Federal control of education. Local jurisdiction and academic freedom must be scrupulously maintained. Local authority was not impaired by the Northwest Ordinances or the Morrill Act. It would not be impaired by making support available to build schools and raise teachers' salaries if the decision on use of the funds is left to the States.

The issue is one of national survival. The Soviets have spent at least $2\frac{1}{2}$ times more of their national income on education than we have, and estimates indicate that within a few years they will have three times as many scientists and engineers.

Civilization, according to the old saying, is "a race between education and catastrophe." It is up to us as a nation to determine the winner of that race. . . .

WASTE OF TALENT BY DISCRIMINATION

Before the student body of Howard University, Kennedy spoke of the disadvantages a Negro child faces from the economic, professional, and educational points of view.

. . . last week on television [I] gave some statistics which I do not think most Americans know or believe strongly enough; the prospects, percentagewise, of a Negro child getting through high school, of that child getting to college, of that child becoming a professional man, of that child when it is born owning its house, of that child being unemployed or the average income that that child will have, . . . the chances of that child getting through high school are about a third. The same per cent getting through college is one-quarter of a white baby being born in the house next door, the chance of owning his house is far less of a percentage, and the chances of being unemployed are far greater.

I think we cannot afford in 1960 to waste any talent which we have. It is a matter of our national survival as well as a matter of national principle, and I believe that the President of the United States must take the leadership in setting the moral tone, the unfinished business in setting the sights of Americans to the goal realizing the talents [in] an equal way of every American. Every American's talents are not equal. Every American will not finish school or college or own a house but that should be on the basis of his contribution to society, his energy, his vitality, his intelligence, his motivations, not based on the color of his skin. That is the goal of the society which I think we should work toward in the 1960's. . . .

"Remarks of Senator John F. Kennedy, Howard University, Washington, D.C., October 7, 1960." *Freedom of Communications*, I, 518.

AID TO MEDICAL TRAINING

As a candidate, Kennedy called attention to the shortage of doctors and nurses, asking for financial assistance to medical education. He recognized the need for new medical schools and for student help in the form of scholarships and loans for young men and women who wish to enter the medical and nursing professions.

As President, on September 24, 1963, he signed Public Law 88-129. The act authorized financial assistance for the construction of teaching facilities to train medical personnel, including physicians, dentists, and nurses. In addition, it authorized loans for students of medicine, dentistry, and osteopathy.

. . . we must provide for the development of doctors and nurses. We are graduating 7,500 doctors a year, 7,500 doctors, and yet our population is increasing over 3 million a year. We don't have enough doctors to maintain our present population, and we shall need half again as many by 1975. This will require at least 20 new medical schools and yet our efforts [to] provide those schools and those doctors for your people and your children [have] been held back in the past years.

. . . we must provide loans and scholarships to those who want to study. It costs $12,500, as well as years of work, to become a doctor. How many families can afford to send their sons and daughters through medical school today? Only 1 out of every 10 gets a scholarship of any kind, and the scholarship averaged less than $500 per person.

Low interest loans and fellowships will make it possible for us to meet our responsibility in this area, and in some cities there is one doctor for every 250 people. And in some rural communities, in my State and in your State, there is one doctor for every 3,000 people. I think we can do better and I think we must do better. . . .

"Speech of Senator John F. Kennedy, The Little White House, Warm Springs, Ga., October 10, 1960." *Freedom of Communications*, I, 545–546.

PROMOTING DESEGREGATION

John Kennedy answered an inquiry by the *Washington Daily News* concerning the powers of the Presidency to speed the desegregation of public schools.

Q. How would you use the implied or specific powers of the Presidency to hasten the end of racial segregation in public schools and other public facilities?

A. The President must be prepared to move forward on three broad fronts—as a legislative leader, as Chief Executive, and as a moral leader.

As a legislative leader, he cannot wait for others to act or for problems to solve themselves. . . .

I will support such action and work for legislation to provide technical assistance to schools facing special problems in the process of transition to desegregation. We must thus continually strengthen the legal framework which will allow us to move toward economic, educational, and political equality.

As Chief Executive, the next President must be prepared to put an end to racial and religious discrimination in every field of Federal activity. He must issue Executive orders which will do so. He must be willing to use the full resources of the executive agencies—from the Commission on Civil Rights to the Department of Health, Education, and Welfare to explore every means of progress in this field, by conference, consultation, and technical assistance.

Finally, as a moral leader, the next President must play an active creative role in interpreting the great human and moral issues involved. He cannot stand above the battle. He must exert the great moral and educational force of his office to create an affirmative new atmosphere in which further steps forward can be taken. The President, the representative of all interests and all sections, can promote the understanding and tolerance which is necessary if we are to complete the transition to a completely free society.

The Washington Daily News, October 11, 1960.

In a letter to the National Association of Educational Broadcasters on the occasion of its thirty-sixth convention, Kennedy cited the importance of educational television. He acknowledged the role ETV has played and will play in teaching more things to more people in less time. And he expressed dissatisfaction with the slow expansion of educational television facilities, promising federal assistance if elected.

On May 1, 1962, President Kennedy signed Public Law 87-477. The measure provided assistance for the construction of educational television broadcasting facilities.

You are meeting at a time when American leadership is challenged as never before in its history: at a time when our well-being as a nation is in jeopardy. If we are to defend ourselves effectively in a world of international tension and move ahead, we must rely no less upon the strength of our educational system than upon the strength of our Military Establishment. Jefferson attached the utmost importance to "the diffusion of knowledge among the people. No other sure foundation can be devised," he said, "for the preservation of freedom and happiness." The issue of education is clearly bound up with our national stature: one cannot and has not through American history been achieved without the other.

Today our schools and colleges face a crisis of appalling proportions in terms of deficits in dollars, teachers, classrooms, and services. American progress and even our national survival is directly dependent on what we as a nation do now about the shameful weaknesses and deficiencies of our educational system.

We must seize all means at hand to help education cope with these dire shortages and improve both the quality and quantity of educational opportunities available to our citizens at all levels, both in and out of school.

Television, a device which has the potential to teach more things to more people in less time than anything yet devised, seems a provi-

"Letter to the National Association of Educational Broadcasters, Washington, D.C., October 14, 1960." *Freedom of Communications*, IV, 555–556.

EDUCATIONAL TELEVISION

dential instrument to come to education's aid. Educational television has already proved it can be a valuable supplement to formal education and a direct medium for nonformal education.

Despite the heroic efforts of people such as yourselves to establish educational television stations across the United States, only a small part of the total potential has been achieved. To date, only 50 of the 256 channels reserved for education have been activated and two-thirds of the population still has no access to educational television service. This is not for lack of zeal or interest on the part of educators or State or local officials, but, primarily, for lack of funds for the initial capital investment required for construction of stations.

Since education is a matter of national concern, the Federal Government should assist in expediting and accelerating the use of television, as a tested aid to education in the schools and colleges of the Nation and as a means of meeting the needs of adult education. A useful start has already been made in this direction by the Government through the National Defense Education Act; more should be done to assist the development of educational television for the benefit of all our people. I pledge you that I will back actively suitable legislation aimed at this objective in the next session of the Congress and will urge its support by my Democratic colleagues. . . .

Senator Kennedy underscored the importance of adult education in supporting the objectives of the Adult Education Association and commending its work. The candidate acknowledged the importance of continuing education in an age of rapid change and innovation, recognizing that formal education is not enough and that the process of education must be continuous in order to insure the nation's progress.

. . . in my view the role of adult education in our national life is so important that I wish to take advantage of your invitation to extend my personal greetings and best wishes to those who are engaged in this rapidly growing segment of our educational system.

It is important to note that in the platform hearings of the Democratic Party, your association, together with other important professional organizations, provided direct testimony about the importance of continuing education if we are to develop informed citizens who can participate effectively in the decisionmaking processes of our society.

It is a source of pride to me that the Democratic platform includes a pledge of "further Federal support for all phases of vocational education for youth and adults; for libraries and adult education; for realizing the potential of educational television; and for the exchange of students and teachers with other nations." Our party has also gone on record in support of "encouraging and expanding participation in and appreciation of our cultural life," and we have proposed a Federal advisory agency to assist in the evaluation, development, and expansion of the cultural resources of the United States. . . .

. . . If our people are to live happy, prosperous, and fruitful lives in this urban age, we need educational programs as bold in concept and broad in scope as the cooperative extension movement which has done so much for rural America.

We need programs that will help all citizens to understand the problems created by urbanization. We need to find better ways to use

"Statement of Senator John F. Kennedy to the Adult Education Association of the U.S.A., Denver, Colo., October 14, 1960." *Freedom of Communications,* I, 1142–1143.

the research and the educational experience of our institutions of learning in solving these problems. Adult educators in our universities and colleges, our schools, libraries and civic organizations, have a vital role to play in getting this job done.

We live in an age of rapid social change and unprecedented increase of new knowledge and scientific invention. In such an age we must do all in our power to strengthen our great system of formal education. But we must not stop there. We must also recognize that a free society today demands that we keep on learning or face the threat of national deterioration. We must educate people today for a future in which the choices to be faced cannot be anticipated by even the wisest now among us. We are on the frontier of an era which holds the possibilities of a new Golden Age in which the inroads of poverty, hunger, and disease will be lessened, in which through the extension of educational opportunities, men and women everywhere will have it within their power to develop their potential capacities to the maximum.

The agenda before the American people is great. The problems are complex. I believe that an America that understands the importance of "lifelong learning" will be able to deal with those problems more wisely and more vigorously.

I am, therefore, pleased to express my support of those who are working to strengthen the adult education programs of our universities and colleges, our schools, our libraries, and our voluntary citizen organizations. Your efforts are helping America to move forward toward greater strength and cultural vitality which can make our Nation once again a beacon light among freedom-loving people everywhere.

FEDERAL AID AND LOCAL AUTONOMY

Many fear that the concomitant of federal aid to education is federal control. In remarks at the home of the University of Michigan, John Kennedy challenged this fear. He noted that the federal government has rendered aid to education since 1785, without limitations being placed on local control; and in his conclusion Kennedy suggested the incorporation in future education legislation of several safeguards to insure the continuation of local authority over education.

A nation which seeks to lead the world must put its own house in order. We have fallen seriously behind . . . in the education of our young people. . . .

Ten years ago we in the United States graduated 52,000 engineers from our universities while the Russians graduated 28,000. Last year they graduated 106,000, more than twice as many as our 47,000. Ten years ago Russians were already spreading their new colonialism throughout Asia and Africa and working hand in glove with the Red Chinese. To this day few American universities teach the Chinese language and the African tongues that soon will fall every day on Western ears. But we must improve our education, not only to compete with the Russians but for the sake of education itself. We must teach not only engineering but the humanities, for in our world, engineering skill has outrun philosophical wisdom and moral judgment and human understanding. We must encourage that free spirit of inquiry which alone produces new ideas—the bold new thinking that we need in our brave new world. We must cultivate brainpower as well as airpower. Above all, we must improve our educational system for the sake of our children. For if one child's mind is not improved, is not cultivated to the utmost, we have wasted our most precious national resource.

I am concerned, and deeply concerned, because too many children are attending double-shift schools, too many children are not given the incentive to finish high school, too few teachers are at work in our school systems, and too many teachers are underpaid. Too many

"Excerpts of remarks by Senator John F. Kennedy, Railroad Station, Ann Arbor, Mich., October 14, 1960 (Advance release text)." *Freedom of Communications*, I, 1125–1126.

FEDERAL AID AND LOCAL AUTONOMY

mothers spend their days chauffeuring back and forth their children who have to go to school in shifts. . . .

The U.S. Office of Education is already spending hundreds of millions to aid local education—$33 million for vocational education, $2½ million for land-grant colleges, $63 million for construction, and $187 million for maintenance and operation of schools in federally affected areas—and the Federal Government has not sought to impose any unreasonable controls.

Moreover, Federal aid to education is nothing new. Throughout our history, the Federal Government has helped to finance educational systems at times when local resources were unequal to the task. The land ordinance of 1785 provided that the 16th section of each township of public lands should be granted to the States for the benefit of common schools. No so-called Federal controls resulted.

The Morrill Act of 1862 gave to the States public lands to aid in establishing agricultural colleges. As a result, agricultural colleges have been established in every State—and no so-called Federal controls resulted.

Through the years special land grants have been given by the Federal Government to endow normal schools, schools of mines, military institutes, reform schools, and girls' colleges—the total acreage granted by the Federal Government for educational purposes is 118 million acres of public lands, an area four times the size of New York State—and no so-called Federal controls have resulted.

Your own great University of Michigan, the first of the Western State universities, was rechartered by the State in 1837 and endowed with proceeds from the educational land reserves—and no so-called Federal controls resulted.

Today, if safeguards are needed, they are simple to erect. The Congress can appropriate funds to be distributed to local school boards and used by those boards to construct more classrooms or pay teachers' salaries, according to their own local needs and at their own local discretion. And if further assurances are deemed desirable, the Congress can specifically declare that the Federal Government shall exercise no control over textbook content, curriculum, teacher selection and tenure, and the like; it can renounce Federal authority in such matters and place authority in the hands of local boards. . . .

IMPROVING UNIVERSITY EDUCATION

In a statement to the Association for Higher Education, Kennedy recognized the urgent need for qualified individuals capable of coping with the highly complex demands of our nation and world. He acknowledged the essential role that higher education must play in this effort and recommended expansion and improvement of college and university facilities with the help of government funds. In addition, the candidate advocated programs for scholarship aid and support for basic research.

Over the next generation there is no challenge facing our country that is more urgent or significant than that of providing better university education to more of our citizens.

But it is a challenge we must face today—not a generation from now. America's New Frontier demands many pioneers of many talents and tools. We are standing on that frontier. It is not something that we will face in the nebulous future. If we are to accept its challenges —if we are not to abandon its promise through default—we must begin moving today.

The new pioneer must be a man who knows where he is going and how he is going about it. Trial and error is a perilous process when a single misstep can bring the holocaust that can end our efforts. We must have trained people—many trained people—their finest talents brought to the keenest edge. We must have not only scientists, mathematicians, and technicians. We must have people skilled in the humanities. For this is not only the age of the missile and space vehicle and thermonuclear power. This is the age that can become man's finest hour in his search for companionship and understanding and brotherhood.

Our challenge—and our promise—is that great today.

I think we are ready to accept both.

This means, at the college and university level, a massive effort to expand both physical facilities and educational and research opportunities. Tens of thousands of qualified students are turned away each year by our crowded colleges. Others are unable to avail

College and University Bulletin, XIII (October 15, 1960), 1–2, 4.

themselves of higher learning or to pursue research for which they have a talent because of lack of money.

The effort will have to be massive just to catch up with current needs. It will have to be pursued with equal vigor as we move on in the sixties. For college enrollment, now estimated at 3.8 million, is expected to double by 1970—to 7.6 million. And our colleges will have to build more new buildings in the next 10 years than have been built on all American campuses since the American Revolution. . . .

As a member of the Senate Labor and Public Welfare Committee, which has jurisdiction over education matters, I have been close to the problem for a long time.

I was a sponsor both of the National Defense Education Act and of the college housing loan program.

I would like to see the National Defense Education Act continued and expanded into a general scholarship program for needy and qualified students, both graduate and undergraduate. Such a program, supplementing the energetic efforts our colleges and universities are already making to raise scholarship funds, would help at least 25,000 of our best high school students each year to go on to a college education they could not otherwise afford. . . .

I was a sponsor of the loan program for college housing facilities which passed Congress last year and was vetoed by the President. I favor a system of loans and matching grants through which not only dormitory facilities but classrooms, libraries, and laboratories may be provided.

Additionally, as we move to meet the challenge and the promise of the New Frontier, we must expand our support of basic research. . . . We need new concepts of man and matter for the future.

During the 1960 Presidential campaign, the publication *Scholastic Teacher* submitted a questionnaire to each candidate. Some of the responses by Senator Kennedy appear below. He supplemented his answers with an additional comment on the state of American education, emphasizing the necessity of upgrading the teaching profession by increasing teachers' salaries.

Q. Do you favor Federal aid for school construction? If so, in what amount and over how many years?

A. Yes. I believe that grants for classroom construction and teachers' salaries should be combined, so that States can determine for themselves how to allocate funds among competing needs. In the Senate this year, I sponsored a 4-year program totaling approximately $4 billion for this purpose.

Q. If so, how should funds be allocated?

A. Funds should go to all States, based on each State's pupil population.

Q. How would the tax funds be raised to support this program?

A. General taxation.

Q. Do you believe that Federal aid funds should be withheld from those areas which have refused court orders to desegregate their schools?

A. No.

Q. Do you believe that each State should have exclusive supervision over funds allotted to it, making reports of fund disposition to the Federal Government?

A. Yes, within the general framework of the [proposed] law.

Q. Do you believe the Federal Government should set up a scholarship program for talented young people who cannot afford to go to college?

A. Yes.

Q. If "yes," how many scholarships per year? Over how many years? How much would each scholarship be worth? How would the scholarship tax money be raised?

Scholastic Teacher (October 19, 1960), pp. 1T–3T, 6T.

FINANCING EDUCATION

A. The original scholarship program of the National Defense Education Act, which I supported, provided for approximately 20,000 scholarships per year. Our needs have not diminished since then. Such a scholarship program should be retained as long as the need persists. The amount of each scholarship could range between $600 and $1,000. Money would be raised through general revenue.

Q. Do you favor proposals to make the United States Office of Education an independent agency under the control of a National Board of Education?

A. No, at the present time.

[ADDITIONAL COMMENTS]

. . . The old system of financing schools primarily from property taxes is no longer sufficient. The old attitudes toward teachers and teachers' colleges, diminishing the quality of that honored profession, can no longer prevail. The old philosophy of leaving the financing of public school education to state and local taxpayers, and the financing of college education primarily to parents, is no longer sufficient.

It is time for action in public education. No one wants Federal control or Federal replacement of local efforts; what we need is emergency Federal action to help halt the decline in American education.

We must launch a massive construction program for both our public schools and our colleges—to make up our present shortage and to prepare for the coming wave of new students. . . .

. . . Most of the Nation's teachers receive outrageously low pay. Nearly one-half of our teachers earn less than $4,500 a year. Beginning salaries for all teachers average $10 a day. Many are forced to take a second job, even during the school year, to give their families bare security.

No profession of such importance in the United States today is so poorly paid. No other occupational group in the country is asked to do so much for so little. No amount of new classrooms, television, training, and recruitment techniques can attract and retain good teachers so long as their salaries are beneath the responsibility and dignity of their profession. . . .

If positive steps in the field of education are not taken we will bequeath a staggering burden to our children—one that can be measured in terms of human waste, loss of talent, unfulfilled lives.

Ninety years ago Ralph Waldo Emerson wrote: "The true test of a civilization is not the census, nor the size of cities, nor the crops—no, but the kind of men the country turns out."

Education is our hope for men and women of excellence. We must move ahead vigorously to fulfill this hope.

"THE BEDROCK OF DEMOCRACY"

Kennedy spoke of the urbanization of the United States and of the rapid growth of our suburbs. He expressed concern about the conditions of our schools and their inability to teach effectively the children of an expanding population. The Senator cited double-shift schools, overcrowded classrooms, and the neglected teacher as prime examples of a desperate situation. He urged immediate action and said that federal aid must be an integral part of any solution to our educational problems.

We live in the midst of a population explosion that is remaking the face of America. The country is filling up, recreation areas are overcrowded, our cities are jammed, our highways are clogged, and on the edges of our great cities the shopping center and ranchhouse have replaced the silo and the haystack until today more than a fourth of all Americans live in suburbs.

The question we have to ask ourselves is: What kind of children, what kind of future men and women, are we raising in our new American homes?

I think the answer will depend to a great extent on the kind of education we provide for them. And I say that today our children's schools are not good enough. . . .

The school crisis has gotten out of control. It is time we stopped talking about it and did something about it.

I favor Federal aid to education. I have spoken for it, worked for it, and most important of all I have voted for it in the United States Senate. . . .

We don't want our children going to school half-time. We don't want our children half-educated. We owe it to each individual child to give him the best education he is capable of absorbing. And we owe it to our Nation to educate our children, for the bedrock of democracy is a constantly rising level of the education of its citizens. And the cause of freedom around the world depends upon the strength of our democracy.

"Remarks by Senator John F. Kennedy, Meadowdale Shopping Center, Carpentersville, Ill., October 25, 1960 (Advance release text)." *Freedom of Communications*, I, 1192–1194.

". . . WHERE EVERY CHILD IS EDUCATED"

In Philadelphia, the birthplace of the nation, John Kennedy spoke of the kind of America he believed in, of his hopes for the citizens of this nation: a full week's pay for a full week's work; medical care for the aged; decent living accommodations; fair farm prices; a sound free-enterprise system; and education for all.

. . . I believe in an America where every child is educated not according to his means or his race, but according to his capacity; where there are no longer literacy tests for voting, because there are no illiterates; where children go to school for a full school day in a well-lit, well-heated, well-equipped classroom, . . . taught by well-trained, well-paid teachers; where there are enough colleges and classrooms and dormitories to make it possible for every young man and woman of talent to go to college. . . .

"Speech by Senator John F. Kennedy, Convention Hall, Philadelphia, Pa., October 31, 1960 (from the *New York Times*)." *Freedom of Communications*, I, 1224.

AN INFORMED PEOPLE

Kennedy often quoted Thomas Jefferson when discussing education. In a speech in Los Angeles a few days before the election, he quoted the third President on ignorance and freedom and reminded his audience that a successful democratic government was largely dependent on an informed and educated people.

. . . Thomas Jefferson once said, "If you expect a nation to be ignorant and free, you expect what never was and never will be." . . .

We need in a free society, where the responsibility lies with the people, with their own good judgment and sense of responsibility and restraint, we want the best educated people in the world. We are at the mercy, and the cause of freedom is at the mercy, of a majority of our citizens, and as one of those citizens who is so involved, as you all are, all of us want those citizens to be well educated. . . .

Here is what I think we ought to do in the next Congress. . . . we ought to pass a bill which will provide assistance to the States, the States then to make the judgment of what percentage of the aid should be turned over to the teachers' salaries and school construction. In that way we can insure local control over education, local control over curriculum, and all the rest, but at the same time make sure that our schools are built and our teachers are compensated. Once we do that, we have a right to expect that our teachers will be well trained, will be imaginative, will be dedicated. We must search for new teaching methods. . . .

In addition, we have to make sure that our schools meet their responsibility, which is a responsibility of yours. In some States of the United States, . . . every graduate from high school, regardless of the standards of the high school, is admitted automatically to college, and then 45 to 50 percent of them flunk out after the first year. We ought to have a right to expect that every high school in the country will meet high school standards, and will make it possible for any

"Speech of Senator John F. Kennedy at the Beverly Hilton Hotel, Los Angeles, Calif., November 2, 1960." *Freedom of Communications,* I, 854–856.

child that graduates from that high school, who has talent, who has ability, who has motivation, who desires to go to college, will have the skills, study and application applied to [him] in [his] earlier years so that [he is] able to make the grade when [he enters] college. . . .

A CONCERN OF ALL

Too often those without children ignore the problems and needs of education. In another speech in Los Angeles, Kennedy challenged this attitude and spelled out the reasons why education must be the concern of all Americans.

. . . Federal aid to education is not merely of importance to those with children in school. . . . We live under majority rule and if that majority is not well educated in its responsibilities, the whole Nation suffers. We live in an era of growth and change, and if our educational system is not producing enough doctors or enough engineers or enough teachers, the whole Nation suffers. And finally, we live in a world of shifting tides and opinion and if we cannot outstrip the Russians in space and science, in technicians to under-developed countries, in the language training of our Foreign Service officers, then our prestige suffers, our influence suffers, and the whole Nation suffers. Ten years ago our colleges were producing twice as many scientists and engineers as the Russians; now they produce twice as many as we do. It is not because our colleges are empty—they are already overcrowded. And those who are counting on sending their children to college in 1970 may find that decision was already made in 1959–60. . . . I say a better educated America is a stronger America. . . .

"Excerpts of Speech by Senator John F. Kennedy, East Los Angeles College Stadium, Los Angeles, Calif., November 1, 1960 (Advance release text)." *Freedom of Communications*, I, 1230.

The campaign was almost over. Kennedy made his last swing through the East as he prepared to return to Boston for Election Day. Speaking on Long Island, he linked the success and security of our nation with our progress in higher education. He spoke of the role of the university and how essential it is to our well-being both at home and abroad. He felt that ideas and trained personnel must flow in unprecedented numbers from our universities to meet the challenges confronting us.

Finally, to all Americans he pledged a system of education that would guarantee higher education to all who qualify.

We pledge ourselves to seek a system of higher education where every young American can be educated, not according to his race or his means, but according to his capacity.

Never in the life of this country has the pursuit of that goal been more important or more urgent. For our universities have become the research and training centers on which American defense and industry and agriculture and the professions depend. Our progress in all these fields depends upon a constant flow of high-caliber and skilled manpower, upon new ideas and creative applications of old ideas, upon the acquisition of skills and the ability to apply those skills. Thus, today, the university is, in the words of Woodrow Wilson, "the root of our intellectual life as a nation."

And our universities are not only essential to a strong society here at home, they are vital to the cause of freedom throughout the world.

Our universities are our hope for success in the intense and serious competition for supremacy in ideas, in military technology, in space, in science, and all the rest in which we are now engaged with the Soviet Union. Other nations will look to us for leadership; our prestige will rise only if we are a vital and progressing society.

"Speech by Senator John F. Kennedy, Commack Arena, Commack, Long Island, N.Y., November 6, 1960 (Advance release text)." *Freedom of Communications*, I, 1261–1262.

"OUR HOPE FOR SUCCESS"

And, today, the basis of vitality and progress is the trained capacity of the human mind.

Our universities must train men and women who can bring the benefits of modern technology to the developing nations of the world, who can help create the framework of economic advance on which freedom in these lands depends.

And our universities must serve as centers in which the youth of other lands can acquire the knowledge to run the factories, teach in the schools, and staff the governments of their own countries.

But American universities are more than a source of strength, here and abroad, they are the great catalyst of the democratic way of life. Through the gateway of a university education young men and women of all backgrounds, of all races and religions, of every economic group, can find opportunity—opportunity to develop their own capacities, and opportunity to find a fruitful and satisfying outlet for their skills and interests.

And that is why we intend to work until a college education is available to every young man and woman with the talent to pursue it. . . .

THREE

THE PRESIDENTIAL
YEARS 1961-1963

On February 20, 1961, President Kennedy set the goals for his education program in a message to Congress in which he stressed the progress of education—excellent education—as the key to the progress of the nation. The President outlined his recommendations with regard to assistance to public schools, construction of college and university facilities, assistance to college and university students, and vocational education.

Our progress as a nation can be no swifter than our progress in education. Our requirements for world leadership, our hopes for economic growth, and the demands of citizenship itself in an era such as this all require the maximum development of every young American's capacity.

The human mind is our fundamental resource. A balanced Federal program must go well beyond incentives for investment in plant and equipment. It must include equally determined measures to invest in human beings—both in their basic education and training and in their more advanced preparation for professional work. Without such measures, the Federal Government will not be carrying out its responsibilities for expanding the base of our economic and military strength.

Our progress in education over the last generation has been substantial. We are educating a greater proportion of our youth to a higher degree of competency than any other country on earth. One-fourth of our total population is enrolled in our schools and colleges. This year $26 billion will be spent on education alone.

But the needs of the next generation—the needs of the next decade and the next school year—will not be met at this level of effort. More effort will be required—on the part of students, teachers, schools, colleges, and all 50 States—and on the part of the Federal Government.

"Special Message to the Congress on Education." Doc. 46, February 20, 1961. *Public Papers of the Presidents: John F. Kennedy* (hereafter cited as *Public Papers*), 1961 (Washington, D.C.: Government Printing Office, 1962), pp. 107–111.

AMERICAN EDUCATION

Education must remain a matter of State and local control, and higher education a matter of individual choice. But education is increasingly expensive. Too many State and local governments lack the resources to assure an adequate education for every child. Too many classrooms are overcrowded. Too many teachers are underpaid. Too many talented individuals cannot afford the benefits of higher education. Too many academic institutions cannot afford the cost of, or find room for, the growing number of students seeking admission in the sixties.

Our twin goals must be: A new standard of excellence in education—and the availability of such excellence to all who are willing and able to pursue it.

I. ASSISTANCE TO PUBLIC ELEMENTARY AND SECONDARY SCHOOLS

A successful educational system requires the proper balance, in terms of both quality and quantity, of three elements: students, teachers, and facilities. The quality of the students depends in large measure on both the quality and the relative quantity of teachers and facilities.

Throughout the 1960's there will be no lack in the quantity of students. An average net gain of nearly 1 million pupils a year during the next 10 years will overburden a school system already strained by well over a half million pupils in curtailed or half day sessions, a school system financed largely by a property tax incapable of bearing such an increased load in most communities.

But providing the quality and quantity of teachers and facilities to meet this demand will be major problems. Even today, there are some 90,000 teachers who fall short of full certification standards. Tens of thousands of others must attempt to cope with classes of unwieldly size because there are insufficient teachers available.

We cannot obtain more and better teachers—and our children should have the best—unless steps are taken to increase teachers' salaries. At present salary levels, the classroom cannot compete in financial rewards with other professional work that requires similar academic background.

It is equally clear that we do not have enough classrooms. In order to meet current needs and accommodate increasing enrollments, if every child is to have the opportunity of a full-day education in an adequate classroom, a total of 600,000 classrooms must be constructed during the next 10 years.

These problems are common to all States. They are particularly severe in those States which lack the financial resources to provide a better education, regardless of their own efforts. Additional difficulties, too often overlooked, are encountered in areas of special educational need, where economic or social circumstances impose special burdens and opportunities on the public school. These areas of special educational need include our depressed areas of chronic unemployment and the slum neighborhoods of our larger cities, where underprivileged children are overcrowded into substandard housing. . . . The proportion of dropouts, delinquency, and classroom disorders in such areas is alarmingly high.

I recommend to the Congress a 3-year program of general Federal assistance for public elementary and secondary classroom construction and teachers' salaries. . . .

II. CONSTRUCTION OF COLLEGE AND UNIVERSITY FACILITIES

Our colleges and universities represent our ultimate educational resource. In these institutions are produced the leaders and the other trained persons whom we need to carry forward our highly developed civilization. If the colleges and universities fail to do their job, there is no substitute to fulfill their responsibility. The threat of opposing military and ideological forces in the world lends urgency to their task. But that task would exist in any case.

The burden of increased enrollments—imposed upon our elementary and secondary schools already in the fifties—will fall heavily upon our colleges and universities during the sixties. By the autumn of 1966, an estimated 1 million more students will be in attendance at institutions of higher learning than enrolled last fall—for a total more than twice as high as the total college enrollment of 1950. Our colleges, already hard pressed to meet rising enrollments since 1950 during a period of rising costs, will be in critical straits merely to provide the necessary facilities, much less the cost of quality education. . . .

The national interest requires an educational system on the college level sufficiently financed and equipped to provide every student with adequate physical facilities to meet his instructional, research, and residential needs.

I therefore recommend legislation which will—

(1) *Extend the current college housing loan program with a 5-year, $250 million a year program designed to meet the Federal Government's appropriate share of residential housing for students and faculty. As a start, additional lending authority is necessary to speed action during fiscal 1961 on approvable loan applications already at hand.*

(2) *Establish a new, though similar, long-term, low-interest rate loan program for academic facilities, authorizing $300 million in loans each year for 5 years to assist in the construction of classrooms, laboratories, libraries, and related structures—sufficient to enable public and private higher institutions to accommodate the expanding enrollments they anticipate over the next 5 years; and also to assist in the renovation, rehabilitation, and modernization of such facilities.*

III. ASSISTANCE TO COLLEGE AND UNIVERSITY STUDENTS

This Nation a century or so ago established as a basic objective the provision of a good elementary and secondary school education to every child, regardless of means. In 1961, patterns of occupation, citizenship, and world affairs have so changed that we must set a higher goal. We must assure ourselves that every talented young person who has the ability to pursue a program of higher education will be able to do so if he chooses, regardless of his financial means.

Today private and public scholarship and loan programs established by numerous States, private sources, and the Student Loan Program under the National Defense Education Act are making substantial contributions to the financial needs of many who attend our colleges. But they still fall short of doing the job that must be done. An estimated one-third of our brightest high school graduates are unable to go on to college, principally for financial reasons.

While I shall subsequently ask the Congress to amend and expand the Student Loan and other provisions of the National Defense Education Act, it is clear that even with this program many talented but needy students are unable to assume further indebtedness in order to continue their education.

I therefore recommend the establishment of a 5-year program with an initial authorization of $26,250,000 of State-administered scholarships for talented and needy young people which will supplement but not supplant those programs of financial assistance to students which are now in operation. . . .

IV. VOCATIONAL EDUCATION

The National Vocational Education Acts, first enacted by the Congress in 1917 and subsequently amended, have provided a program of training for industry, agriculture, and other occupational areas. The basic purpose of our vocational education effort is sound and sufficiently broad to provide a basis for meeting future needs. However, the technological changes which have occurred in all occupations call for a review and re-evaluation of these acts, with a view toward their modernization.

To that end, *I am requesting the Secretary of Health, Education, and Welfare to convene an advisory body drawn from the educational profession, labor-industry, and agriculture, as well as the lay public, together with representation from the Departments of Agriculture and Labor, to be charged with the responsibility of reviewing and evaluating the current National Vocational Education Acts, and making recommendations for improving and redirecting the program.*

CONCLUSION

These stimulatory measures represent an essential though modest contribution which the Federal Government must make to American education at every level. One-sided aid is not enough. We must give attention to both teachers' salaries and classrooms, both college academic facilities and dormitories, both scholarships and loans, both vocational and general education.

We do not undertake to meet our growing educational problems merely to compare our achievements with those of our adversaries. These measures are justified on their own merits—in times of peace as well as peril—to educate better citizens as well as better scientists and soldiers. The Federal Government's responsibility in this area has been established since the earliest days of the Republic—it is time now to act decisively to fulfill that responsibility for the sixties.

FEDERAL AID TO SCHOOLS AND STUDENTS

Legislation providing federal aid to education has traditionally met with strong opposition in Congress. Resistance has focused on federal control, segregation, and the issue of aid to private and parochial schools. With regard to the last, some constitutional lawyers have distinguished between the constitutionality of aiding public schools and the unconstitutionality of assisting private schools. Further distinctions have been drawn between primary and secondary education and higher education, the thought being that there are fewer constitutional restrictions on aid to colleges and universities. A further distinction has often been drawn between aid directly to a student who attends a private college or school and aid to the school proper. During a press conference on March 1, 1961, the President discussed this distinction.

. . . Q. Sir, in view of the criticism that has occurred, could you elaborate on why you have not recommended Federal aid to public and—to private and parochial elementary and secondary schools?

A. Well, the Constitution clearly prohibits aid to the school, to parochial schools. I don't think there is any doubt of that.

The Everson case, which is probably the most celebrated case, provided only by a 5 to 4 decision was it possible for a local community to provide bus rides to nonpublic school children. But all through the majority and minority statements on that particular question there was a very clear prohibition against aid to the school direct. The Supreme Court made its decision in the Everson case by determining that the aid was to the child, not to the school. Aid to the school is—there isn't any room for debate on that subject. It is prohibited by the Constitution, and the Supreme Court has made that very clear. And therefore there would be no possibility of our recommending it.

"The President's News Conference of March 1, 1961." Doc. 62, March 1, 1961. *Public Papers*, 1961, pp. 142–143. In *Everson v Board of Education*, 330 U.S. 1 (1947), the United States Supreme Court ruled that legislation providing tax funds for the transportation of children from their homes to private schools was not a violation of the religion clause of the First Amendment. The Court considered the statute in question to be public welfare legislation and similar to police and fire protection afforded to all schools without regard to their public or private nature.

Q. But you are free to make the recommendations you have made which will affect private and parochial colleges and universities?

A. Well, the aid that we have recommended to colleges is in a different form. We are aiding the student in the same way the GI bill of rights aided the student. The scholarships are given to the students who have particular talents and they can go to the college they want. In that case it is aid to the student, not to the school or college, and, therefore, not to a particular religious group. That is the distinction between them, except in the case of aid to medical schools, and that has been done for a number of years. Because that is a particular kind of technical assistance the constitutional question has not arisen on that matter. . . .

THE NEED FOR THE COLLEGE GRADUATE

On receiving an honorary degree from George Washington University, President Kennedy spoke of the link between great American patriots and higher education. He referred to the Adamses, Robert E. Lee, Woodrow Wilson, and others who have contributed to the growth of university life in this country. The President went on to remind his audience that the duty of the educated man and woman is to oversee the maintenance of our society in critical times.

. . . I don't think that there has ever been a time when we have had greater need for those qualities which a university produces. I know that many people feel that a democracy is a divided system, that where the Communists are certain in purpose and certain in execution, we debate and talk and are unable to meet their consistency and their perseverance.

I do not hold that view. There are many disadvantages which a free society bears with it in a cold war struggle, but I believe over the long run that people do want to be free, that they desire to develop their own personalities and their own potentials, that democracy permits them to do so. And that it is the job of schools and colleges such as this to provide the men and women who will, with their sense of discipline and purpose and understanding, contribute to the maintenance of free societies here and around the world. . . .

"Remarks at George Washington University Upon Receiving an Honorary Degree." Doc. 162, May 3, 1961. *Public Papers,* 1961, p. 347.

EDUCATION FOR SERVICE

The 1961 graduating class of the United States Naval Academy heard its Commander-in-Chief speak of the revolutionary character of the age and of the corresponding increasing demand on the Annapolis graduates. The President emphasized the duty of the modern officer to represent the American people, a dedication involving constant struggles and difficulties. "The battle for freedom takes many forms," and this form—commitment of young men involved in national defense—is desperately needed and deeply appreciated by the nation.

I am proud as a citizen of the United States to come to this institution and this room where there is concentrated so many men who have committed themselves to the defense of the United States. I am honored to be here.

In the past I have had some slight contact with this Service, though I never did reach the state of professional and physical perfection where I could hope that anyone would ever mistake me for an Annapolis graduate.

I know that you are constantly warned during your days here not to mix, in your Naval career, in politics. I should point out, however, on the other side, that my rather rapid rise from a Reserve Lieutenant, of uncertain standing, to Commander-in-Chief, has been because I did not follow that very good advice.

I trust, however, that those of you who are Regulars will, for a moment, grant a retired civilian officer some measure of fellowship.

Nearly a half century ago, President Woodrow Wilson came here to Annapolis on a similar mission, and addressed the Class of 1914. On that day, the graduating class numbered 154 men. There has been, since that time, a revolution in the size of our military establishment, and that revolution has been reflected in the revolution in the world around us.

When Wilson addressed the class in 1914, the Victorian structure of power was still intact, the world was dominated by Europe, and

"Remarks at Annapolis to the Graduating Class of the United States Naval Academy." Doc. 232, June 7, 1961. *Public Papers,* 1961, pp. 446–448.

EDUCATION FOR SERVICE

Europe itself was the scene of an uneasy balance of power between dominant figures and America was a spectator on a remote sideline.

The autumn after Wilson came to Annapolis, the Victorian world began to fall to pieces, and our world one-half a century later is vastly different. Today we are witnesses to the most extraordinary revolution, nearly, in the history of the world, as the emergent nations of Latin America, Africa, and Asia awaken from long centuries of torpor and impatience.

Today the Victorian certitudes which were taken to be so much a part of man's natural existence are under siege by a faith committed to the destruction of liberal civilization, and today the United States is no longer the spectator, but the leader.

This half century, therefore, has not only revolutionized the size of our military establishment, it has brought about also a more striking revolution in the things that the Nation expects from the men in our Service.

Fifty years ago the graduates of the Naval Academy were expected to be seamen and leaders of men. They were reminded of the saying of John Paul Jones, "Give me a fair ship so that I might go into harm's way."

When Captain Mahan began to write in the nineties on the general issues of war and peace and naval strategy, the Navy quickly shipped him to sea duty. Today we expect all of you—in fact, you must, of necessity—be prepared not only to handle a ship in a storm or a landing party on a beach, but to make great determinations which affect the survival of this country.

The revolution in the technology of war makes it necessary in order that you, when you hold positions of command, may make an educated judgment between various techniques, that you also be a scientist and an engineer and a physicist, and your responsibilities go far beyond the classic problems of tactics and strategy.

In the years to come, some of you will serve as your Commandant did last year, as an adviser to foreign governments; some will negotiate as Admiral Burke did, in Korea, with other governments on behalf of the United States; some will go to the far reaches of space and some will go to the bottom of the oceans. Many of you from one time or another, in the positions of command, or as members of staff, will participate in great decisions which go far beyond the narrow reaches of professional competence.

You gentlemen, therefore, have a most important responsibility, to recognize that your education is just beginning, and to be prepared, in the most difficult period in the life of our country, to play the role that the country hopes and needs and expects from you. You must understand not only this country but other countries. You must know something about strategy and tactics and logic—logistics, but also economics and politics and diplomacy and history. You must know everything you can know about military power, and you must also understand the limits of military power. You must understand that few of the important problems of our time have, in the final analysis, been finally solved by military power alone. When I say that officers today must go far beyond the official curriculum, I say it not because I do not believe in the traditional relationship between the civilian and the military, but you must be more than the servants of national policy. You must be prepared to play a constructive role in the development of national policy, a policy which protects our interests and our security and the peace of the world. Woodrow Wilson reminded your predecessors that you were not serving a government or an administration, but a people. In serving the American people, you represent the American people and the best of the ideals of this free society. Your posture and your performance will provide many people far beyond our shores, who know very little of our country, the only evidence they will ever see as to whether America is truly dedicated to the cause of justice and freedom.

In my inaugural address, I said that each citizen should be concerned not with what his country can do for him, but what he can do for his country. What you have chosen to do for your country, by devoting your life to the service of our country, is the greatest contribution that any man could make. It is easy for you, in a moment of exhilaration today, to say that you freely and gladly dedicate your life to the United States. But the life of service is a constant test of your will.

It will be hard at times to face the personal sacrifice and the family inconvenience, to maintain this high resolve, to place the needs of your country above all else. When there is a visible enemy to fight, the tide of patriotism in this country runs strong. But when there is a long, slow struggle, with no immediate visible foe, when you watch your contemporaries indulging the urge for material gain and comfort and personal advancement, your choice will seem hard, and you will recall, I am sure, the lines found in an old sentry box at Gibraltar, "God and the soldier all men adore in time of trouble and no more, for when war is over, and all things righted, God is neglected and the old soldier slighted."

Never forget, however, that the battle for freedom takes many forms. Those who through vigilance and firmness and devotion are the great servants of this country—and let us have no doubt that the United States needs your devoted assistance today.

The answer to those who challenge us so severely in so many parts of the globe lies in our willingness to freely commit ourselves to the maintenance of our country and the things for which it stands.

This ceremony today represents the kind of commitment which you are willing to make. For that reason, I am proud to be here. This nation salutes you as you commence your service to our country in the hazardous days ahead. And on behalf of all of them, I congratulate you and thank you.

Kennedy always advocated a partnership between politicians and educators. On several occasions while in the Senate, he had urged greater cooperation between the two groups and had predicted national profit as a result.

The reception of an honorary Doctor of Laws degree at the University of North Carolina in the fall of 1961 was the occasion for remarks on the importance of liberal arts and, particularly, the need for respect and appreciation of political life. The need for educated men and women to solve the problems of the modern world has never been greater; and he concluded that they must be prepared to make constructive suggestions rather than destructive criticism.

. . . I want to emphasize, in the great concentration which we now place upon scientists and engineers, how much we still need the men and women educated in the liberal traditions, willing to take the long look, undisturbed by prejudices and slogans of the moment, who attempt to make an honest judgment on difficult events. . . .

But more than that, I hope that you will realize that from the beginning of this country . . . there has been the closest link between educated men and women and politics and government.

I would urge you, therefore, regardless of your specialty, and regardless of your chosen field or occupation, and regardless of whether you bear office or not, that you recognize the contribution which you can make as educated men and women to intellectual and political leadership in these difficult days, when the problems are infinitely more complicated and come with increasing speed, with increasing significance, in our lives than they were a century ago when so many gifted men dominated our political life. The U.S. Senate had more able men serving in it, from the period of 1830 to 1850, than probably any time in our history, and yet they dealt with three or four problems which they had dealt with for over a generation.

Now they come day by day, from all parts of the world. Even the

"Address at the University of North Carolina Upon Receiving an Honorary Degree." Doc. 418, October 12, 1961. *Public Papers*, 1961, pp. 666–669.

experts find themselves confused, and therefore in a free society such as this, where the people must make an educated judgment, they depend upon those of you who have had the advantage of the scholar's education. . . .

It is not enough to lend your talents to deploring present solutions. Most educated men and women on occasions prefer to discuss what is wrong, rather than suggest alternative courses of action. . . .

I do not suggest that our political and public life should be turned over to college-trained experts, nor would I give this university a seat in the Congress, as William and Mary was once represented in the Virginia House of Burgesses, nor would I adopt from the Belgian Constitution a provision giving three votes instead of one to college graduates—at least not until more Democrats go to college. But I do hope that you will join them.

The centennial celebration of the establishment of land-grant colleges prompted the President to praise the effects of two acts signed by Abraham Lincoln during the Civil War. The Homestead Act provided farm land for the settlers, and the Morrill Act provided for federally supported universities. The nation is still reaping benefits from this legislation.

In July 1862, in the darkest days of the Civil War, President Abraham Lincoln signed two acts which were to help to mold the future of the Nation which he was then struggling to preserve.

The first of these, the Homestead Act, provided, in Carl Sandburg's words, "a farm free to any man who wanted to put a plow into unbroken sod."

The second, the Morrill Act, donated more than 1 million acres of Federal land to endow at least one university in every State of the Union.

Thus, even as the Nation trembled on the brink of destruction, the vast lands of the American West were open to final settlement. A new America of unparalleled abundance began to grow, and the most ambitious and fruitful system of higher education in the history of the world was developed. Today more than 68 land-grant institutions located in each of the 50 States and in Puerto Rico are a monument to the visions of those who built the foundations of peace in a time of war. Over one-half of our Ph.D. degrees in science and engineering are awarded by these schools. Twenty-four out of 40 Nobel Prize winners in our country are among their graduates. One-fourth of all high school and elementary teachers and over one-third of our college teachers are their products.

These universities have grown as our Nation's needs have grown. The original endowment called for instruction which emphasized agricultural and mechanized arts, and with their help the strongest agricultural community on earth was built. Today these schools teach

"Message Recorded for the Centennial Convocation of the Association of Land-Grant Colleges and State Universities." Doc. 462, November 12, 1961. *Public Papers,* 1961, pp. 714–715.

subjects ranging from philosophy to science and the conduct of foreign relations—the whole broad spectrum of knowledge upon which the future of this country and freedom depends, and upon which the well-being of Americans who will come after us is so richly intertwined.

In the history of land-grant schools can be read much of the history of our country, a history they have played no small part in shaping. In addition, these schools are one of the finest examples of our Federal system: the fruitful cooperation between National and State Governments in the pursuit of a decent education for all of our citizens. Founded at Federal initiative, strongly supported by Federal funds—funds which were specifically appropriated for instruction rather than the construction of buildings or facilities—these institutions have built a proud tradition of independence and academic integrity untroubled by governmental interference of any kind. They are a monument to the fact that the cooperative effort of Federal and State Governments is the best way to insure an independent educational system of the highest quality.

I congratulate the land-grant colleges on the centennial of their birth. I assure you of my vigorous and continued support. I bring you the thanks of a grateful nation for what you have done in the past. And I bring you the hope of all of our people that you will continue to light the way for our country and for future generations.

A message from the President on February 6, 1962, embodied his desire to realize the ideal of equal opportunity for education for all Americans. Education promotes enrichment and growth of a country, and Kennedy wished to rectify the flaws in the system which allow so many to drop out of school and so many to go illiterate and untrained. In order to prevent further problems in the future, federal funds must be made available for the achievement of educational excellence and for the availability of this excellence to all willing and able to pursue it—the two goals set at the beginning of Kennedy's administration.

The President saw the passage of the specific proposals he enumerated as both a national investment and a means of combating threats against freedom.

No task before our Nation is more important than expanding and improving the educational opportunities of all our people. The concept that every American deserves the opportunity to attain the highest level of education of which he is capable is not new to this administration—it is a traditional ideal of democracy. But it is time that we moved toward the fulfillment of this ideal with more vigor and less delay.

For education is both the foundation and the unifying force of our democratic way of life—it is the mainspring of our economic and social progress—it is the highest expression of achievement in our society, ennobling and enriching human life. In short, it is at the same time the most profitable investment society can make and the richest reward it can confer.

Today, more than at any other time in our history, we need to develop our intellectual resources to the fullest. But the facts of the matter are that many thousands of our young people are not educated to their maximum capacity—and they are not, therefore, making the maximum contribution of which they are capable to themselves, their families, their communities, and the Nation. Their talents lie wasted—

"Special Message to the Congress on Education." Doc. 37, February 6, 1962. *Public Papers*, 1962, pp. 110–117.

their lives are frequently pale and blighted—and their contribution to our economy and culture are lamentably below the levels of their potential skills, knowledge and creative ability. Educational failures breed delinquency, despair, and dependence. They increase the costs of unemployment and public welfare. They cut our potential national economic output by billions. They deny the benefits of our society to large segments of our people. They undermine our capability as a nation to discharge world obligations. All this we cannot afford—better schools we can afford.

To be sure, Americans are still the best educated and best trained people in the world. But our educational system has failed to keep pace with the problems and needs of our complex technological society. Too many are illiterate or untrained, and thus either unemployed or underemployed. Too many receive an education diminished in quality in thousands of districts which cannot or do not support modern and adequate facilities, well-paid and well-trained teachers, or even a sufficiently long school year.

Too many—an estimated 1 million a year—leave school before completing high school—the bare minimum for a fair start in modern-day life. Too many high school graduates with talent—numbering in the hundreds of thousands—fail to go on to college; and 40 per cent of those who enter college drop out before graduation. And too few, finally, are going on to graduate studies that modern society requires in increasing number. The total number of graduates receiving doctorate degrees has increased only about one-third in 10 years; in 1960 they numbered less than 10,000, including only 3,000 in mathematics, physical science, and engineering.

An educational system which is inadequate today will be worse tomorrow, unless we act now to improve it. . . .

THE ROLE OF THE FEDERAL GOVERNMENT

The control and operation of education in America must remain the responsibility of State and local governments and private institutions. This tradition assures our educational system of the freedom, the diversity, and the vitality necessary to serve our free society fully. But the Congress has long recognized the responsibility of the Nation as a whole—that additional resources, meaningful encouragement, and vigorous leadership must be added to the total effort by the Federal Government if we are to meet the task before us. For education in this country is the right—the necessity—and the responsibility—of all. Its advancement is essential to national objectives and dependent on the greater financial resources available at the national level.

Let us put to rest the unfounded fears that "Federal money means Federal control." . . . Since the end of the Korean War, Federal funds for constructing and operating schools in districts affected by Federal installations have gone directly to over 5,500 districts without any sign or complaint of interference or dictation from Washington. In the last decade, over $5 billion of Federal funds have been channeled to aid higher education without in any way undermining local administration.

While the coordination of existing Federal programs must be improved, we cannot meanwhile defer action on meeting our current pressing needs. Every year of further [delay] means a further loss of the opportunity for quality instruction to students who will never get that opportunity back. I therefore renew my urgent request of last year to the Congress for early action on those measures necessary to help this Nation achieve the twin goals of education: a new standard of educational excellence—and the availability of such excellence to all who are willing and able to pursue it.

I. ASSISTANCE TO ELEMENTARY AND SECONDARY EDUCATION

Elementary and secondary schools are the foundation of our educational system. There is little value in our efforts to broaden and improve our higher education, or increase our supply of such skills as science and engineering, without a greater effort for excellence at this basic level of education. With our mobile population and demanding needs, this is not a matter of local or State action alone—this is a national concern.

Since my Message on Education of last year, our crucial needs at this level have intensified and our deficiencies have grown more critical. We cannot afford to lose another year in mounting a national effort to eliminate the shortage of classrooms, to make teachers' salaries competitive, and to lift the quality of instruction. . . .

A NATIONAL INVESTMENT

The President then went on to point out the need for classroom construction and the necessity for improving teachers' salaries. In order to provide better educational quality and development, he recommended that Congress authorize—

(1) The award each year of up to 2,500 scholarships to outstanding elementary and secondary school teachers for a year of full-time study;

(2) The establishment of institutes at colleges and universities for elementary and secondary school teachers of those subjects in which improved instruction is needed;

(3) Grants to institutions of higher education to pay part of the cost of special projects designed to strengthen teacher preparation programs through better curriculums and teaching methods;

(4) Amendment of the Cooperative Research Act to permit support of extensive, multipurpose educational research, development, demonstration, and evaluation projects; and

(5) Grants for local public school systems to conduct demonstration or experimental projects of limited duration to improve the quality of instruction or meet special educational problems in elementary and secondary schools.

II. ASSISTANCE TO HIGHER EDUCATION

. . . Increasing student enrollments in this decade will place a still greater burden on our institutions of higher education than that imposed on our elementary and secondary schools where the cost of education per student is only a fraction as much. Between 1960 and 1970 it is expected that college enrollments will double, and that our total annual operating expenditures for expanding and improving education must increase 2½ times by nearly $10 billion.

In order to accommodate this increase in enrollments, the Office of Education estimates that nearly $22 billion of college facilities will have to be built during the 1960's—three times the construction achieved in the last 10 years. . . .

But I want to take this opportunity to stress that buildings alone are not enough. In our democracy every young person should have an equal opportunity to obtain a higher education, regardless of his station in life or financial means. Yet more than 400,000 high school seniors who graduated in the upper half of their classes last June failed to enter college this fall. In this group were 200,000 who . . . failed to go on to college principally because of a lack of finances. Others lack the necessary guidance, incentive, or the opportunity to attend the college of their choice. But whatever the reason, each of these 400,000 students represents an irreplaceable loss to the Nation.

Student loans have been helpful to many. But they offer neither incentive nor assistance to those students who, by reason of family or other obligations, are unable or unwilling to go deeper into debt. . . . Federal scholarships providing up to $1000 a year can fill part of this gap. It is, moreover, only prudent economic and social policy for the public to share part of the costs of the long period of higher education for those whose development is essential to our national economic and social well-being. All of us share in the benefits—all should share in the costs. . . .

III. SPECIAL EDUCATION AND TRAINING PROGRAMS

1. *Medical and dental education*

The health needs of our Nation require a sharp expansion of medical and dental education in the United States. We do not have an adequate supply of physicians and dentists today—we are in fact importing many from abroad where they are urgently needed—and the shortage is growing more acute, as the demand for medical services mounts and our population grows. Even to maintain the present ratio of physicians and dentists to population we must graduate 50 per cent more physicians and 90 per cent more dentists per year by 1970, requiring not only the expansion of existing schools but the construction of at least 20 new medical schools and 20 new dental schools.

But here again more buildings are not enough. It is an unfortunate and disturbing fact that the high costs of the prolonged education necessary to enter these professions deprives many highly competent young people of an opportunity to serve in these capacities. Over 40 per cent of all medical students now come from the 12 per cent of our families with income of $10,000 or more a year, while only 14 per cent of the students come from the 50 per cent of the Nation's

A NATIONAL INVESTMENT

families with incomes under $5,000. This is unfair and unreasonable. A student's ability—not his parents' income—should determine whether he has the opportunity to enter medicine or dentistry.

I recommend that Congress enact the Health Professions Educational Assistance Act which I proposed last year to (a) authorize a 10-year program of matching grants for the construction of new medical and dental schools and (b) provide 4-year scholarships and cost-of-education grants for one-fourth of the entering students in each medical and dental school in the United States.

2. Scientists and engineers

Our economic, scientific, and military strength increasingly requires that we have sufficient numbers of scientists and engineers to cope with the fast-changing needs of our time—and the agency with general responsibility for increasing this supply today is the National Science Foundation. At the elementary and secondary school level, I have recommended in the 1963 budget an expansion of the Science Foundation program to develop new instructional materials and laboratory apparatus for use in a large number of secondary schools and to include additional subjects and age groups; an expansion of the experimental summer program permitting gifted high school students to work with university research scientists; and an expansion in the number of National Science Foundation supported institutes offering special training in science and mathematics for high school teachers throughout the country. The budget increase requested for this latter program would permit approximately 36,000 high school teachers, representing about 30 per cent of the secondary school teachers of science and mathematics in this country, to participate in the program.

At the higher education level, I am recommending similar budget increases for institute programs for college teachers; improvement in the content of college science, mathematics, and engineering courses; funds for laboratory demonstration apparatus; student research programs; additional top level graduate fellowships in science, mathematics, and engineering; and $61,500,000 in grants to our colleges and universities for basic research facilities.

3. *Reduction of adult illiteracy*

Adult education must be pursued aggressively. Over 8 million American citizens aged 25 or above attended school for less than 5 years, and more than a third of these completely lack the ability to read and write. The economic result of this lack of schooling is often chronic unemployment, dependency, or delinquency, with all the consequences this entails for these individuals, their families, their communities, and the Nation. The twin tragedies of illiteracy and dependency are often passed on from generation to generation.

There is no need for this. Many nations—including our own—have shown that this problem can be attacked and virtually wiped out. Unfortunately, our State school systems—overburdened in recent years by the increasing demands of growing populations and the increasing handicaps of insufficient revenues—have been unable to give adequate attention to this problem. I recommend the authorization of a 5-year program of grants to institutions of higher learning and to the States, to be coordinated in the development of programs which will offer every adult who is willing and able the opportunity to become literate.

4. *Education of migrant workers*

The neglected educational needs of America's 1 million migrant agricultural workers and their families constitute one of the gravest reproaches to our Nation. The interstate and seasonal movement of migrants imposes severe burdens on those school districts which have the responsibility for providing education to those who live there temporarily. I recommend authorization of a 5-year Federal-State program to aid States and school districts in improving the educational opportunities of migrant workers and their children.

5. *Educational television*

The use of television for educational purposes—particularly for adult education—offers great potentialities. The Federal Government has sought to further this through the reservation of 270 television channels for education by the Federal Communications Commission and through the provision of research and advisory services by the Office of Education. Unfortunately, the rate of construction of new broadcasting facilities has been discouraging. Only 80 educational TV channels have been assigned in the last decade. It is apparent that further Federal stimulus and leadership are essential if the vast educational potential of this medium is to be realized. . . .

6. *Aid to handicapped children*

Another longstanding national concern has been the provision of specially trained teachers to meet the educational needs of children afflicted with physical and mental disabilities. The existing program providing Federal assistance to higher education institutions and to State education agencies for training teachers and supervisory personnel for mentally retarded children was supplemented last year to provide temporarily for training teachers of the deaf. I recommend broadening the basic program to include assistance for the special training needed to help all our children afflicted with the entire range of physical and mental handicaps. . . .

IV. CONCLUSION

The problems to which these proposals are addressed would require solution whether or not we were confronted with a massive threat to freedom. The existence of that threat lends urgency to their solution— to the accomplishment of those objectives which, in any case, would be necessary for the realization of our highest hopes and those of our children. . . .

The education of our people is a national investment. It yields tangible returns in economic growth, and improved citizenry, and higher standards of living. But even more importantly, free men and women value education as a personal experience and opportunity— as a basic benefit of a free and democratic civilization. It is our responsibility to do whatever needs to be done to make this opportunity available to all and to make it of the highest possible quality.

THE MOST VITAL FUNCTION

Ten days after the President's education message was delivered to Congress, he said farewell to a group of visiting foreign educators, expressing the hope that his country would achieve a higher level of excellence in education, perhaps urged on by the remarks, questions, and observations of these visitors who have similar desires for their homelands.

I want to say how proud we have been that you chose to come to this country to examine our educational system, and I am sure that you taught us during your visit here more than you learned.

There is, I know, a great tendency in every country, including my own, to consider education important but perhaps not so vital. We are so concerned in so many parts of the world with the problems that are coming today, next year, and the year after—and it does take 5 or 10 or 15 years to educate a boy or girl—and therefore there is a tendency to concentrate available resources on the problems we face now, and perhaps ignore what the potentialities and capabilities will be of our people 10 or 15 years from now.

. . . from the beginning of this country, in order to maintain a very difficult discipline which is self-government, we have placed a major emphasis on education.

My own feeling is, we have to do better—not only in quantity but also in quality, and I am hopeful that we can develop in this country a cult of excellence in regard to education and intellectual development, which will make this country more equipped to meet its problems. What is true of us I'm sure is true of you. In some of your countries your problems are entirely different, and that is, making it possible for, in the mass, to educate great numbers of your people who today do not have that advantage, and also making sure that at the higher level we can train and then usefully employ men and women to serve not only their own interests but that of their country.

I want you to know we are very proud to have you here. Our

"Remarks to a Group of Visiting Foreign Educators." Doc. 51, February 16, 1962. *Public Papers*, 1962, p. 142.

THE MOST VITAL FUNCTION

educational system has represented the devoted efforts of our citizenry, but I think we can always do better. And perhaps by your presence here, and your questions, and your concerns, you have been able to stimulate us to move more forward along what I consider to be the most vital function of society: educating our people—making it possible for them to realize their potentials, and by serving their own personalities and development, serving the national interest.

So we're glad to see you and we hope that when you go home you will be able to communicate to them not only things that you may have liked here, or disliked, but also the sense of a people desiring to improve themselves and their country. . . .

THE INTERDEPENDENCE OF KNOWLEDGE

Interdependence of all knowledge was the theme of an address by Kennedy on Charter Day at the University of California at Berkeley in March of 1962. Each scholar and scientist is dependent in some way on the work of others, and realization of this cooperation in knowledge could pave the way to cooperation in the drive for peace. Cooperation with the Soviet government in the exploration of space would be, the President said, an auspicious start that could lead to other projects of shared learning.

. . . We may be proud as a nation of our record in scientific achievement—but at the same time we must be impressed by the interdependence of all knowledge. I am certain that every scholar and scientist here today would agree that his own work has benefited immeasurably from the work of the men and women in other countries. The prospect of a partnership with Soviet scientists in the exploration of space opens up exciting prospects of collaboration in other areas of learning. And cooperation in the pursuit of knowledge can hopefully lead to cooperation in the pursuit of peace.

Yet the pursuit of knowledge itself implies a world where men are free to follow out the logic of their own ideas. It implies a world where nations are free to solve their own problems and to realize their own ideals. It implies, in short, a world where collaboration emerges from the voluntary decisions of nations strong in their own independence and their own self-respect. It implies, I believe, the kind of world which is emerging before our eyes—the world produced by the revolution of national independence which has today, and has been since 1945, sweeping across the face of the world. . . .

Wisdom requires the long view. And the long view shows us that the revolution of national independence is a fundamental fact of our era. This revolution will not be stopped. As new nations emerge from the oblivion of centuries, their first aspiration is to affirm their national identity. Their deepest hope is for a world where, within a framework

"Address in Berkeley at the University of California." Doc. 109, March 23, 1962. *Public Papers*, 1962, pp. 263–266.

of international cooperation, every country can solve its own problems according to its own traditions and ideals.

It is in the interests of the pursuit of knowledge—and it is in our own national interest—that this revolution of national independence succeed. For the Communists rest everything on the idea of a monolithic world—a world where all knowledge has a single pattern, all societies move toward a single model, all problems and roads have a single solution and a single destination. The pursuit of knowledge, on the other hand, rests everything on the opposite idea—on the idea of a world based on diversity, self-determination, and freedom. And that is the kind of world to which we Americans, as a nation, are committed by the principles upon which the great Republic was founded.

As men conduct the pursuit of knowledge, they create a world which freely unites national diversity and international partnership. This emerging world is incompatible with the Communist world order. It will irresistibly burst the bonds of the Communist organization and the Communist ideology. And diversity and independence, far from being opposed to the American conception of world order, represent the very essence of our view of the future of the world.

. . . No one who examines the modern world can doubt that the great currents of history are carrying the world away from the monolithic idea toward the pluralist idea—away from communism and toward national independence and freedom. No one can doubt that the wave of the future is not the conquest of the world by a single dogmatic creed but the liberation of the diverse energies of free nations and free men. No one can doubt that cooperation in the pursuit of knowledge must lead to freedom of the mind and freedom of the soul.

. . . Nothing is more stirring than the recognition of great public purpose. Every great age is marked by innovation and daring—by the ability to meet unprecedented problems with intelligent solutions. In a time of turbulence and change, it is more true than ever that knowledge is power; for only by true understanding and steadfast judgment are we able to master the challenge of history.

If this is so, we must strive to acquire knowledge—and to apply it with wisdom. We must reject oversimplified theories of international life—the theory that American power is unlimited, or that the American mission is to remake the world in the American image. We must seize the vision of a free and diverse world—and shape our policies to speed progress toward a more flexible world order. . . .

As we press forward on every front to realize the flexible world order, the role of the university becomes ever more important, both as a reservoir of ideas and as a repository of the long view of the shore dimly seen.

"Knowledge is the great sun of the firmament," said Senator Daniel Webster. "Life and power are scattered with all its beams."

In its light, we must think and act not only for the moment but for our time. I am reminded of the story of the great French Marshal Lyautey, who once asked his gardener to plant a tree. The gardener objected that the tree was slow-growing and would not reach maturity for a hundred years. The marshal replied, "In that case, there is no time to lose, plant it this afternoon."

Today a world of knowledge—a world of cooperation—a just and lasting peace—may be years away. But we have no time to lose. Let us plant our trees this afternoon.

INVESTMENTS IN THE FUTURE

> With characteristic warmth and hospitality, President Kennedy welcomed foreign students to Washington, noted the compliment the United States felt at their presence, and encouraged them to return to their countries as profitable investments in the future. The President also called on his fellow citizens to help the students feel at home.

. . . We had an earlier occasion last year in which we welcomed the students from abroad who were studying in Washington. And I hope that in other cities a similar effort will be made to bring together on an occasion the students from different countries who come here to study.

We regard this as a great compliment. I hope you will permit us to do so. And we regard it also as an indication of your curiosity and interest in this free society which we believe develops an intellectual atmosphere which permits progress. The other night we had a reception in the White House in which we had those people from this country who had won the Nobel prize. And though these aren't national prizes, I am pleased, as a believer in a free society, that over 40 per cent of all the prizes given in the last 30 years have been given to people who studied here—and [are] working here. They are not all Americans. Ten or twelve of them grew up in other countries and came here. But I like to believe that this society, which we are attempting to build—and obviously we have not succeeded yet in building it, and I suppose never will, but we are working towards it—permits maximum intellectual development.

All of us, at least many of us, have been foreign students. The Secretary of State, the Under Secretary of State, the head of the Policy Planning were all Rhodes scholars; the Deputy Attorney General and others; the Chairman of the Senate Foreign Relations Committee. My wife was a student in Paris for a year. I studied at the London School of Economics—my brother did. I am a great believer in the effort which we make to understand each other, and to learn, and to develop.

"Remarks at a Reception for Foreign Students on the White House Lawn." Doc. 180, May 10, 1962. *Public Papers*, 1962, pp. 383–384.

146

INVESTMENTS IN THE FUTURE

We have had a lot of foreign students in this country. A lot of them came in the thirties, and many of them went back to be leaders of their country. They may have gotten an impression of the United States, in those days, which may not have been as sympathetic as we would hope it would be today. Those were the days of the depression, when we were meeting many serious challenges at home.

I hope that when you go back—and you will be the future leaders of the country—many of you come from countries which have only a handful, as newly independent countries, of educated men and women. You are their investment in the future. And I know you will go home, and I know that you will regard this great effort which has been made, to bring you here and which you have made, not merely as an opportunity to advance your economic interest but to advance the welfare of your country. . . .

The last point I want to make, and that's really addressed to my fellow Americans, I think a good many foreign students come here and are left alone, and feel alone—see other foreign students—don't see many Americans. I hope that we are making progress in that area. This is not an organized society, we treat our own students that way. When I was at Harvard, no one spoke to me for the first nine months. And I suppose if I hadn't been staying, I might have gone back to another country, and had a conclusion about this country which wouldn't have been accurate.

I hope that those Americans who are desirous of doing something for their country will think of the thousands of foreign students who are here and give them a chance to see American life intimately. That's one of the reasons that you are here. And I hope you will feel that even though your "fun and games" is not organized by the United States Government, fortunately, that that is part of living in a free society: to be left alone, and to sink or swim. And if anybody wants it differently, then of course the Government's responsibilities would have to change. So I'm sure you understand that. . . .

We know that some other President, in other days, will be greeting you as either the Prime Ministers or the Presidents or the First Ladies of significant countries. And I hope when you do that, you will say that you were at the White House once before. . . .

147

PUBLIC SERVICE

Each summer the Federal Government sponsors programs beckoning young people to jobs in Washington, hoping that ultimately their experience will lead them into careers in government work.

June of 1962 found President Kennedy welcoming student participants and hoping that they would learn as much as possible about their government during the months they would be in the nation's capital. He urged them to consider public service as a career possibility. The zeal of young people of the present generation led him to believe that the desire to serve was present in many; the opportunities were many, the need great; and the President hoped to see these students in responsible capacities in the future.

I am glad to see you in Washington. I appreciate your willingness to come down and submit yourselves to the living on the bull's-eye here. I sometimes wish I just had a summer job here!

I do want to say what an opportunity it is for us in the Federal Government to have you here. These programs of bringing young Americans, particularly college students, to Washington every summer to work in the various departments have been going on for a great many years. The Federal Government does not do this out of largess. It does it because it hopes that in the 1 or 2 months that you come to Washington and work with us that you will become sufficiently interested in Government as a career that many of you will come back; and in that way we can attract to the national governmental service the best of the talents of our country, those who are most interested, those who are most committed. This has been going on, as I have said, for a great many years.

What we have been attempting to do this year, however, is to spread your interests. Those who may work in the State Department or the Department of Defense, those who may work in the White House or in the Executive Office do get a very clear idea, whether it may be because of carrying messages from one part of the building to another

"Remarks of Welcome to Participants in the Summer Intern Program for College Students." Doc. 250, June 20, 1962. *Public Papers*, 1962, pp. 499–501.

or working in more sophisticated jobs, they get some idea of what the work of the Government department in their area may be. But what we are anxious to do is use this time while you are here to give you as much information as broadly based and as sophisticated as is possible. And therefore during the next 2 months, with your help and cooperation, we will attempt to bring to your attention some of the many facets of governmental service.

It is my judgment that there is no career that could possibly be open to you in the 1960's that will offer to you as much satisfaction, as much stimulus, as little compensation perhaps financially, as being a servant of the United States Government.

I think within all of us, and really in a sense, I suppose endowed almost by nature in addition to a natural desire to advance our own interests, there is also a parallel desire, and that is to be part of this great enterprise of public service. The totalitarian powers have exploited that. Even in Cuba, Mr. Castro's emphasis, certainly at the beginning, was on a desire to improve the lot of the Cuban people. In China we had all of these examples of people spending their days off going out on illiteracy, health, building dams, doing all the things to build a better country. This is in all of us.

I think that it is a more difficult and subtle problem in a democracy, with a great deal of emphasis, of course, on individual liberty, on the right of pursuing our private interests, and so on, so that while there is this desire, frequently it does not have a chance to express itself. But the desire is there, and it is our hope that the desire is there stronger in these years than ever before. And I think the response to the Peace Corps indicates how real this feeling is, the willingness of thousands of young Americans, and some not so young, to volunteer to serve their country and a much larger constituency than their country in dozens of countries overseas. I hope and in fact I know you would not be here if you did not feel the same way.

When you leave here in August I hope that you will come back in other days when you have finished your studies and be willing to give part of your time and life to the service of our country. When I say come back, I do not mean it in the geographic sense. It may be that your service will take place in your own community or your own county or your own State, but to contribute part of your lives, part of your effort, if not all, to the advancement of the great interests of this country. . . .

So I am glad you have come to Washington. This Government needs your assistance. It needs the disciplines which you have acquired. . . .

Recently I heard a story of a young Peace Corpsman named Tom Scanlon who is working in Chile. He works in a village about 40 miles from an Indian village which prides itself on being Communist. The village is up a long, winding road which Scanlon has gone on many occasions to see the chief. Each time the chief avoided seeing him. Finally he saw him and said, "You are not going to talk us out of being Communists." Scanlon said, "I am not trying to do that, only to talk to you about how I can help." The chief looked at him and replied, "In a few weeks the snow will come. Then you will have to park your jeep 20 miles from here and come through 5 feet of snow on foot. The Communists are willing to do that. Are you?"

When a friend saw Scanlon recently and asked him what he was doing, he said, "I am waiting for the snow."

Well, I hope that spirit motivates all of you. You are most welcome here. And I want to say come rain or shine, I hope that when you leave in August you will have a chance to come to the White House and say goodby.

LOYALTY OATHS AND DISCLAIMERS

The original National Science Foundation and National Defense Education acts required applicants for loans to sign a Communist disclaimer affidavit. This requirement, which was coupled with that of a loyalty oath, caused a number of colleges to refuse to participate in the programs and prompted complaints from both students and college personnel. President Kennedy, on October 17, 1962, expressed strong approval of legislation directed toward doing away with the disclaimer; he reiterated the argument that the chances of its having prevented a Communist from receiving aid were slight, but that it did prevent deserving students from receiving federal financial aid. Kennedy had introduced similar legislation while in the Senate.

I have given my approval to the action of the Congress eliminating from the National Science Foundation and National Defense Education Acts the section which required any scientist, teacher, or other student who applied for a loan or grant thereunder to execute an affidavit declaring that he does not believe in, belong to, or support any organization which believes in or teaches the overthrow of the United States Government by force or by an illegal method. It substitutes a provision making it illegal for anyone to apply for or receive any such loan or grant if he is a member of a Communist organization registered under the Subversive Activities Control Act. It also requires recipients of National Defense Education Act fellowships or of advanced foreign language training stipends and recipients of National Science Foundation scholarships or fellowships to furnish a list of their crimes and criminal charges, pending against them, of a serious nature.

The affidavit requirement caused [a number] of our colleges to refuse to participate in the National Defense Education Act student loan program. Many others who participated did so reluctantly. Representatives of many of our colleges testified that the affidavit discriminated against college students and was offensive to them.

"Statement by the President Upon Signing Bill Modifying the Anti-Communist Oath Requirement of Student Loans." Doc. 469, October 17, 1962. *Public Papers*, 1962, p. 788.

LOYALTY OATHS AND DISCLAIMERS

It is highly unlikely that the affidavit requirement kept any Communist out of the programs. It did, however, keep out those who considered the disclaimer affidavit a bridle upon freedom of thought.

I am glad to approve the legislation.

A NEW COMMISSIONER

Francis Keppel was sworn in as United States Commissioner of Education on December 10, 1962, and the President found the occasion a fitting time to restate the federal government's place in providing the best possible education for the most people.

I want to express our very warm welcome to Mr. Keppel. We are very glad to have present with us today representatives of some of the distinguished American organizations who have made their life's work the advancement of education in the United States.

This is a matter which has been of concern to the National Government since our inception. The Northwest Ordinance, the Land Grant College Act, and all the rest indicate the strong belief of our Founding Fathers and this present administration that no free society can possibly survive unless it has an educated citizenry.

And therefore it is natural that the National Government, representing all the people, the State governments, the private community, the local communities both private and public—all will combine to provide the best education for the most informed citizenry in this great free country.

We are particularly fortunate to have Mr. Keppel to give leadership to this cause, working with Secretary Celebrezze. This office can be most important and I think that he undertook this job recognizing that he would have the strong support of the Secretary—and my strong support. I believe that he's rendering a distinguished service. And while Harvard University, under his leadership, played a most important role in the field of education, we believe that this office has wide horizon and has great opportunity to develop responsibilities. We are very glad to have you down here and to express our appreciation. . . .

"Remarks at the Swearing In of Francis Keppel as Commissioner of Education." Doc. 540, December 10, 1962. *Public Papers*, 1962, pp. 857–858.

THE KEYSTONE IN THE ARCH

In January of John F. Kennedy's third year in the Presidency, he again addressed Congress on his education program. His thesis that the pace of education sets the pace of the country had not changed during his term in office, and he believed that the federal government still had not met its responsibilities in the field. Social and economic growth are proportionate to educational growth—which, given the demands on the modern man, must be increased. Despite the fine job of state and local governments, the job is much too extensive for their finances, and the national government must make funds available to achieve the goals of American education. By helping the schools to be more stable financially, federal aid will encourage independence. In order to improve the quality of education, and the ability to cope with the vast numbers desiring education, the President proposed a comprehensive program, formally entitled the National Education Improvement Act of 1963. The proposals in this omnibus bill ranged from aid to higher education to encouragement of elementary, secondary, vocational, and special education, along with federal funds for libraries and extension courses so that the education of Americans might be an unending process.

Education is the keystone in the arch of freedom and progress. Nothing has contributed more to the enlargement of this Nation's strength and opportunities than our traditional system of free, universal elementary and secondary education, coupled with widespread availability of college education.

For the individual, the doors to the schoolhouse, to the library and to the college lead to the richest treasures of our open society: to the power of knowledge—to the training and skills necessary for productive employment—to the wisdom, the ideals, and the culture which enrich life—and to the creative, self-disciplined understanding of society needed for good citizenship in today's changing and challenging world.

For the Nation, increasing the quality and availability of educa-

"Special Message to the Congress on Education." Doc. 43, January 29, 1963. *Public Papers,* 1963, pp. 105–116.

tion is vital to both our national security and our domestic well-being. A free nation can rise no higher than the standard of excellence set in its schools and colleges. Ignorance and illiteracy, unskilled workers and school dropouts—these and other failures of our educational system breed failures in our social and economic system: delinquency, unemployment, chronic dependence, a waste of human resources, a loss of productive power and purchasing power and an increase in tax-supported benefits. The loss of only 1 year's income due to unemployment is more than the total cost of 12 years of education through high school. Failure to improve educational performance is thus not only poor social policy, it is poor economics.

At the turn of the century, only 10 per cent of our adults had a high school or college education. Today such an education has become a requirement for an increasing number of jobs. Yet nearly 40 per cent of our youths are dropping out before graduating from high school; only 43 per cent of our adults have completed high school; only 8 per cent of our adults have completed college; and only 16 per cent of our young people are presently completing college. As my Science Advisory Committee has reported, one of our most serious manpower shortages is the lack of Ph. D.'s in engineering, science, and mathematics; only about one-half of 1 per cent of our school-age generation is achieving Ph. D. degrees in all fields.

This Nation is committed to greater investment in economic growth; and recent research has shown that one of the most beneficial of all such investments is education, accounting for some 40 per cent of the Nation's growth and productivity in recent years. It is an investment which yields a substantial return in the higher wages and purchasing power of trained workers, in the new products and techniques which come from skilled minds and in the constant expansion of this Nation's storehouse of useful knowledge.

In the new age of science and space, improved education is essential to give new meaning to our national purpose and power. In the last 20 years, mankind has acquired more scientific information than in all of previous history. Ninety per cent of all the scientists that ever lived are alive and working today. Vast stretches of the unknown are being explored every day for military, medical, commercial and other reasons. And finally, the twisting course of the cold war requires a citizenry that understands our principles and problems. It requires skilled manpower and brainpower to match the power of totalitarian discipline. It requires a scientific effort which demonstrates the superiority of freedom. And it requires an electorate in every State with sufficiently broad horizons and sufficient maturity of judgment to guide this Nation safely through whatever lies ahead.

In short, from every point of view, education is of paramount concern to the national interest as well as to each individual. Today we need a new standard of excellence in education, matched by the fullest possible access to educational opportunities, enabling each citizen to develop his talents to the maximum possible extent.

Our concern as a Nation for the future of our children—and the growing demands of modern education which Federal financing is better able to assist—make it necessary to expand Federal aid to education beyond the existing limited number of special programs. We can no longer afford the luxury of endless debate over all the complicated and sensitive questions raised by each new proposal on Federal participation in education. To be sure, these are all hard problems— but this Nation has not come to its present position of leadership by avoiding hard problems. We are at a point in history when we must face and resolve these problems.

State and local governments and private institutions, responsive to individual and local circumstances, have admirably served larger national purposes as well. They have written a remarkable record of freedom of thought and independence of judgment; and they have, in recent years, devoted sharply increased resources to education. . . .

But all this has not been enough. And the Federal Government— despite increasing recognition of education as a nationwide challenge, and despite the increased financial difficulties encountered by States, communities, and private institutions in carrying this burden—has clearly not met its responsibilities in education. It has not offered sufficient help to our present educational system to meet its inadequacies and overcome its obstacles.

I do not say that the Federal Government should take over responsibility for education. That is neither desirable nor feasible. Instead its participation should be selective, stimulative and, where possible, transitional.

A century of experience with land-grant colleges has demonstrated that Federal financial participation can assist educational progress and growth without Federal control. In the last decade, experience with the National Science Foundation, with the National Defense Education Act, and with programs for assisting federally affected school districts has demonstrated that Federal support can benefit education without leading to Federal control. The proper Federal role is to identify national education goals and to help local, State, and private authorities build the necessary roads to reach those goals. Federal aid will enable our schools, colleges and universities to be more stable financially and therefore more independent.

These goals include the following:

First, we must improve the *quality* of instruction provided in all of our schools and colleges. We must stimulate interest in learning in order to reduce the alarming number of students who now drop out of school or who do not continue into higher levels of education. This requires more and better teachers—teachers who can be attracted to and retained in schools and colleges only if pay levels reflect more adequately the value of the services they render. It also requires that our teachers and instructors be equipped with the best possible teaching materials and curriculums. They must have at their command methods of instruction proven by thorough scientific research into the learning process and by careful experimentation.

Second, our educational system faces a major problem of *quantity* —of coping with the needs of our expanding population and of the rising educational expectations for our children which all of us share as parents. Nearly 50 million people were enrolled in our schools and colleges in 1962—an increase of more than 50 per cent since 1950. By 1970, college enrollment will nearly double, and secondary schools will increase enrollment by 50 per cent—categories in which the cost of education, including facilities, is several times higher than in elementary schools.

Third, we must give special attention to increasing the *opportunities* and *incentives* for all Americans to develop their talents to the utmost—to complete their education and to continue their self-development throughout life. This means preventing school dropouts, improving and expanding special educational services, and providing better education in slum, distressed and rural areas where the educational attainment of students is far below par. It means increased opportunities for those students both willing and intellectually able to advance their education at the college and graduate levels. It means increased attention to vocational and technical education, which have long been underdeveloped in both effectiveness and scope, to the detriment of our workers and our technological progress.

In support of these three basic goals, I am proposing today a comprehensive, balanced program to enlarge the Federal Government's investment in the education of its citizens—a program aimed at increasing the educational opportunities of potentially every American citizen, regardless of age, race, religion, income, and educational achievement.

This program has been shaped to meet our goals on the basis of three fundamental guidelines:

(a) An appraisal of the entire range of educational problems, viewing educational opportunity as a continuous lifelong process, starting with preschool training and extending through elementary and secondary schools, college, graduate education, vocational education, job training and retraining adult education, and such general community educational resources as the public library;

(b) A selective application of Federal aid—aimed at strengthening, not weakening, the independence of existing school systems and aimed at meeting our most urgent education problems and objectives, including quality improvement; teacher training; special problems of slum, depressed, and rural areas; needy students; manpower shortage areas such as science and engineering; and shortages of educational facilities; and

(c) More effective implementation of existing [education] laws. . . .

To enable the full range of educational needs to be considered as a whole, I am transmitting to the Congress with this message a single, comprehensive education bill—the National Education Improvement Act of 1963. For education cannot easily or wisely be divided into separate parts. Each part is linked to the other. The colleges depend on the work of the schools; the schools depend on the colleges for teachers; vocational and technical education is not separate from general education. This bill recalls the posture of Jefferson: "Nobody can doubt my zeal for the general instruction of the people. I never have proposed a sacrifice of the primary to the ultimate grade of instruction. Let us keep our eye steadily on the whole system."

In order that its full relation to economic growth, to the new age of science, to the national security, and to human and institutional freedom may be analyzed in proper perspective, this bill should be considered as a whole, as a combination of elements designed to solve problems that have no single solution.

This is not a partisan measure—and it neither includes nor rejects all of the features which have long been sought by the various educational groups and organizations. It is instead an attempt to launch a prudent and balanced program drawing upon the efforts of many past Congresses and the proposals [of] many Members of both Houses and both political parties. It is solely an educational program, without trying to solve all other difficult domestic problems. It is clearly realistic in terms of its cost—and it is clearly essential to the growth and security of this country.

I. THE EXPANSION OF OPPORTUNITIES FOR INDIVIDUALS IN HIGHER EDUCATION

. . . Now a veritable tidal wave of students is advancing inexorably on our institutions of higher education, where the annual costs per student are several times as high as the cost of a high school education, and where these costs must be borne in large part by the student or his parents. . . . The future of these young people and the Nation rests in large part on their access to college and graduate education. For this country reserves its highest honors for only one kind of aristocracy —that which the Founding Fathers called "an aristocracy of achievement arising out of a democracy of opportunity."

Well over half of all parents with school-age children expect them to attend college. But only one-third do so. Some 40 per cent of those who enter college do not graduate, and only a small number continue into graduate and professional study. The lack of adequate aid to students plays a large part in this disturbing record.

Federal aid to college students is not new. More than 3 million World War II and Korean conflict veterans have received $6 billion in Federal funds since 1944 to assist them to attend college.

Additionally, the National Defense Education Act college student loan program has aided more than 300,000 students in more than 1,500 institutions who have borrowed nearly $220 million dollars. In four years of operations, defaults have totaled only $700 while repayment rates are more than twice that required by law.

But as effective as this program has been, it has not fulfilled its original objective of assuring that "no student of ability will be denied an opportunity for higher education because of financial need." The institutional ceiling of $250,000 per year on the Federal contribution limits loan funds in at least 98 of the presently participating institutions. The annual statutory ceiling of $90 million on Federal appropriations restricts the size of the program. As a result, only about 5 per cent of the students enrolled in participating colleges are assisted. . . . This proven program must be enlarged and strengthened.

Other types of assistance are needed. For students who cannot meet the financial criteria under the National Defense Education Act loan program, a loan insurance program . . . would encourage banks and other institutions to loan more money for educational purposes.

Moreover, many students from families with limited incomes cannot and should not carry a heavy burden of debt. They must rely largely on income from employment while in college. For these students, the Federal Government should . . . help colleges provide additional student work opportunities of an educational character.

A serious barrier to increased graduate study is the lack of adequate financial aid for graduate students. Only 1,500 fellowships are permitted annually under the National Defense Education Act program, upon which we are dependent for urgently needed increases in the number of college teachers and the number of graduate students pursuing other courses essential to the Nation's advancement and security. . . . In all fields the need exceeds the supply of doctoral recipients. The shortage is particularly acute in college teaching, where at present rates the Nation will lack 90,000 doctoral degree holders by 1970. It is clearly contrary to the national interest to have the number of graduate students limited by the financial ability of those able and interested in pursuing advanced degrees. Fellowship programs can ease much of the financial burden and, most importantly, encourage and stimulate a fuller realization and utilization of our human resources.

The welfare and security of the Nation require that we increase our investment in financial assistance for college students both at undergraduate and graduate levels. In keeping with present needs and our traditions of maximum self-help, *I recommend that the Congress enact legislation to—*

(1) *Extend the National Defense Education Act student loan program, liberalize the repayment forgiveness for teachers, raise the ceiling on total appropriations and eliminate the limitation on amounts available to individual institutions.*

(2) *Authorize a supplementary new program of Federal insurance for commercial loans made by banks and other institutions to college students for educational purposes.*

(3) *Establish a new work-study program for needy college students unable to carry too heavy a loan burden, providing up to half the pay for students employed by the colleges in work of an educational character—as, for example, laboratory, library, or research assistants.*

(4) *Increase the number of National Defense Education Act fellowships to be awarded by the Office of Education from 1,500 to 12,000, including summer session awards.*

(5) *Authorize a thorough survey and evaluation of the need for scholarships or additional financial assistance to undergraduate students so that any further action needed in this area can be considered by the next Congress.*

(6) In addition, as part of this program to increase financial assistance to students, . . . expand the number of [National Science Foundation] fellowships and new teaching grants for graduate study from 2,800 in 1963 to 8,700 in fiscal 1964.

II. EXPANSION AND IMPROVEMENT OF HIGHER EDUCATION

Aid to college students will be to no avail if there are insufficient college classrooms. The long-predicted crisis in higher education facilities is now at hand. For the next 15 years, even without additional student aid, enrollment increases in colleges will average 340,000 each year. . . . This means that, unless we are to deny higher education opportunities to our youth, American colleges and universities must expand their academic facilities at a rate much faster than their present resources will permit.

In many colleges, students with adequate modern dormitories and living quarters—thanks to the College Housing Act—are crammed in outmoded, overcrowded classrooms, laboratories, and libraries. Even now it is too late to provide these facilities to meet the sharp increases in college enrollment expected during the next 2 years. Further delay will aggravate an already critical situation.

I recommend, therefore, the prompt enactment of a program to provide loans to public and nonprofit private institutions of higher education for construction of urgently needed academic facilities.

The opportunity for a college education is severely limited for hundreds of thousands of young people because there is no college in their own community. Studies indicate that the likelihood of going to college on the part of a high school graduate who lives within 20 to 25 miles of a college is 50 per cent greater than it is for the student who lives beyond commuting distance. This absence of college facilities in many communities causes an unfortunate waste of some of our most promising youthful talent. A demonstrated method of meeting this particular problem effectively is the creation of 2-year community colleges—a program that should be undertaken without delay and which will require Federal assistance for the construction of adequate facilities.

I recommend, therefore, a program of grants to States for construction of public community junior colleges.

There is an especially urgent need for college-level training of technicians to assist scientists, engineers, and doctors. Although ideally one scientist or engineer should have the backing of two or three technicians, our institutions today are not producing even one technician for each three science and engineering graduates. This shortage results in an inefficient use of professional manpower—the occupation of critically needed time and talent to perform tasks which could be performed by others—an extravagance which cannot be tolerated when the Nation's demand for scientists, engineers, and doctors continues to grow. Failure to give attention to this matter will impede the objectives of the graduate and postgraduate training programs mentioned below.

I recommend, therefore, a program of grants to aid public and private nonprofit institutions in the training of scientific, engineering, and medical technicians in 2-year, college-level programs, covering up to 50 per cent of the cost of constructing and equipping as well as operating the necessary academic facilities.

Special urgency exists for expanding the capacity for the graduate training of engineers, scientists, and mathematicians. The President's Science Advisory Committee has recently reported that an unprecedented acceleration in the production of advanced degrees is immediately necessary to increase our national capability in these fields. Added facilities, larger faculties, and new institutions are needed. *I have recommended, therefore, . . . a strengthening of the National Science Foundation matching-grant program for institutions of higher education to expand and improve graduate and undergraduate science facilities.*

Because today's trend in colleges and universities is toward less lecturing and more independent study, the college and university library becomes even more essential in the life of our students. Today, as reported by the American Library Association, nearly all college libraries are urgently in need of additional books, periodicals, scientific reports and similar materials to accommodate the growing number of students and faculty. Additionally, they need buildings, equipment, and publications to serve their academic communities, whether public or private.

I recommend the authorization of Federal grants to institutions of higher education for library materials and construction, on a broad geographic basis, with priority to those most urgently requiring expansion and improvement.

Expansion of high quality graduate education and research in all fields is essential to national security and economic growth. Means of increasing our supply of highly trained professional personnel to match the rapidly growing demands of teaching, industry, government, and research warrants our interest and support.

We need many more graduate centers, and they should be better distributed geographically. Three-quarters of all doctoral degrees are granted by a handful of universities located in 12 States. The remaining States with half our population produce only one-fourth of the Ph. D.'s.

New industries increasingly gravitate to or are innovated by strong centers of learning and research. The distressed area of the future may well be one which lacks centers of graduate education and research. It is in the national interest to encourage establishment of these critically needed centers of advanced learning, especially in parts of the Nation now lacking them.

I recommend enactment of a Federal grant program . . . for the development and expansion of new graduate centers. I also urge appropriation of the increased funds . . . for expansion of the National Science Foundation program of science development grants, which will also contribute to strengthening of graduate education.

Our experience under the National Defense Education Act with respect to modern language and area centers has demonstrated that Federal aid can spur development of intellectual talent. They deserve our continuing support, with assurance that resources will be available for orderly expansion in keeping with availability of teaching talent.

I recommend that the current modern foreign language program aiding public and private institutions of higher learning be extended and expanded.

III. IMPROVEMENT OF EDUCATIONAL QUALITY

A basic source of knowledge is research. Industry has long realized this truth. Health and agriculture have established the worth of systematic research and development. But research in education has been astonishingly meager and frequently ignored. A fraction of 1 per cent of this Nation's total expenditures for education is now devoted to such research. It is appalling that so little is known about the level of performance, comparative value of alternative investments and specialized problems of our educational system—and that it lags behind, sometimes by as much as 20 or even 50 years, in utilizing the result of research and keeping abreast of man's knowledge in all fields, including education itself.

Highest priority must be given to strengthening our educational research efforts, including a substantial expansion of the course content improvement programs which the Government has supported, particularly through the National Science Foundation. Two interrelated actions are necessary:

1. *I have recommended appropriations . . . for substantially expanding the National Science Foundation science and mathematics course materials program and the Office of Education educational research program.*

2. *I recommend legislation to broaden the Cooperative Research Act to authorize support of centers for multipurpose educational research, and for development and demonstration programs; and to broaden the types of educational agencies eligible to conduct research.*

The second step to improvement of educational quality is *teacher training.* The quality of education is determined primarily by the quality of the teacher. . . . In the field of English, between 40 and 60 per cent of the secondary school teachers lack even the minimum requirement of a college major in that subject. Thus it is not surprising that, largely because of unsatisfactory elementary and secondary school instruction, our colleges and universities are now required to spend over $10 million annually on remedial English courses.

The lack of teacher quality and preparation in other fields is equally disturbing. More than two-thirds of our 1.6 million teachers completed their degree work more than 5 years ago. Yet, within the past 5 years, major advances have been made—not only in the physical, biological, engineering, and mathematical sciences, but also in specialized branches of the social sciences, the arts and humanities, and in the art of teaching itself.

In addition, we lack sufficient trained teachers for 6 million handicapped children and youth, including 1.5 million mentally retarded and another 1.5 million with very serious social and emotional problems. Only through special classes, taught by specially trained teachers, can these children prepare for rehabilitation, employment, and community participation. Yet less than one-fourth of these children now have access to the special education they require, primarily because of the lack of qualified special teachers, college instructors, research personnel, and supervisors. It is estimated that 75,000 special teachers —55,000 more than presently available—are needed for the mentally retarded alone.

The teacher training support programs of the National Science Foundation and the Office of Education have demonstrated their value.

I recommend, therefore—

That the National Science Foundation program for training institutes for teachers in the natural sciences, mathematics, engineering, and social sciences be expanded to provide for upgrading the knowledge and skills of 46,000 teachers. . . .

That new legislation be enacted to (a) broaden authority for teacher institutes financed by the Office of Education, now restricted to school guidance counselors and language teachers, to other academic fields; (b) authorize a program of project grants to help colleges and universities improve their teacher preparation programs by upgrading academic courses and staff, by encouraging the selection and retention of their most talented prospective teachers, and by attracting and training teachers from new sources such as retired military personnel or women whose family responsibilities permit them to teach; and (c) authorize training grants through colleges and universities for teachers and other educational personnel requiring specialized training, with particular emphasis on the training of teachers of the mentally retarded and other handicapped children, teachers of gifted or culturally deprived children, teachers of adult literacy, librarians, and educational researchers.

IV. STRENGTHENING PUBLIC ELEMENTARY AND SECONDARY EDUCATION

Improved research and teacher training are not enough, if good teachers do not choose to teach. Yet present salary schedules in some cases are too low at the start to compete against other positions available to college graduates. In almost all cases, they are too low at the top to retain our ablest young teachers. Without sufficient incentive to make teaching a lifetime career, teachers with valuable training and experience but heavy family responsibilities too often become frustrated and drop out of the profession. Their children may never try to enter. Although teachers' salaries have generally improved in the Nation in recent years, there are still districts which have starting salaries below $3,000.

Good teachers, moreover, need good schools. Last year, over 1,500,000 children were in overcrowded classrooms and an estimated 2 million others were studying amid grossly substandard health and safety conditions. In many areas school dropouts, or the education of the economically disadvantaged, the culturally deprived, the physically or mentally handicapped, and the gifted require specially designed programs which simply are not available.

I am not the first, but I hope to be the last, President to be compelled to call these needless shortcomings to the Nation's attention. These are national problems crossing State boundaries, and deserving of national attention. In our mobile population—where every year one out of five families moves, sometimes across the street, but often across State lines—every family has reason to make teaching in every State a more rewarding and productive profession, and to help every State strengthen its public elementary and secondary education, particularly in those school districts that are financially unable to keep up.

Yet let us face the fact that the Federal Government cannot provide all the financial assistance needed to solve all of the problems mentioned. Instead of a general aid approach that could at best create a small wave in a huge ocean, our efforts should be selective and stimulative, encouraging the States to redouble their efforts under a plan that would phase out Federal aid over a 4-year period.

I recommend, therefore, a 4-year program to provide 1.5 billion dollars to assist States in undertaking under their own State plans selective and urgent improvements in public elementary and secondary education including: (1) increasing starting and maximum teacher salaries, and increasing average teacher salaries in economically disadvantaged areas; (2) constructing classrooms in areas of critical and dangerous shortage; and (3) initiating pilot, experimental, or demonstration projects to meet special educational problems, particularly in slums and depressed rural and urban areas.

I also recommend extension of the National Defense Education Act programs which contribute to improving the quality of elementary and secondary education. Grants for testing, guidance, and counseling programs should be expanded and continued beyond the 1964 expiration date. This program has great relevance for the detection of incipient problems which inhibit learning and for development of the talents of our youth. National Defense Education Act assistance for science, mathematics, and foreign language laboratory equipment—which is essentially for adequate educational programs using newly developed teaching methods—should also be continued beyond 1964.

Finally, in regard to elementary and secondary schools, *I recommend a 4-year continuation of those portions of the federally affected area laws which expire June 30, 1963.* These statutes now assist some 4,000 school districts located in every State, which together enroll one-third of all public elementary and secondary school pupils in the Nation. Almost 60,000 critically needed classrooms have been constructed at a cost of $1.15 billion to house more than 1,700,000 pupils; and school operating budgets have been supplemented by more than $1.7 billion. For fiscal 1964 the present provisions would be extended. Limited modifications of the existing provisions, which would take effect beginning in 1965, would overcome certain inequities demonstrated by past experience. Also, the District of Columbia should be added to the jurisdictions eligible to participate.

V. VOCATIONAL AND SPECIAL EDUCATION

Since the wartime administration of President Woodrow Wilson, Congress has recognized the national necessity of widespread vocational education. Although revised and extended frequently since 1917, the national vocational education acts are no longer adequate. Many once-familiar occupations have declined or disappeared and wholly new industries and jobs have emerged from economic growth and change. The complexities of modern science and technology require training at a higher level than ever before.

For this reason, 2 years ago I requested the Secretary of Health, Education, and Welfare to convene an expert and representative committee to review and evaluate the present vocational education laws and to make recommendations for their modernization. The report of that committee shows the need for providing new training opportunities—in occupations which have relevance to contemporary

America—to 21 million youth now in grade school who will enter the labor market without a college degree during the 1960's. These youth—representing more than 80 per cent of the population between the ages of 16 and 21—will be entering the labor market at a time when the need for unskilled labor is sharply diminishing. It is equally necessary to provide training or retraining for the millions of workers who need to learn new skills or whose skills and technical knowledge must be updated.

Both budgetary action and enactment of new legislation is called for. In my 1964 budget *I have recommended funds which would permit doubling the number of workers to be trained by the Manpower Development and Training Act programs.* These programs have, in their brief existence, already enrolled more than 18,000 men, women, and out-of-school youths who are being trained in occupations where jobs are available.

In addition, I recommend legislation to—

(a) Expand the scope and level of vocational education programs supported through the Office of Education by replacing the Vocational Education Act of 1946 with new grant-in-aid legislation aimed at meeting the needs of individuals in all age groups for vocational training in occupations where they can find employment in today's diverse labor markets, and

(b) Provide employment and training opportunities for unemployed youth in conservation and local public service projects. . . .

VI. CONTINUING EDUCATION

Education need not and should not end upon graduation at any level. An increasing number of Americans recognize the need and the value of continuing education. The accountant, the salesman, the merchant, the skilled and semiskilled worker, all interested in self-improvement, should all be afforded the opportunity of securing up-to-date knowledge and skills. Only one American in eight has even taken as much as one college course. Yet the State universities and land-grant colleges which offer the majority of extension or part-time courses enroll less than a half million people. Due to inadequate finances and facilities, these colleges can offer only a very limited adult education program.

I recommend legislation authorizing Federal grants to States for expanding university extension courses in land-grant colleges and State universities. Despite our high level of education opportunity and attainment, nearly 23 million adult Americans lack an eighth-grade education. They represent a staggering economic and cultural loss to their families and the Nation. *I recommend again, as part of this comprehensive bill, a program to assist all States in offering literacy and basic education courses to adults.*

The public library is also an important resource for continuing education. But 18 million people in this Nation still have no access to any local public library service and over 110 million more have only inadequate service.

Advanced age, lack of space, and lack of modern equipment characterize American public library buildings in 1963. Their rate of replacement is barely noticeable: 2 per cent in a decade. There are now no Carnegie funds available for libraries, nor have there been for 40 years.

The public library building is usually one of the oldest governmental structures in use in any community. In one prosperous midwestern State, for example, 30 per cent of all public library buildings were built before the year 1910, and 85 per cent were erected before 1920. Many other States are in a similar situation.

I recommend enactment of legislation to amend the Library Services Act by authorizing a 3-year program of grants for urban as well as rural libraries and for construction as well as operation.

VII. CONCLUSION

In all the years of our national life, the American people, in partnership with their governments, have continued to insist that "the means of education shall forever be encouraged," as the Continental Congress affirmed in the Northwest Ordinance. Fundamentally, education is and must always be a local responsibility, for it thrives best when nurtured at the grassroots of our democracy. But in our present era of economic expansion, population growth, and technological advance, State, local, and private efforts are insufficient. These efforts must be reinforced by national support if American education is to yield a maximum of individual development and national well-being.

The necessity of this program does not rest on the course of the cold war. Improvement in education is essential to our Nation's development without respect to what others are doing. Nevertheless, it is worthwhile noting that the Soviet Union recognizes that educational effort in the 1960's will have a major effect on a nation's power, progress, and status in the 1970's and 1980's. According to a recent report prepared for the National Science Foundation, Soviet institutions of higher education are graduating three times as many engineers and four times as many physicians as the United States. While trailing behind this country in aggregate annual numbers of higher education graduates, the Soviets are maintaining an annual flow of scientific and technical professional manpower more than twice as large as our own. At the same time, they have virtually eliminated illiteracy, with a 23-fold increase since the turn of the century in the proportion of persons with an education beyond the seventh grade. This Nation's devotion to education is surely sufficient to excel the achievements of any other nation or system.

The program here proposed is reasonable and yet far reaching. It offers Federal assistance without Federal control. It provides for economic growth, manpower development, and progress toward our educational and humanitarian objectives. It encourages the increase of the knowledge, skills, attitudes, and critical intelligence necessary for the preservation of our society. It will help keep America strong and safe and free. I strongly recommend it to the Congress for high priority action.

CULTIVATING YOUNG TALENT

Early in the first session of the Eighty-eighth Congress, President Kennedy submitted a Special Message on the Nation's Youth to the House and Senate. The message covered the problems of youth employment, a national service corps (domestic peace corps), family welfare, youth education, and the physical fitness of young people. The President encouraged interest in youth as the best possible investment of a nation economically, socially, and culturally. On youth education, he urged Congress to enact his omnibus education bill.

"The youth of a nation," said Disraeli, "are the trustees of posterity." The future promise of any nation can be directly measured by the present prospects of its youth. This Nation—facing increasingly complex economic, social and international challenges—is increasingly dependent on the opportunities, capabilities and vitality of those who are soon to bear its chief responsibilities. Such attributes as energy, a readiness to question, imagination and creativity are all attributes of youth that are also essential to our total national character. To the extent that the Nation is called upon to promote and protect the interests of our younger citizens, it is an investment certain to bring a high return, not only in basic human values but in social and economic terms. . . .

YOUTH EDUCATION

The most direct, rewarding and important investment in our children and youth is education. A high rate of investment in education is essential for our national economic growth, our scientific advancement and our national security. Maintaining the broadest possible opportunities in education is essential to the maintenance of democratic government and to the attainment of our social, cultural and economic aspirations.

Yet millions of our young men and women do not have proper educational opportunities. As a result they do not fully develop their

"Special Message to the Congress on the Nation's Youth." Doc. 64, February 14, 1963. *Public Papers*, 1963, pp. 164, 170–171.

intellectual capacities and take their proper place as productive, adult members of society. To strengthen our educational system, we must increase both the quantity and the quality of our educational facilities and services, providing an opportunity for every young American to achieve the highest level of his capacity. It is to these problems that the program outlined in my recent message on Education was addressed: I again urge action on a comprehensive Federal program to meet critical education needs. . . .

EQUAL OPPORTUNITY

The centennial of the issuance of the Emancipation Proclamation was the occasion of Kennedy's message to Congress on civil rights on February 28, 1962. In retrospect, the step taken by Lincoln was the first of a series; unfortunately, though it abolished slavery, it did not eliminate discrimination. One section of the President's proposed civil rights bill was devoted to equal rights in education. The Chief Executive vowed to continue efforts to bring about equal educational opportunity for all. Progress had been too slow, and federal technical and financial assistance was proposed by the President to facilitate desegregation in the schools.

"Our Constitution is color blind," wrote Mr. Justice Harlan before the turn of the century, "and neither knows nor tolerates classes among citizens." But the practices of the country do not always conform to the principles of the Constitution. And this message is intended to examine how far we have come in achieving first-class citizenship for all citizens regardless of color, how far we have yet to go, and what further tasks remain to be carried out by the executive and legislative branches of the Federal Government, as well as by State and local governments and private citizens and organizations.

One hundred years ago the Emancipation Proclamation was signed by a President who believed in the equal worth and opportunity of every human being. That proclamation was only a first step, a step which its author unhappily did not live to follow up, a step which some of its critics dismissed as an action which "frees the slave but ignores the Negro." Through these long 100 years, while slavery has vanished, progress for the Negro has been too often blocked and delayed. Equality before the law has not always meant equal treatment and opportunity. And the harmful, wasteful, and wrongful results of racial discrimination and segregation still appear in virtually every aspect of national life, in virtually every part of the Nation. . . .

No American who believes in the basic truth that "all men are

"Special Message to the Congress on Civil Rights." Doc. 82, February 28, 1963. *Public Papers,* 1963, pp. 221–222, 225–226, 230.

created equal, that they are endowed by their Creator with certain unalienable rights," can fully excuse, explain, or defend the picture these statistics portray. Race discrimination hampers our economic growth by preventing the maximum development and utilization of our manpower. It hampers our world leadership by contradicting at home the message we preach abroad. It mars the atmosphere of a united and classless society in which this Nation rose to greatness. It increases the costs of public welfare, crime, delinquency, and disorder. Above all, it is wrong.

Therefore, let it be clear, in our own hearts and minds, that it is not merely because of the cold war, and not merely because of the economic waste of discrimination, that we are committed to achieving true equality of opportunity. The basic reason is because it is right.

The cruel disease of discrimination knows no sectional or State boundaries. The continuing attack on this problem must be equally broad. It must be both private and public, it must be conducted at National, State, and local levels, and it must include both legislative and executive action.

In the last two years, more progress has been made in securing the civil rights of all Americans than in any comparable period in our history. Progress has been made through executive action, litigation, persuasion, and private initiative in achieving and protecting equality of opportunity in education, voting, transportation, employment, housing, government, and the enjoyment of public accommodations.

But pride in our progress must not give way to relaxation of our effort. Nor does progress in the executive branch enable the legislative branch to escape its own obligations. On the contrary, it is in the light of this nationwide progress, and in the belief that Congress will wish once again to meet its responsibilities in this matter, that I stress in the following agenda of existing and prospective action important legislative as well as administrative measures. . . .

EDUCATION

Nearly 9 years have elapsed since the Supreme Court ruled that State laws requiring or permitting segregated schools violate the Constitution. That decision represented both good law and good judgment—it was both legally and morally right. Since that time it has become increasingly clear that neither violence nor legalistic evasions will be tolerated as a means of thwarting court-ordered desegregation, that closed schools are not an answer, and that responsible communities are able to handle the desegregation process in a calm and sensible manner. . . .

. . . State-supported universities in Georgia and South Carolina met this test in recent years with calm and maturity, as did the State-supported universities of Virginia, North Carolina, Florida, Texas, Louisiana, Tennessee, Arkansas, and Kentucky in earlier years. In addition, progress toward the desegregation of education at all levels has made other notable and peaceful strides, including the following forward moves in the last 2 years alone:

—Desegregation plans have been put into effect peacefully in the public schools of Atlanta, Dallas, New Orleans, Memphis, and elsewhere, with over 60 school districts desegregated last year—frequently with the help of Federal persuasion and consultation, and in every case without incident or disorder.

—Teacher training institutes financed under the National Defense Education Act are no longer held in colleges which refuse to accept students without regard to race, and this has resulted in a number of institutions opening their doors to Negro applicants voluntarily.

—The same is now true of institutes conducted by the National Science Foundation;

—Beginning in September of this year, under the Aid to Impacted Area School Program, the Department of Health, Education, and Welfare will initiate a program of providing on-base facilities so that children living on military installations will no longer be required to attend segregated schools at Federal expense. These children should not be victimized by segregation merely because their fathers chose to serve in the armed forces and were assigned to an area where schools are operated on a segregated basis.

—In addition, the Department of Justice and the Department of Health, Education, and Welfare have succeeded in obtaining voluntary desegregation in many other districts receiving "impacted area" school assistance; and, representing the Federal interest, have filed lawsuits to end segregation in a number of other districts.

The Department of Justice has also intervened to seek the opening of public schools in the case of Prince Edward County, Virginia, the only county in the Nation where there are no public schools, and where a bitter effort to thwart court decrees requiring desegregation has caused nearly 1,500 out of 1,800 school age Negro children to go without any education for more than 3 years.

In these and other areas within its jurisdiction, the executive branch will continue its efforts to fulfill the constitutional objective of an equal nonsegregated, educational opportunity for all children.

Despite these efforts, however, progress toward primary and secondary school desegregation has still been too slow, often painfully so. Those children who are being denied their constitutional rights are suffering a loss which can never be regained, and which will leave scars which can never be fully healed. I have in the past expressed my belief that the full authority of the Federal Government should be placed behind the achievement of school desegregation, in accordance with the command of the Constitution. One obvious area of Federal action is to help facilitate the transition to desegregation in those areas which are conforming or wish to conform their practices to the law.

Many of these communities lack the resources necessary to eliminate segregation in their public schools while at the same time assuring that educational standards will be maintained and improved. The problem has been compounded by the fact that the climate of mistrust in many communities has left many school officials with no qualified source to turn to for information and advice.

There is a need for technical assistance by the Office of Education to assist local communities in preparing and carrying out desegregation plans, including the supplying of information on means which have been employed to desegregate other schools successfully. There is also need for financial assistance to enable those communities which desire and need such assistance to employ specialized personnel to cope with problems occasioned by desegregation and to train school personnel to facilitate the transition to desegregation. While some facilities for providing this kind of assistance are presently available in the Office of Education, they are not adequate to the task.

I recommend, therefore, a program of Federal technical and financial assistance to aid school districts in the process of desegregation in compliance with the Constitution.

Finally, it is obvious that the unconstitutional and outmoded concept of "separate but equal" does not belong in the Federal statute books. This is particularly true with respect to higher education, where peaceful desegregation has been underway in practically every State for some time. I repeat, therefore, this administration's recommendation of last year that this phrase be eliminated from the Morrill Land-Grant College Act. . . .

CONCLUSION

. . . it is my hope that this message will lend encouragement to those state and local governments—and to private organizations, corporations, and individuals—who share my concern over the gap between our precepts and our practices. This is an effort in which every individual who asks what he can do for his country should be able and willing to take part. It is important, for example, for private citizens and local governments to support the State Department's effort to end the discriminatory treatment suffered by too many foreign diplomats, students, and visitors to this country. But it is not enough to treat those from other lands with equality and dignity—the same treatment must be afforded to every American citizen.

The program outlined in this message should not provide the occasion for sectional bitterness. No state or section of this Nation can pretend a self-righteous role, for every area has its own civil rights problems.

Nor should the basic elements of this program be imperiled by partisanship. The proposals put forth are consistent with the platforms of both parties and with the positions of their leaders. Inevitably there will be disagreement about means and strategy. But I would hope that on issues of constitutional rights and freedom, as in matters affecting our national security, there is a fundamental unity among us that will survive partisan debate over particular issues.

The centennial of the issuance of the Emancipation Proclamation is an occasion for celebration, for a sober assessment of our failures, and for rededication to the goals of freedom. Surely there could be no more meaningful observance of the centennial than the enactment of effective civil rights legislation and the continuation of effective executive action.

At ceremonies marking the centennial of Boston College, Kennedy emphasized again the growing importance of higher education in the modern world. He outlined four leading roles that the university must fill.

. . . Learned men have been talking here of the knowledge explosion, and in all that they have said I am sure that they have implied the heavy present responsibility of institutions like this one. Yet today I want . . . to impress upon you as urgently as I can the growing and insistent importance of universities in our national life.

. . . most of what I say applies to liberal arts colleges as well. My theme is not limited to any one class of universities, public or private, religious or secular. Our national tradition of variety in higher education shows no sign of weakening, and it remains the task of each of our institutions to shape its own role among its differing sisters.

In this hope I am much encouraged by a reading in this last week of the remarkable encyclical, "Pacem in Terris." In its penetrating analysis of today's great problems, of social welfare and human rights, or disarmament and international order and peace, that document surely shows that on the basis of one great faith and its traditions there can be developed counsel on public affairs that is of value to all men and women of good will. As a Catholic, I am proud of it; and as an American, I have learned from it. It only adds to the impact of this message that it closely matches notable expressions of conviction and aspiration from churchmen of other faiths, as in recent documents of the World Council of Churches, and from outstanding world citizens with no ecclesiastical standing. We are learning to talk the language of progress and peace across the barriers of sect and creed. It seems reasonable to hope that a similar process may be taking place across the quite different barriers of higher learning.

From the office that I hold, in any case, there can be no doubt today of the growing meaning of universities in America. That, of

"Address at the Boston College Centennial Ceremonies." Doc. 136, April 20, 1963. *Public Papers,* 1963, pp. 335–337.

course, is one basic reason for the increasing urgency with which those who care most for the progress of our society are pressing for more adequate programs in higher education and in education generally. It is for this reason that I urge upon everyone here and in this country the pressing need for national attention and a national decision in the national interest upon the national question of education. In at least four ways, the new realities of our day have combined to intensify the focal role of the university in our Nation's life.

First, and perhaps most obvious, the whole world has come to our doorstep and the universities must be its student. In the strange geometry of modern politics, the distant Congo can be as close to us as Canada, and Canada, itself, is worth more attention than we have sometimes given. Cultures not our own press for understanding. Crises we did not create require our participation. Accelerating change is the one universal human prospect.

Second, there is indeed an explosion of knowledge and its outward limits are not yet in sight. In some fields, progress seems very fast; in others, distressingly slow. It is no tribute to modern science to jump lightly to the conclusion that all its secrets of particle physics, of molecular life, of heredity, of outer space, are now within easy reach. The truth is more massive and less magical. It is that wherever we turn, in defense, in space, in medicine, in industry, in agriculture, and most of all in basic sciences, itself, the requirement is for better work, deeper understanding, higher education. And while I have framed this comment in the terms of the natural sciences, I insist, as do all those who live in this field, that at every level of learning there must be an equal concern for history, for letters and the arts, and for man as a social being in the widest meaning of Aristotle's phrase. This also is the work of the university.

And third, as the world presses in and knowledge presses out, the role of interpreter grows. Men can no longer know everything themselves; the 20th century has no universal man. All men today must learn to know through one another—to judge across their own ignorance—to comprehend at second hand. These arts are not easily learned. Those who would practice them must develop intensity of perception, variety of mental activity, and the habit of open concern for truth in all its forms. Where can we expect to find a training ground for this modern maturity, if not in our universities?

Fourth and finally, these new requirements strengthen still further what has always been a fundamental element in the life of American colleges and universities—that they should be dedicated to "the Nation's service." The phrase is Woodrow Wilson's, and no one has discussed its meaning better. What he said in 1896 is more relevant today than ever before, and I close with a quotation from him. . . .

"It is not learning," said President Wilson, "but the spirit of service that will give a college place in the public annals of the Nation. It is indispensable," he said, "if it is to do its right service, that the air of affairs should be admitted to all its classrooms . . . the air of the world's transactions, the consciousness of the solidarity of the race, the sense of the duty of man toward man . . . the promise and the hope that shine in the face of all knowledge. . . . The days of glad expansion are gone, our life grows tense and difficult; our resource for the future lies in careful thought, providence, and a wise economy; and the school must be of the Nation." . . .

THE EDUCATED CITIZEN

Rights and responsibilities go hand in hand, and the President made
this point clear when speaking at the ninetieth anniversary convocation of Vanderbilt University. Each citizen has the responsibility
to benefit society with the gifts he has cultivated, and this responsibility takes many forms.

. . . this Nation was not founded solely on the principle of citizen
rights. Equally important, although too often not discussed, is the citizen's responsibility, for our privileges can be no greater than our
obligations. The protection of our rights can endure no longer than
the performance of our responsibilities. Each can be neglected only at
the peril of the other. I speak to you today, therefore, not of your
rights as Americans, but of your responsibilities. They are many in
number, and different in nature. They do not rest with equal weight
upon the shoulders of all. Equality of opportunity does not mean
equality of responsibility. All Americans must be responsible citizens,
but some must be more responsible than others, by virtue of their
public or their private position, their role in the family or community,
their prospects for the future, or their legacy from the past.

Increased responsibility goes with increased ability, for of those to
whom much is given, much is required. . . .

You have responsibilities, in short, to use your talents for the benefit of the society which helped develop those talents. You must decide
. . . whether you will give to the world in which you are reared and
educated the broadest possible benefits of that education. . . .

If the pursuit of learning is not defended by the educated citizen,
it will not be defended at all, for there will always be those who scoff
at intellectuals, who cry out against research, who seek to limit our
educational system. Modern cynics and skeptics see no more reason
for landing a man on the moon, which we shall do, than the cynics
and skeptics of half a millenium ago saw for the discovery of this
country. They see no harm in paying those to whom they entrust the

"Remarks in Nashville at the 90th Anniversary Convocation of Vanderbilt
University." Doc. 192, May 18, 1963. *Public Papers,* 1963, pp. 406–409.

minds of their children a smaller wage than is paid to those to whom they entrust the care of their plumbing.

But the educated citizen knows how much more there is to know. He knows that knowledge is power, more so today than ever before. He knows that only an educated and informed people will be a free people, that the ignorance of one voter in a democracy impairs the security of all, and that if we can, as Jefferson put it, "enlighten the people generally . . . tyranny and the oppression of mind and body will vanish like evil spirits at the dawn of day." And, therefore, the educated citizen has a special obligation to encourage the pursuit of learning, to promote exploration of the unknown, to preserve the freedom of inquiry, to support the advancement of research, and to assist at every level of government the improvement of education for all Americans from grade school to graduate school.

Secondly, the educated citizen has an obligation to serve the public. He may be a precinct worker or President. He may give his talents at the courthouse, the State house, the White House. He may be a civil servant or a Senator, a candidate or a campaign worker, a winner or a loser. But he must be a participant and not a spectator.

"At the Olympic games," Aristotle wrote, "it is not the finest and strongest men who are crowned, but they who enter the lists—for out of these the prize-men are elected. So, too, in life, of the honorable and the good, it is they who act who rightly win the prizes."

I urge all of you today, especially those who are students, to act, to enter the lists of public service and rightly win or lose the prize. For we can have only one form of aristocracy in this country, as Jefferson wrote long ago in rejecting John Adams' suggestion of an artificial aristocracy of wealth and birth. It is, he wrote, the natural aristocracy of character and talent, and the best form of government, he added, was that which selected these men for positions of responsibility.

I would hope that all educated citizens would fulfill this obligation—in politics, in Government, . . . in the Peace Corps, in the Foreign Service, in the Government service, . . . in the world. You will find the pressures greater than the pay. You may endure more public attacks than support. But you will have the unequaled satisfaction of knowing that your character and talent are contributing to the direction and success of this free society.

THE EDUCATED CITIZEN

Third, and finally, the educated citizen has an obligation to uphold the law. This is the obligation of every citizen in a free and peaceful society. But the educated citizen has a special responsibility by the virtue of his greater understanding. For whether he has ever studied history or current events, ethics or civics, the rules of a profession or the tools of a trade, he knows that only a respect for the law makes it possible for free men to dwell together in peace and progress.

He knows that law is the adhesive force of the cement of society, creating order out of chaos and coherence in place of anarchy. He knows that for one man to defy a law or court order he does not like is to invite others to defy those which they do not like, leading to a breakdown of all justice and all order. He knows, too, that every fellow man is entitled to be regarded with decency and treated with dignity. Any educated citizen who seeks to subvert the law, to suppress freedom, or to subject other human beings to acts that are less than human and degrade his inheritance, ignores his learning and betrays his obligation.

Certain other societies may respect the rule of force—we respect the rule of law. . . .

EDUCATION FOR MILITARY LEADERSHIP

The Commander-in-Chief addressed the 1963 graduating class of the Air Force Academy and commended its members on their fine academic and military records and on their promise for the future.

. . . I am impressed by the extraordinary scholastic record, unmatched by any new college or university in this country, which has been made by the students and graduates of this Academy. Four Rhodes scholarships last year, two this year, and other selected scholarships, and also your record in the graduate record examination makes the people of this country proud of this Academy and Air Force which made it possible.

This country is proud of the fact that more than one out of five of your all-military faculty has a doctor's degree, and all the rest have master's degrees. This is what we need for leadership in our military services, for the Air Force officer of today and tomorrow requires the broadest kind of scholarship to understand a most complex and changing world. He requires understanding and learning unmatched in the days before World War II. Any graduate of this Academy who serves in our Armed Forces will need to know economics and history, and international affairs, and languages. You will need an appreciation of other societies, and an understanding of our own Nation's purposes and policy. . . .

"Remarks at Colorado Springs to the Graduating Class of the U.S. Air Force Academy." Doc. 221, June 5, 1963. *Public Papers*, 1963, pp. 441–442.

THE HIGHER PURPOSE

Speaking at the commencement exercises of San Diego State College, President Kennedy reiterated a favorite theme—the necessary commitment by each college graduate to a higher service than his individual economic gain. The graduate has his part to play in the attainment and maintenance of peace and security; and it is within his power to see that opportunity similar to his is available to all Americans.

In the course of the ceremonies, the President received the first honorary doctorate conferred by the college.

. . . No country can possibly move ahead, no free society can possibly be sustained, unless it has an educated citizenry whose quality of mind and heart permit it to take part in the complicated and sophisticated decisions that pour not only upon the President and upon the Congress, but upon all the citizens who service the ultimate power. . . .

I am sure that the graduates of this college recognize that the . . . concentrated effort of mind and scholarship to educate the young citizens of this State has not been done merely to give this school's graduates an economic advantage in the life struggle. Quite obviously, there is a higher purpose, and that is the hope that you will turn to the service of the State, the scholarship, the education, the qualities which society has helped develop in you; that you will render on the community level or on the State level or on the national level or the international level a contribution to the maintenance of freedom and peace and the security of our country and those associated with it in a most critical time.

In so doing, you will follow a great and laudable tradition which combined American scholarship and American leadership in political affairs. It is an extraordinary fact of history, I think, unmatched since the days of early Greece, that this country should have produced during its founding days in a population of a handful of men such an extraordinary range of scholars and creative thinkers who helped build this country—Jefferson, Franklin, Morris, Wilson, and all the rest.

"Commencement Address at San Diego State College." Doc. 226, June 6, 1963. *Public Papers*, 1963, pp. 445–448.

This is a great tradition which we must maintain in our time with increasing strength and increasing vigor.

Those of you who are educated, those of us who recognize the responsibilities of an educated citizen, should now concern ourselves with whether we are providing an adequate education for all Americans, whether all Americans have an equal chance to develop their intellectual qualities, and whether we are preparing ourselves today for the educational challenges which are going to come before this decade is out.

The first question, and the most important—does every American boy and girl have an opportunity to develop whatever talents they have? All of us do not have equal talent, but all of us should have an equal opportunity to develop those talents. . . .

American children today do not yet enjoy equal educational opportunities for two primary reasons: One is economic and the other is racial. If our Nation is to meet the goal of giving every American child a fair chance, because an uneducated child makes an uneducated parent who in another day produces another uneducated child, we must move ahead swiftly in both areas. And we must recognize that segregation and education, and I mean *de facto* segregation in the North as well as the proclaimed segregation in the South, brings with it serious handicaps to a large proportion of the population. It does no good . . . to say that that is the business of another State. . . .

The second question relates to the quality of our education. . . .

. . . our current educational programs, much as they represent a burden upon the taxpayers of this country, do not meet the responsibility. The fact of the matter is that this is a problem which faces us all, no matter where we live, no matter what our political views must be. . . .

We have to improve, and we have so recommended, the quality of our teachers by expanding teacher training institutes, by improving teacher preparation programs, by broadening educational research and authorizing—and this is one of our greatest needs—increased training for teachers for the handicapped—the deaf, and those who can't speak, and those who are otherwise handicapped. . . . [We have] to strengthen public elementary and secondary education through grants to the states for better teachers' salaries, to relieve critical classroom shortages, to meet the special educational problems of depressed areas, and the continuing expansion of vocational education and counsel.

And finally, we must make a massive attack upon illiteracy in the year 1963 in the United States by an expansion of university extension courses and by a major effort to improve our libraries in every community of our country.

I recognize that this represents a difficult assignment for us all, but I do not think it is an assignment from which we should shrink. I believe that education comes at the top of the responsibilities of any government, at whatever level. It is essential to our survival as a nation in a dangerous and hazardous world, and it is essential to the maintenance of freedom at a time when freedom is under attack.

I have traveled in the last 24 hours from Washington to Colorado, to Texas, to here, and on every street I see mothers standing with two or three or four children. They are going to pour into our schools and our colleges in the next 10 or 20 years and I want this generation of Americans to be as prepared to meet this challenge as our forefathers did in making it possible for all of us to be here today.

We are the privileged, and it should be the ambition of every citizen to express and expand that privilege so that all of our countrymen and women share it.

At the beginning of his commencement address at American University, the President noted the deep appreciation he felt for the beauty held within university walls: the beauty of a place where "those who hate ignorance may strive to know." Ignorance has played its part in preventing world peace, and he saw a university campus as the appropriate place to speak of an end to war and of peace for all people.

The President's speech on that day had international impact. It led to the drafting of the nuclear test ban treaty, ratified by the United States Senate on September 24, 1963.

. . . "There are few earthly things more beautiful than a university," wrote John Masefield, in his tribute to English universities—and his words are equally true today. He did not refer to spires and towers, to campus greens and ivied walls. He admired the splendid beauty of the university, he said, because it was "a place where those who hate ignorance may strive to know, where those who perceive truth may strive to make others see."

I have, therefore, chosen this time and this place to discuss a topic on which ignorance too often abounds and the truth is too rarely perceived—yet it is the most important topic on earth: World peace. . . .

"Commencement Address at American University in Washington." Doc. 232, June 10, 1963. *Public Papers*, 1963, p. 460.

A SENSE OF JUSTICE

The President regretted the slow pace at which Congress was working on the civil rights bill, and on June 19, 1963, he urged the legislative branch to view the plight of the nation and act as necessary. As he had done previously, the President emphasized the fact that the problem is not sectional but nationwide, and he called for bipartisan cooperation to overcome the crisis.

. . . while commending the progress already made in achieving desegregation of education at all levels as required by the Constitution, I [am] compelled to point out the slowness of progress toward primary and secondary school desegregation. The Supreme Court has recently voiced the same opinion. Many Negro children entering segregated grade schools at the time of the Supreme Court decision in 1954 will enter segregated high schools this year, having suffered a loss which can never be regained. Indeed, discrimination in education is one basic cause of the other inequities and hardships inflicted upon our Negro citizens. The lack of equal educational opportunity deprives the individual of equal economic opportunity, restricts his contribution as a citizen and community leader, encourages him to drop out of school, and imposes a heavy burden on the effort to eliminate discriminatory practices and prejudices from our national life.

The Federal courts, pursuant to the 1954 decision of the U.S. Supreme Court and earlier decisions on institutions of higher learning, have shown both competence and courage in directing the desegregation of schools on the local level. It is appropriate to keep this responsibility largely within the judicial arena. But it is unfair and unrealistic to expect that the burden of initiating such cases can be wholly borne by private litigants. Too often those entitled to bring suit on behalf of their children lack the economic means for instituting and maintaining such cases or the ability to withstand the personal, physical, and economic harassment which sometimes descends upon those who do insti-

"Special Message to the Congress on Civil Rights and Job Opportunities." Doc. 248, June 19, 1963. *Public Papers*, 1963, pp. 487–488, 493–494.

tute them. The same is true of students wishing to attend the college of their choice but unable to assume the burden of litigation.

These difficulties are among the principal reasons for the delay in carrying out the 1954 decision; and this delay cannot be justified to those who have been hurt as a result. Rights such as these, as the Supreme Court recently said, are "present rights. They are not merely hopes to some future enjoyment of some formalistic constitutional promise. The basic guarantees of our Constitution are warrants for the here and now. . . ."

In order to achieve a more orderly and consistent compliance with the Supreme Court school and college desegregation decisions, therefore, I recommend that the Congress assert its specific constitutional authority to implement the 14th Amendment by including in the Civil Rights Act of 1963 a new title providing the following:

(A) Authority would be given the Attorney General to initiate in the Federal district courts appropriate legal proceedings against local public school boards or public institutions of higher learning— or to intervene in existing cases—whenever—

(1) he has received a written complaint from students or from the parents of students who are being denied equal protection of the laws by a segregated public school or college; and

(2) he certifies that such persons are unable to undertake or otherwise arrange for the initiation and maintenance of such legal proceedings for lack of financial means or effective legal representation or for fear of economic or other injury; and

(3) he determines that his initiation of or intervention in such suit will materially further the orderly progress of desegregation in public education. For this purpose, the Attorney General would establish criteria to determine the priority and relative need for Federal action in those districts from which complaints have been filed.

(B) As previously recommended, technical and financial assistance would be given to those school districts in all parts of the country which, voluntarily or as the result of litigation, are engaged in the process of meeting the educational problems flowing from desegregation or racial imbalance but which are in need of guidance, experienced help, or financial assistance in order to train their personnel for this changeover, cope with new difficulties and complete the job satisfactorily (including in such assistance loans to a district where State or local funds have been withdrawn or withheld because of desegregation).

Public institutions already operating without racial discrimination, of course, will not be affected by this statute. Local action can always make Federal action unnecessary. Many school boards have peacefully and voluntarily desegregated in recent years. And while this act does not include private colleges and schools, I strongly urge them to live up to their responsibilities and to recognize no arbitrary bar of race or color—for such bars have no place in any institution, least of all one devoted to the truth and to the improvement of all mankind. . . .

CONCLUSION

Many problems remain that cannot be ignored. The enactment of the legislation I have recommended will not solve all our problems of race relations. This bill must be supplemented by action in every branch of government at the Federal, State, and local level. It must be supplemented as well by enlightened private citizens, private businesses, and private labor and civil organizations, by responsible educators and editors, and certainly by religious leaders who recognize the conflict between racial bigotry and the Holy Word.

This is not a sectional problem—it is nationwide. It is not a partisan problem. The proposals set forth above are based on a careful consideration of the views of leaders of both parties in both Houses of Congress. In 1957 and 1960, members of both parties rallied behind the civil rights measures of my predecessor; and I am certain that this tradition can be continued, as it has in the case of world crises. A national domestic crisis also calls for bipartisan unity and solutions.

We will not solve these problems by blaming any group or section for the legacy which has been handed down by past generations. But neither will these problems be solved by clinging to the patterns of the past. Nor, finally, can they be solved in the streets, by lawless acts on either side, or by physical actions or presence of any private group or public official, however appealing such melodramatic devices may seem to some. . . .

I therefore ask every Member of Congress to set aside sectional and political ties, and to look at this issue from the viewpoint of the Nation. I ask you to look into your hearts, not in search of charity, for the Negro neither wants nor needs condescension, but for the one plain, proud, and priceless quality that unites us all as Americans: a sense of justice. . . .

A CALLING TO PARTICIPATE

Two months before the President's assassination, students at the University of North Dakota heard John Kennedy explain the position he hoped each of them would fill, emphasizing again—as he had done so often before similar groups—the importance of bearing responsible citizenship and helping others to do likewise.

. . . What I urge upon those of you who are students here is to make determinations based on life as it is, on facts as they are, not merely here in this community, not merely in North Dakota, not merely in the United States, but in this varied and dangerous world of ours in which we play such a leading and responsible part. Unless the United States can demonstrate a sound and vigorous democratic life, a society which is not torn apart by friction and faction, an economy which is steadily growing—unless it can do all those things we cannot continue to bear the responsibilities of leadership which I think almost alone have prevented this world of ours from being overrun. . . .

. . . I urge those of you who are students here to recognize the obligation which any educated man or woman must bear to society as a whole. . . . We do not seek merely, I am sure, at this school to graduate lawyers, or farmers, or doctors who may lead their communities in income. What we seek to advance, what we seek to develop in all of our colleges and universities, are educated men and women who can bear the burdens of responsible citizenship, who can make judgments about life as it is, and as it must be, and encourage the people to make those decisions which can bring not only prosperity and security, but happiness to the people of the United States and those who depend upon it.

So in that great effort, I urge you to participate. Nothing will give you more satisfaction. No need is greater. . . .

"Address at the University of North Dakota." Doc. 379, September 25, 1963. *Public Papers,* 1963, pp. 718–719.

THE EXPLOSION OF KNOWLEDGE

From North Dakota, the President went to his second university address of the day, in which he spelled out to students at the University of Wyoming the uniqueness of our era and the corresponding responsibility it places on the shoulders of college graduates.

The Chief Executive's primary purpose in visiting the Western states was to emphasize the need for conserving our natural resources. In his university talks, Kennedy dealt with the importance of conserving and utilizing human resources.

. . . What we are attempting to do is to develop the talents in our country which require, of course, education which will permit us in our time, when the conservation of our resources requires entirely different techniques than were required fifty years ago, when the great conservation movement began under Theodore Roosevelt—and these talents, scientific and social talents, must be developed at our universities.

I hope that all of you who are students here will recognize the great opportunity that lies before you in this decade, and in the decades to come, to be of service to our country. The Greeks once defined happiness as full use of your powers along lines of excellence, and I assure you that there is no area of life where you will have an opportunity to use whatever powers you have, and to use them along more excellent lines, bringing ultimately, I think, happiness to you and those whom you serve.

What I think we must realize is that the problems which now face us and their solution are far more complex, far more difficult, far more subtle, require a far greater skill and discretion of judgment, than any of the problems that this country has faced in its comparatively short history, or any, really, that the world has faced in its long history. The fact is that almost in the last thirty years the world of knowledge has exploded. . . . This last generation has produced nearly all of the scientific breakthroughs, at least relatively, that this world of ours has ever experienced. . . .

"Address at the University of Wyoming." Doc. 381, September 25, 1963.
Public Papers, 1963, p. 720.

THE EXPLOSION OF KNOWLEDGE

There is really not much use in having science and its knowledge confined to the laboratory unless it comes out into the mainstream of American and world life, and only those who are trained and educated to handle knowledge and the disciplines of knowledge can be expected to play a significant part in the life of their country. . . .

AN INVALUABLE ASSET

During an address at the University of Maine, the President drew a perceptive analogy to emphasize the importance of the university in American life.

. . . In the year 1715, King George I of England donated a very valuable library to Cambridge University—and at very nearly the same time had occasion to dispatch a regiment to Oxford. The King, remarked one famous wit, had judiciously observed the condition of both universities—one was a learned body in need of loyalty, and the other was a loyal body in need of learning.

Today some observers may feel that very little has changed in two centuries. We are asking the Congress for funds to assist our college libraries, including those in Cambridge, Mass., and it was regrettably necessary on one occasion to send troops to Oxford, Miss. And, more generally speaking, critics of our modern universities have often accused them of producing either too little loyalty or too little learning. But I cannot agree with either charge. I am convinced that our universities are an invaluable national asset which must be observed, conserved, and expanded. . . .

"Address at the University of Maine." Doc. 426, October 19, 1963. *Public Papers,* 1963, p. 795.

TRIBUTE TO A FRIEND

In late October, 1963, President Kennedy took the opportunity to pay tribute to a great American at the ground-breaking for the Robert Frost Library at Amherst College. Frost had been an honored guest at the President's inauguration, and Kennedy considered a library the best possible memorial to his friend.

. . . I knew Mr. Frost quite late in his life, in really the last 4 or 5 years, and I was impressed, as I know all you were who knew him, by a good many qualities, but also by his toughness. He gives the lie, as a good many other poets have, to the fact that poets are rather sensitive creatures who live in the dark of the garret. He was very hardboiled in his approach to life, and his desires for our country. He once said that America is the country you leave only when you want to go out and lick another country. He was not particularly belligerent in his relations, his human relations, but he felt very strongly that the United States should be a country of power, of force, to use that power and force wisely. But he once said to me not to let the Harvard in me get to be too important. So we have followed that advice.

Home, he once wrote, is the place where when you have to go there they have to take you in. And Amherst took him in. This was his home off and on for 22 years. The fact that he chose this college, this campus, when he could have gone anywhere and would have been warmly welcomed, is a tribute to you as much as it is to Mr. Frost. When he was among you, he once said, "I put my students on the operating table" and proceeded to take ideas they didn't know they had out of them. The great test of a college student's chances, he also wrote, is when we know the sort of work for which he will neglect his studies.

In 1937 he said of Amherst, "I have reason to think they like to have me here." And now you are going to have him here for many, many years. Professor Kittredge, at Harvard, once said that they could take down all the buildings of Harvard, and if they kept Widener Library, Harvard would still exist.

"Remarks at the Ground Breaking for the Robert Frost Library at Amherst College." Doc. 440, October 26, 1963. *Public Papers*, 1963, p. 818.

Libraries are memories and in this library you will have the memory of an extraordinary American; much more than that, really—an extraordinary human being. And also you will have the future, and all the young men who come into this library will touch something of distinction in our national life, and, I hope, give something to it.

I am proud to be associated with this great enterprise.

FOUR

THE PEACE CORPS

THE PEACE CORPS

Speaking especially to the nation's new voters during the 1960 presidential campaign, Senator John F. Kennedy said on October 5:

Should I be selected to provide the Presidential leadership of our Nation for the next four years, I would explore thoroughly the possibility of utilizing the services of the very best of our trained and qualified young people to give of from three to five years of their lives to the cause of world peace by forming themselves into a Youth Peace Corps, going to the places that really need them and doing the sort of jobs that need to be done. Such an example of young Americans helping young nations to pioneer new fields on the world's underdeveloped frontiers would, in my opinion, be not only a great assistance to such nations and a great example to the world, but the greatest possible growing experience of the new generation of American leadership which must inevitably lead the free world coalition.[1]

With these words the Peace Corps idea became part of the New Frontier. Today, the Peace Corps stands as a proud memorial to John F. Kennedy, representing much of the idealism the late President conveyed to American youth.

Of the many Kennedy achievements, the Peace Corps is no doubt the most significant from the standpoint of capturing the imagination of the nation and the world. The Peace Corps has had unprecedented success in its brief existence. Its volunteers have reflected the very essence of the American way by quietly doing their job and doing it well. Their example has given incentive to other nations, and many have started or encouraged Peace Corps-type programs. It can fairly be said that no other government experiment in this century has received such acclaim.

Others had suggested the Peace Corps idea, but John F. Kennedy's imaginative approach ignited the enthusiasm and support of the American people for such a project. During the 1960 campaign he challenged Americans of every age, and especially young Americans, to help the less fortunate of the world help themselves. The response was immediate and far beyond expectation. Inquiries and expressions of willingness to join were forthcoming even before the formal commencement of the program. Youngsters, oldsters, students, business

---

[1] *Freedom of Communications*, I, 1084.

executives, doctors, lawyers, teachers, farmers, and mechanics responded to the call for Peace Corps recruits.

Politically the idea was not so warmly received. Many politicians had reservations. The project was often referred to as "Kennedy's Kiddie Korps," and one politician ventured to say that the Peace Corps was a "juvenile experiment." Others adopted an extremely cautious attitude and felt that the program should receive limited funds and operate on an experimental basis.

Despite these criticisms, Kennedy moved ahead with his Peace Corps program even before the Inauguration. Shortly after the November election a task force was appointed to appraise and plan the project. When President Kennedy moved into the White House, he appointed his brother-in-law, Sargent Shriver, Jr., as the director of the tentative pilot plan. On March 1, 1961, the President signed an executive order establishing a Peace Corps on a temporary basis.[2] At the same time, he sent a message to Congress recommending the permanent adoption of the Peace Corps plan.

To finance the program while Congress was acting on his proposal, President Kennedy used funds from his foreign aid contingency fund. Over $1.6 million was allocated from the fund to support the Peace Corps in its infancy. Director Shriver anticipated placing 500 to 1,000 volunteers in the field by the end of 1961, to be increased to 2,700 overseas or in training by June, 1962. The first Peace Corps examination was set for May 27, 1961. Requests for Peace Corps workers had been received from Tanganyika, the Philippines, and Colombia. Several requests were pending, and the headquarters office in Washington anticipated many more. To fill these requests, it was decided that the first volunteers would undergo training during the summer months of 1961.

Strict standards were established to guide the Peace Corps operation. The selection of projects depended on the following: (1) a request for Peace Corps assistance from the potential host; (2) balanced geographical distribution of personnel throughout the world; (3) clear need for Peace Corps help; (4) indication of recipient countries to undertake measures for economic and social reform; (5) necessity to

---

[2] Executive Order 10924, March 1, 1961.

provide skills not already sufficiently available in the host country; (6) participation of host country in the project and ability to carry on with it after departure of Peace Corps volunteers; and (7) reasonable assurance of a significant psychological and educational impact on the host country—which, it was hoped, would stimulate related activities.[3]

It was often said that President Kennedy selected his brother-in-law as Director of the Peace Corps because it would be easier to fire a relative if the program did not succeed. Of course, the reasons for appointing him were far more compelling. Robert Sargent Shriver, Jr., was born in Westminster, Maryland, in 1915. The son of a banker, he graduated from Yale *cum laude* in 1938 and from the Yale Law School in 1941. During the war he rose from an apprentice seaman to lieutenant commander, serving in both the Atlantic and Pacific theaters. After the war, he worked as an assistant editor for *Newsweek*. In 1946 he met Eunice Kennedy; her father was attracted to young Shriver and approached him on the feasibility of editing the letters of his late son Joseph P. Kennedy, Jr., who was killed in action during the war. Joseph Kennedy brought Shriver to Chicago in 1948 to help manage one of the Kennedy enterprises—the Merchandise Mart. In 1953 Shriver married Eunice Kennedy.

In addition to his responsibilities at the Mart, the young executive found time to serve as a member of the Chicago Board of Education and as a trustee of DePaul, Chicago, and Loyola universities. He was named national chairman of the Yale Alumni Board and elected vice-president of the Chicago Council on Foreign Relations.

In 1960, he left the Merchandise Mart to help with his brother-in-law's campaign for the Presidency. He never returned. Shortly after the Inauguration, he was named Director of the Peace Corps. To this demanding job Shriver brought both his wide executive experience and his driving, forceful, magnetic personality. He converted an idea into a highly effective day-to-day operation. His imaginative and exciting approach made the Peace Corps the fulfillment of Kennedy's promises. Perhaps the most important aspect in making this venture what it is today was Shriver's frankness and friendliness in dealing with members of Congress. The legislative branch had been less than enthu-

[3] *Congressional Quarterly Almanac, 1961* (Washington, D.C.: Congressional Quarterly, 1962), p. 325.

siastic about the Peace Corps idea. Shriver's personality and his ability to meet congressional opposition with basic realistic facts made the legislative journey of the Peace Corps bill much smoother than was expected.

When signing the Peace Corps bill, President Kennedy paid a supreme compliment to his Peace Corp director, saying that Shriver was "the most effective lobbyist on the Washington scene." [4] For a newcomer to the political world of Washington, this was a remarkable endorsement.

From the beginning, the standard of selection was based on the applicant's motivation. This is determined through the use of the Peace Corps questionnaire and a non-competitive, aptitude interest examination. Those selected undergo extensive training lasting two to three months. Instruction in the host country's language, geography, government, and culture is mandatory. In addition the volunteers refresh their knowledge of American history and institutions. No special privilege is afforded the volunteer in the foreign country. No diplomatic immunities nor PX privileges are allowed. U.S. Public Health Service doctors assigned to each country see that the best medical care is made available to Peace Corps workers around the world. Beyond this, the volunteer is expected to live at the social and economic level of his or her counterpart in the host country. It was agreed that the volunteer should receive living, travel, and subsistence allowances. To facilitate readjustment after completion of the tour of duty, it was further decided to give each Peace Corp volunteer a readjustment allowance payable at the end of service. Under this arrangement, a volunteer receives $75.00 for each month of satisfactory service.

The first year of Peace Corps operation was an overwhelming success. Over 3,000 took the first Peace Corps exam in May, 1961. By the end of 1961 approximately 750 volunteers had been assigned to foreign duty. The number of Peace Corps workers in foreign lands by October 31, 1962, was 4,178. Of these 1,446 were on duty or training for service in Africa, 875 for the Far East, 1,396 for Latin America, and 461 for the Near East and South Asia.[5] Close to 7,000 workers were overseas

---

[4] *Public Papers*, 1961, p. 615.

[5] *Congressional Quarterly Almanac, 1962* (Washington, D.C.: Congressional Quarterly, 1963), p. 341.

by the end of 1963, and the number was increased to 10,000 by September, 1964. The demands from foreign countries for Peace Corps personnel far exceed the supply. Peace Corps workers today are situated in 46 countries and two dozen nations are now on the waiting list, which is expected to grow.

The Honorable Thanat Khoman, Foreign Minister of Thailand, at Chulalongkorn University awarding Shriver an honorary degree, said:

It is indeed striking that this important idea, the most powerful idea in recent times, of a Peace Corps, of youth mingling, living, working with youth, should come from this mightiest nation on earth, the United States. Many of us who did not know about the United States thought of this great nation as a wealthy nation, a powerful nation, endowed with great material strength and many powerful weapons. But how many of us know that in the United States ideas and ideals are also powerful? This is the secret of greatness, of your might, which is not imposing or crushing people, but is filled with the hope of future goodwill and understanding.[6]

Organizations modeled on the Peace Corps are now operating in twelve foreign countries. The entire concept of the American Peace Corps displays what American leadership can do to help a world torn by conflict. It shows that Americans are willing to put idealism to work in a realistic way and take one step forward towards a better life for all people.

John F. Kennedy's mortal enemies were poverty, ignorance, and disease. With the inception of the Peace Corps, he struck a staggering blow to eliminate these deadly burdens of mankind. The Peace Corps, reflecting his leadership and image, has set its course to continue the struggle of its fallen leader.

[6] Quoted by R. C. Parrott, Director, National Voluntary Service Programs, Peace Corps, in a speech to the Soap and Detergent Association, January 27, 1965, New York City.

A CHALLENGE TO GO FORTH

The idea of a Peace Corps was growing in Senator Kennedy's mind well before his election to the Presidency. His immediate image of the Corps was that of service to underdeveloped nations; but at the same time he saw the returning participants as excellent candidates for government and Foreign Service careers. On October 14, 1960, he presented a challenge to University of Michigan students, placing responsibility for the future growth of our country on those willing to sacrifice part of their lives for the success of a democracy.

How many of you are willing to spend 10 years in Africa or Latin America or Asia working for the United States and working for freedom? How many of you [who] are going to be doctors are willing to spend your days in Ghana? Technicians or engineers: how many of you are willing to work in the Foreign Service and spend your lives travelling around the world? On your willingness to do that, not merely to serve one or two years in the service, but on your willingness to contribute part of your life to this country I think will depend the answer whether we as a free society can compete. I think we can, and I think Americans are willing to contribute. But the effort must be far greater than we have made in the past. And therefore I am delighted to come to Michigan, this university, because unless we have those resources in this school, unless you are willing to make this sacrifice, this country cannot possibly move ahead during the next 10 years in our period of relative strength.

Quoted in "John F. Kennedy and the Peace Corps Idea." *Peace Corps Volunteer,* II (December, 1963), 4.

A SIMPLE PROPOSAL

The Cow Palace, San Francisco, was the setting for candidate Kennedy's Peace Corps proposal. Though the details had not been developed, Kennedy advocated a volunteer corps of Americans who would, essentially, act as ambassadors of peace—a group trained, as he said on November 4, 1960, in Chicago, to help underdeveloped nations help themselves.

. . . I therefore propose . . . a peace corps of talented young men and women, willing and able to serve their country . . . for 3 years as an alternative or as a supplement to peacetime selective service, well qualified through rigorous standards, well trained in the languages, skills, and customs they will need to know. . . .

We cannot discontinue training our young men as soldiers of war, but we also want them to be ambassadors of peace. . . .

This would be a volunteer corps, and volunteers would be sought among not only talented young men and women, but all Americans, of whatever age, who wished to serve the great Republic and serve the cause of freedom, men who have taught or engineers or doctors or nurses, who have reached the age of retirement, or who in the midst of their work wished to serve their country and freedom, should be given an opportunity and an agency in which their talents could serve our country around the globe.

I am convinced that the pool of people in this country of ours anxious to respond to the public service is greater than it has ever been in our history. I am convinced that our men and women, dedicated to freedom, are able to be missionaries, not only for freedom and peace, but join in a worldwide struggle against poverty and disease and ignorance. . . .

. . . most recently, I have proposed, as a counter to the flood of well-trained and dedicated Communist technicians now helping these

"Speech of Senator John F. Kennedy, Cow Palace, San Francisco, Calif., November 2, 1960." *Freedom of Communications,* I, 865. "Excerpts From Speech by Senator John F. Kennedy, Chicago Auditorium, Chicago, Ill., November 4, 1960." *Ibid.,* p. 1260.

A SIMPLE PROPOSAL

[underdeveloped] nations with their problems, an American "peace corps." . . . A peace corps of Americans trained to help these nations help themselves, to show them modern agriculture, public health, roadbuilding, government and other skills. . . .

The President included in his first State of the Union Message the idea of mobilizing dedicated individuals to help establish world order.

. . . An even more valuable national asset is our reservoir of dedicated men and women—not only on our college campuses but in every age group—who have indicated their desire to contribute their skills, their efforts, and a part of their lives to the fight for world order. We can mobilize this talent through the formation of a National Peace Corps, enlisting the services of all those with the desire and capacity to help foreign lands meet their urgent needs for trained personnel. . . .

"Annual Message to the Congress on the State of the Union." Doc. 11, January 30, 1961. *Public Papers*, 1961, p. 25.

THE PILOT PROJECT

A temporary Peace Corps project was established by executive order on March 1, 1961. In his statement at the signing of the order, the President explained that the life of a volunteer would not be easy, but would provide a means of exercising responsibility in the cause of international development. As well as benefiting other nations, such service would broaden the horizons of our nation while enriching the life of the individual Peace Corps volunteer.

I have today signed an Executive Order [No. 10924] providing for the establishment of a Peace Corps on a temporary pilot basis. I am also sending to Congress a message proposing authorization of a permanent Peace Corps. This Corps will be a pool of trained American men and women sent overseas by the United States Government or through private institutions and organizations to help foreign countries meet their urgent needs for skilled manpower.

It is our hope to have 500 or more people in the field by the end of the year. . . .

In establishing our Peace Corps we intend to make full use of the resources and talents of private institutions and groups. Universities, voluntary agencies, labor unions and industry will be asked to share in this effort—contributing diverse sources of energy and imagination— making it clear that the responsibility for peace is the responsibility of our entire society.

We will only send abroad Americans who are wanted by the host country—who have a real job to do—and who are qualified to do that job. Programs will be developed with care, and after full negotiation, in order to make sure that the Peace Corps is wanted and will contribute to the welfare of other people. Our Peace Corps is not designed as an instrument of diplomacy or propaganda or ideological conflict. It is designed to permit our people to exercise more fully their responsibilities in the great common cause of world development.

Life in the Peace Corps will not be easy. There will be no salary

"Statement by the President Upon Signing Order Establishing the Peace Corps." Doc. 61, March 1, 1961. *Public Papers*, 1961, pp. 134–135.

and allowances will be at a level sufficient only to maintain health and meet basic needs. Men and women will be expected to work and live alongside the nationals of the country in which they are stationed—doing the same work, eating the same food, talking the same language.

But if the life will not be easy, it will be rich and satisfying. For every young American who participates in the Peace Corps—who works in a foreign land—will know that he or she is sharing in the great common task of bringing to man that decent way of life which is the foundation of freedom and a condition of peace.

THE PROPOSED PROGRAM

Kennedy's message to Congress requesting a permanent Peace Corps was sent on the same day he signed the executive order for its temporary establishment. Since the freedom of the United States depends in part on the growth and liberation of other nations, the Chief Executive saw it as the responsibility of capable Americans to help provide the skilled manpower necessary to the development of struggling nations. Encouraged by the interest of Americans of all ages and walks of life, the President presented the proposed Peace Corps to Congress, including a review of the requirements and duties of a volunteer and ending with the wish that eventually other nations would mobilize similar projects to promote international cooperation and brotherhood.

. . . I recommend to the Congress the establishment of a permanent Peace Corps—a pool of trained American men and women sent overseas by the United States Government or through private organizations and institutions to help foreign countries meet their urgent needs for skilled manpower.

I have today signed an Executive Order establishing a Peace Corps on a temporary pilot basis.

The temporary Peace Corps will be a source of information and experience to aid us in formulating more effective plans for a permanent organization. In addition, by starting the Peace Corps now we will be able to begin training young men and women for overseas duty this summer with the objective of placing them in overseas positions by late fall. This temporary Peace Corps is being established under existing authority in the Mutual Security Act and will be located in the Department of State. Its initial expenses will be paid from appropriations currently available for our foreign aid program.

Throughout the world the people of the newly developing nations are struggling for economic and social progress which reflects their deepest desires. Our own freedom, and the future of freedom around the world, depend, in a very real sense, on their ability to build grow-

"Special Message to the Congress on the Peace Corps." Doc. 63, March 1, 1961. *Public Papers*, 1961, pp. 143–146.

ing and independent nations where men can live in dignity, liberated from the bonds of hunger, ignorance and poverty.

One of the greatest obstacles to the achievement of this goal is the lack of trained men and women with the skill to teach the young and assist in the operation of development projects—men and women with the capacity to cope with the demands of swiftly evolving economies, and with the dedication to put that capacity to work in the villages, the mountains, the towns and the factories of dozens of struggling nations.

The vast task of economic development urgently requires skilled people to do the work of the society—to help teach in the schools, construct development projects, demonstrate modern methods of sanitation in the villages, and perform a hundred other tasks calling for training and advanced knowledge.

To meet this urgent need for skilled manpower we are proposing the establishment of a Peace Corps—an organization which will recruit and train American volunteers, sending them abroad to work with the people of other nations.

This organization will differ from existing assistance programs in that its members will supplement technical advisers by offering the specific skills needed by developing nations if they are to put technical advice to work. They will help provide the skilled manpower necessary to carry out the development projects planned by the host governments, acting at a working level and serving at great personal sacrifice. There is little doubt that the number of those who wish to serve will be far greater than our capacity to absorb them.

The Peace Corps or some similar approach has been strongly advocated by Senator Humphrey, Representative Reuss and others in the Congress. It has received strong support from universities, voluntary agencies, student groups, labor unions and business and professional organizations.

Last session, the Congress authorized a study of these possibilities. Preliminary reports of this study show that the Peace Corps is feasible, needed, and wanted by many foreign countries.

Most heartening of all, the initial reaction to this proposal has been an enthusiastic response by student groups, professional organizations and private citizens everywhere—a convincing demonstration

THE PROPOSED PROGRAM

that we have in this country an immense reservoir of dedicated men and women willing to devote their energies and time and toil to the cause of world peace and human progress.

Among the specific programs to which Peace Corps members can contribute are: teaching in primary and secondary schools, especially as part of national English language teaching programs; participation in the worldwide program of malaria eradication; instruction and operation of public health and sanitation projects; aiding in village development through school construction and other programs; increasing rural agricultural productivity by assisting local farmers to use modern implements and techniques. The initial emphasis of these programs will be on teaching. Thus the Peace Corps members will be an effective means of implementing the development programs of the host countries—programs which our technical assistance operations have helped to formulate.

The Peace Corps will not be limited to the young, or to college graduates. All Americans who are qualified will be welcome to join this effort. But undoubtedly the Corps will be made up primarily of young people as they complete their formal education.

Because one of the greatest resources of a free society is the strength and diversity of its private organizations and institutions much of the Peace Corps program will be carried out by these groups, financially assisted by the Federal Government.

Peace Corps personnel will be made available to developing nations in the following ways:

1. Through private voluntary agencies carrying on international assistance programs.

2. Through overseas programs of colleges and universities.

3. Through assistance programs of international agencies.

4. Through assistance programs of the United States government.

5. Through new programs which the Peace Corps itself directly administers.

In the majority of cases the Peace Corps will assume the entire responsibility for recruitment, training and the development of overseas projects. In other cases it will make available a pool of trained applicants to private groups who are carrying out projects approved by the Peace Corps.

In the case of Peace Corps programs conducted through voluntary agencies and universities, these private institutions will have the option of using the national recruitment system—the central pool of trained manpower—or developing recruitment systems of their own.

In all cases men and women recruited as a result of Federal assistance will be members of the Peace Corps and enrolled in the central organization. All private recruitment and training programs will adhere to Peace Corps standards as a condition of Federal assistance.

In all instances the men and women of the Peace Corps will go only to those countries where their services and skills are genuinely needed and desired. United States Operations Missions, supplemented where necessary by special Peace Corps teams, will consult with leaders in foreign countries in order to determine where Peace Corpsmen are needed, the types of job they can best fill, and the number of people who can be usefully employed. The Peace Corps will not supply personnel for marginal undertakings without a sound economic or social justification. In furnishing assistance through the Peace Corps careful regard will be given to the particular country's developmental priorities.

Membership in the Peace Corps will be open to all Americans, and applications will be available shortly. Where application is made directly to the Peace Corps—the vast majority of cases—they will be carefully screened to make sure that those who are selected can contribute to Peace Corps programs, and have the personal qualities which will enable them to represent the United States abroad with honor and dignity. In those cases where application is made directly to a private group, the same basic standards will be maintained. Each new recruit will receive a training and orientation period varying from six weeks to six months. This training will include courses in the culture and language of the country to which they are being sent and specialized training designed to increase the work skills of recruits. In some cases training will be conducted by participant agencies and universities in approved training programs. Other training programs will be conducted by the Peace Corps staff.

Length of service in the Corps will vary depending on the kind of project and the country, generally ranging from two to three years. Peace Corps members will often serve under conditions of physical

THE PROPOSED PROGRAM

hardship, living under primitive conditions among the people of developing nations. For every Peace Corps member service will mean a great financial sacrifice. They will receive no salary. Instead they will be given an allowance which will only be sufficient to meet their basic needs and maintain health. It is essential that Peace Corpsmen and women live simply and unostentatiously among the people they have come to assist. At the conclusion of their tours, members of the Peace Corps will receive a small sum in the form of severance pay based on length of service abroad, to assist them during their first weeks back in the United States. Service with the Peace Corps will not exempt volunteers from Selective Service.

The United States will assume responsibility for supplying medical services to Peace Corps members and ensuring supplies and drugs necessary to good health.

I have asked the temporary Peace Corps to begin plans and make arrangements for pilot programs. A minimum of several hundred volunteers could be selected, trained and at work abroad by the end of this calendar year. It is hoped that within a few years several thousand Peace Corps members will be working in foreign lands.

It is important to remember that this program must, in its early stages, be experimental in nature. This is a new dimension in our overseas program and only the most careful planning and negotiation can ensure its success.

The benefits of the Peace Corps will not be limited to the countries in which it serves. Our own young men and women will be enriched by the experience of living and working in foreign lands. They will have acquired new skills and experience which will aid them in their future careers and add to our own country's supply of trained personnel and teachers. They will return better able to assume the responsibilities of American citizenship and with greater understanding of our global responsibilities.

Although this is an American Peace Corps, the problem of world development is not just an American problem. Let us hope that other nations will mobilize the spirit and energies and skill of their people in some form of Peace Corps—making our own effort only one step in a major international effort to increase the welfare of all men and improve understanding among nations.

IN THE CAUSE OF PEACE

On the passage of the Peace Corps bill, in September, 1961, the President expressed his pleasure at the bipartisan cooperation involved in the enactment of the legislation. He also spoke of the success of the pilot project, and of the establishment of similar projects in other nations.

With the enactment of this legislation, an avenue is provided by which Americans can serve their country in the cause of world peace and understanding and simultaneously assist other nations toward their legitimate goals of freedom and opportunity.

I want particularly to express pleasure at the bipartisan effort and support in the shaping of this new agency.

Already more than thirteen thousand Americans have offered their services to the Peace Corps. By the end of the year almost one thousand will be serving overseas or completing their training in the United States. . . .

These men and women are going overseas at the request of the host nations. They will be doing specific, needed jobs. They will be working at a level and living at a level comparable to the citizens of the foreign nations. They will be farmers and teachers, craftsmen and nurses, doctors and technicians of all kinds. They will be a cross-section of the finest men and women that this Nation has to offer.

The sure sign of a good idea is that you can follow it, and I am pleased that several other nations have decided to establish Peace Corps agencies of their own.

Much credit for what has been done must go to congressional leaders like the men and women in this room, and the scores of other dedicated Americans who have given their advice and counsel. . . .

"Remarks Upon Signing the Peace Corps Bill." Doc. 380, September 22, 1961. *Public Papers*, 1961, pp. 614–615.

CONGRATULATIONS

At a meeting of the Peace Corps staff, President Kennedy congratulated those involved in the organization and operation of the overseas program, a taxing job which, he hoped, would inspire others to continue their work with equal dedication.

. . . I don't think it is altogether fair to say that I handed [Sargent Shriver] a lemon from which he made lemonade, but I do think that he was handed and you were handed one of the most sensitive and difficult assignments which any administrative group in Washington has been given, almost, in this century.

The concept of the Peace Corps was entirely new. It was subjected to a great deal of criticism at the beginning. If it had not been done with such great care and really, in a sense, loving and prideful care, it could have defeated a great purpose and could have set back the whole cause of public service internationally for a good many years. That it has turned out to be the success that it has been has been due to the tireless work of Sargent Shriver, and to all of you. You have brought to Government service a sense of morale and a sense of enthusiasm and, really, commitment which has been absent from too many governmental agencies for too many years.

So that while the Peace Corpsmen overseas have rendered unusual service, those of you who have worked to make this success here in Washington I think have set an example for Government service which I hope will be infectious. . . .

You remember, in the Second World War, Winston Churchill made one of his speeches—I think at Tripoli, when the 8th Army marched in there—and said, "they will say to you 'What did you do during the great war?' and you will be able to say 'I marched with the 8th Army!' " Well, they may ask you what you have done in the sixties for your country, and you will be able to say, "I served in the Peace Corps, I served in the United States Government," and I think that people will recognize that you have made your contribution. . . .

"Remarks at a Meeting With the Headquarters Staff of the Peace Corps." Doc. 243, June 14, 1962. *Public Papers,* 1962, p. 482.

A GREAT ADVENTURE

Six hundred Peace Corps trainees were invited to the White House on August 9, 1962, and the President expressed to them his deep satisfaction at their commitment in the exciting era of the sixties.

This occasion gives me a particular sense of satisfaction to welcome 600 Americans from all parts of the country who have committed themselves to a great adventure, I think, for our country and more than our country, for really all people.

I think that by the end of this year we will have more than 5,000 peace corpsmen, men and women of all ages, serving abroad in all parts of the world, in countries about which Americans knew little 10 years ago, countries which we did not even know existed 20 years ago.

This is an extraordinary action by this country and I know that you are proud to take part in it. I must say that it gives me the greatest satisfaction that it is taking place at this time. . . .

Well—I must say I wish that all Americans could hear that litany of countries you are going to, your willingness to do it, and I hope that when you come back that we can persuade you to come and serve in the United States Government in other areas, particularly in the Foreign Service, in all of the areas, because I think the United States is so heavily involved in so many parts of the world, we are so in need of dedicated men and women of talent and experience, that I can think of no better recruiting ground than the Peace Corps for our future Foreign Service officers, for those who represent our information services and aid agencies abroad, so that I hope that you will regard this as the first installment in a long life of service in the most exciting career in the most exciting time, and that is serving this country in the sixties and seventies, so we are very proud to have you here.

The White House belongs to all the people, but I think it particularly belongs to you.

"Remarks to a Group of Peace Corps Trainees." Doc. 325, August 9, 1962. *Public Papers*, 1962, pp. 608–609.

RECRUITING RETURNING VOLUNTEERS

In 1963 the first Peace Corps volunteers returned from their two-year tour of duty. President Kennedy, realizing the vast potential of these men and women, signed an executive order to encourage and facilitate their employment in the various departments of the government.

I have today signed an Executive Order designed to encourage returning volunteers who have satisfactorily completed their service under the Peace Corps Act to enter the civilian career services of the Federal Government. Also, I have been pleased to learn that the major agencies employing personnel under the Foreign Service Act already have made arrangements to facilitate the recruitment of returning Peace Corps volunteers into the Foreign Service and Foreign Service Reserve by giving examinations in the field and otherwise expediting the examining process and by providing special examination options which will permit testing and evaluation of the ability of applicants to live, act, and learn in a foreign environment.

The Director of the Peace Corps has stated that more than 35 per cent of the Peace Corps volunteers now serving overseas have expressed an interest in making their careers in various agencies of the Federal Government. As I have stated before, I am most anxious that the valuable experience and the demonstrated capabilities of the men and women who have volunteered to serve under the trying conditions which confront Peace Corps volunteers should not be lost to the Federal service. I anticipate that each of you will take advantage of the opportunity to obtain the services of these dedicated people by making full use of the procedures prescribed by today's Executive Order and the other arrangements which have been provided for under the Foreign Service Act, and I request that you keep me informed, through the chairman of the Civil Service Commission, of the results of your efforts in this regard.

"Memorandum on Recruitment of Former Peace Corps Volunteers for Career Government Service." Doc. 129, April 10, 1963. *Public Papers*, 1963, p. 320. The President referred to Executive Order 11103 "Providing for the Appointment of Former Peace Corps Volunteers to the Civilian Career Services."

PEACE CORPS CHRONOLOGY

1961

Executive Order 10924, by President John F. Kennedy, March 1, 1961
Establishment and administration of the Peace Corps in the Department of State.

H.R. 7500—Public Law 87-293, approved September 22, 1961
Established a Peace Corps of American volunteers to carry America's skills and talents and idealism abroad to help other people help themselves (full text will be found on pp. 253–276).

1962

H.R. 10700—Public Law 87-442, approved April 27, 1962
Authorized an increased appropriation for the Peace Corps for Fiscal Year 1963. Allowed the Peace Corps to increase its volunteers to a maximum of 6,700.

1963

H.R. 9009—Public Law 88-200, approved December 13, 1963
Authorized an increased appropriation for the Peace Corps for Fiscal Year 1964. Allowed the Peace Corps to increase its volunteers to a maximum of 11,300.

APPENDICES

EDUCATION LEGISLATION INTRODUCED
BY JOHN F. KENNEDY

The following is a list of bills sponsored or co-sponsored by John F. Kennedy while in the United States Congress (1947–60) that had bearing on education, training, or youth. Bills are listed giving the date of introduction, a brief description, and legislative history, if any.

EIGHTIETH CONGRESS 1947–48

H.R. 4370—Athletic Equipment
Introduced: July 24, 1947

To aid the associations, groups, organizations, and institutions encouraging participation of the youth of the country in athletic and sports programs by making surplus athletic equipment available to such associations, groups, or organizations, and institutions.

No Action

EIGHTY-FIRST CONGRESS 1949–50

H.R. 1380—College Cooperative Extension Program for Labor
Introduced: January 13, 1949

To promote the general welfare of the people of the United States by establishing a publicly supported labor extension program for wage and salary earners.

Hearing in House July 26, 1949

Reprinted by permission from CONGRESSIONAL INDEX, published by and copyright 1948 through 1960, Commerce Clearing House, Inc., Chicago 46, Illinois.

H.R. 5838—Educational Finance Act
Introduced: August 1, 1949

To authorize the appropriation of funds to assist the states and territories in financing a minimum foundation education program of public elementary and secondary schools, in reducing the inequalities of educational opportunities through public elementary and secondary schools, to provide for essential auxiliary school services for all school children.

No Action

EIGHTY-SECOND CONGRESS 1951–52

H.R. 5253—Service Academies—Appointments
Introduced: August 20, 1951

To establish a Commission on Improvement of Methods for the selection of candidates to the United States Military Academy and the United States Naval Academy.

No Action

House Joint Resolution 381—Tidelands Receipts—Medical Use
Introduced: February 18, 1952

To provide that royalties received under certain mineral leases governing submerged lands of the Continental Shelf shall be set aside in the Treasury for use as grants-in-aid of medical education and research and the construction and operation of hospitals and other community health facilities.

No Action

EIGHTY-THIRD CONGRESS 1953-54

S. 2601—School Construction—Federal Aid
Introduced: August 3, 1953

To provide for Federal assistance to the States and Territories in the construction of public elementary and secondary school facilities.

Hearing in Senate May 11, 1954
Reported—Senate Report 1771, July 9, 1954

S. 2763—Continental Shelf Revenues
Introduced: January 19, 1954

To amend the Outer Continental Shelf Land Act in order to provide that revenues under the provisions of such Act shall be used as grants-in-aid to primary, secondary and higher education.

No Action

Senate Joint Resolution 145—Continental Shelf Lands
Introduced: April 1, 1954

To subject the submerged lands under the marginal seas to the provisions of the Outer Continental Shelf Lands Act, and to amend such Act in order to provide that revenues under its provisions shall be used as grants-in-aid to primary, secondary, and higher education.

No Action

S. 3726—New England Education
Introduced: July 9, 1954

To grant the consent of Congress to certain New England States to enter into a compact relating to higher education in the New England States and to establish the New England Board of Higher Education.

Reported—Senate Report 2202—August 2, 1954
Senate bill tabled but H.R. 9712 passed in lieu
thereof and became P.L. 83-719 on August 30,
1954. H.R. 9712 was similar to S. 3726
Reported—House Report 2565—July 28, 1954
Passed House—July 29, 1954

EIGHTY-FOURTH CONGRESS 1955–56

S. 772—Education—Grants-in-Aid
Introduced: January 27, 1955

To amend the Outer Continental Shelf Lands Act in order to provide that revenues under the provisions of such Act shall be used as grants-in-aid to primary, secondary and higher education.

No Action

S. 1004—Surplus Property
Introduced: February 8, 1955

Amending the Federal Property and Administrative Services Act of 1949, so as to improve the administration of the program for the utilization of surplus property for educational and public health purposes.

Hearing in Senate April 21, 1955

S. 1323—Medical Research Facilities
Introduced: March 4, 1955

To authorize a five year program of grants for construction of medical educational and research facilities.

Hearing in Senate May 5, 1955

S. 2600—Veterans—Education and Training Allowances
Introduced: July 21, 1955

Increase the education and training allowances under the Veterans' Readjustment Assistance Act of 1952.

No Action

S. 3246—National Institute of Dental Research
Introduced: February 21, 1956

Increasing the amount authorized for erection and equipment of suitable and adequate buildings and facilities for the use of the National Institute of Dental Research.

Hearing in Senate February 29, 1956
Reported—Senate Report 1719—March 28, 1956
Passed Senate March 29, 1956
Hearing in House April 17, 1956
Reported—House Report 2144—May 10, 1956
Passed House July 13, 1956
Approved P.L. 84-732 July 19, 1956

S. 3430—National Library of Medicine
Introduced: March 13, 1956

Promoting the progress of medicine and advancing the national health and welfare by creating a National Library of Medicine.

Hearing in Senate April 10, 1956
Reported—Senate Report 2071—May 29, 1956
Passed Senate June 11, 1956
Reported—House Report 2826—July 19, 1956
Passed House July 23, 1956
Approved P.L. 84-941 August 3, 1956

S. 3431—Veterans—Educational Program for Children
Introduced: March 13, 1956

To establish an educational assistance program for children of servicemen who died as a result of a disability incurred in line of duty during World War II and the Korean service period in combat or from an instrumentality of war.

No Action

S. 3958—Mental Health—Improved Methods
Introduced: May 29, 1956

To improve the health of the people by assisting in increasing the number of adequately trained professional and practical nurses and professional public health personnel, assisting in the development of improved methods of care and treatment in the field of mental health.

Reported—Senate Report 2070—May 29, 1956
Passed Senate June 11, 1956
Hearing in House June 13, 1956
Reported—House Report 2569—July 2, 1956
Passed House July 23, 1956
Approved—P.L. 84-911 August 2, 1956

S. 4301—Vocational and Technical Education
Introduced: July 27, 1956

To provide for the extension of vocational education to persons in areas where programs are not fully developed or available and for the development of vocational and technical education, including training and technological developments, by encouraging states to establish area vocational schools and programs for the training and retraining of technicians and skilled workers in industry and agriculture and for training in other occupations essential to the Nation's security and economy.

No Action

EIGHTY-FIFTH CONGRESS 1957–58

S. 1298—Area Vocational Education
Introduced: February 20, 1957

To assist states in providing needed vocational education of less than college grade in essential occupations, including retraining made necessary by scientific and technological developments, through establishment and maintenance of area vocational school programs providing vocational training and retraining for persons residing in the state or area, including related instruction for apprentices.

No Action

S. 1728—State Maritime Academies
Introduced: March 27, 1957

To provide assistance to State and Territorial maritime academies or colleges.

Reported—Senate Report 1013—August 19, 1957
Passed Senate August 26, 1957
Reported—House Report 2343—August 1, 1958
Passed House August 4, 1958
Approved—P.L. 85-672 August 18, 1958

APPENDIX A

S. 1922—Research Facilities—Construction
Introduced: April 18, 1957

To authorize a five-year program of grants for construction of medical and dental educational and research facilities.

Hearing in Senate June 3, 1957

S. 2505—Veterans—Teaching Fellowships
Introduced: July 9, 1957

To provide graduate fellowships for veterans for study, leading to a career in teaching.

No Action

S. 2580—Public Health—Grants-in-Aid
Introduced: July 18, 1957

To amend the Public Health Service Act, so as to authorize the Surgeon General to make certain grants-in-aid for the support of public or non-profit educational institutions which provide training and services in the fields of public health and in the administration of state and local public health programs.

No Action

S. 2911—Communism—Educational Material
Introduced: August 30, 1957

To provide for the preparation of a compilation of educational material concerning Communism, as contrasted with Americanism.

No Action

S. 3070—Milk Program
Introduced: January 23, 1958

To continue the special milk program for children in the interest of improved nutrition by fostering the consumption of fluid milk in the schools.

No Action

S. 3179—School Construction
Introduced: January 28, 1958

To authorize Federal assistance to the State and local communities in financing an expanded program of school construction so as to eliminate the national shortage of classrooms.

No Action

S. 3187—Science and Technology Programs
Introduced: January 30, 1958

To strengthen the national defense, advance the cause of peace, and assure the intellectual preeminence of the United States, especially in science and technology, through programs designed to stimulate the development of these skills.

No Action

S. 3713—Classroom Construction
Introduced: April 28, 1958

Amending Title IV (college housing) of the Housing Act of 1950 to provide loans to educational institutions for the construction and improvement of classroom buildings.

No Action

APPENDIX A

S. 4327—Science and Technology—Promotion
Introduced: August 6, 1958

To provide for the strengthening of the national defense by promoting and encouraging intellectual eminence in science and technology, development of science, engineering, mathematics, language courses and providing additional facilities to promote the development of technical skills and to help teachers to increase their knowledge and improve their effectiveness.

Reported—Senate Report 2242—August 8, 1958
Senate bill indefinitely postponed and H.R. 13247
passed in lieu thereof and became P.L. 85-864
on September 6, 1958
Reported—House Report 2157—July 15, 1958
Passed House—August 8, 1958

EIGHTY-SIXTH CONGRESS—1959–60

S. 194—Construction Loans—Schools
Introduced: January 12, 1959

To amend Title IV of the Housing Act of 1950 (college housing) to authorize loans to educational institutions for the construction, rehabilitation, alteration, conversion, and improvement of classroom buildings and other academic facilities.

Hearing in Senate January 22, 1959

S. 819—Loyalty Affidavits
Introduced: January 29, 1959

To amend the National Defense Education Act of 1958 in order to repeal certain provisions requiring affidavits of loyalty and allegiance.

Hearing in Senate April 29, 1959
Reported—Senate Report 454—June 29, 1959
Defeated by Recommittal Vote July 23, 1959

Senate Joint Resolution 41—International Medical Research
Introduced: February 2, 1959

To establish in the Department of Health, Education, and Welfare the National Advisory Council for International Medical Research, and establishing in the Public Health Service the National Institute for International Medical Research.

No Action

Senate Concurrent Resolution 24—International Educational
Programs
Introduced: April 20, 1959

To encourage the development outside the continental United States of international educational programs.

No Action

Senate Resolution 129—International Health Research
Introduced: June 5, 1959

Favoring continued efforts by all nations to strengthen cooperation in health and research activities.

Reported—Senate Report 905—September 4, 1959
Passed Senate September 9, 1959

Senate Joint Resolution 127—Deaf Children—Teachers
Introduced: August 6, 1959

To help make available to those children in the United States who are handicapped by deafness, the specially trained teachers of the deaf needed to develop their abilities and to help make available to individuals suffering from speech and hearing impairments those specially trained speech pathologists and audiologists needed to help them overcome their handicaps.

No Action

S. 2727—Committee on Education
Introduced: September 15, 1959

To make the Committee on Education established by the Act of July 26, 1954, advisory to the President and available to the states for consultation on means of improving the quality of education.

No Action

S. 2830—Library Services Act
Introduced: January 14, 1960

To amend the Library Services Act in order to extend for five years the authorization of appropriations.

Reported—Senate Report 1412—May 23, 1960
Passed Senate May 26, 1960
Reported—House Report 1622—May 18, 1960
Passed House August 22, 1960
Approved—P.L. 86-679 August 31, 1960

S. 2929—Loyalty Oath—NDEA
Introduced: January 27, 1960

To amend the National Defense Education Act of 1958 in order to repeal certain provisions requiring affidavits of belief.

Reported—Senate Report 1347—May 12, 1960
Passed Senate June 15, 1960

S. 3007—Colleges—Loans
Introduced: February 9, 1960

To authorize Federal loans to colleges and universities for the construction, rehabilitation, alteration, conversion, or improvement of classroom buildings and other academic facilities.

Hearing in Senate June 13, 1960

Senate Resolution 388—Colleges—Federal Aid
Introduced: August 31, 1960

To favor a survey looking to Federal aid for institutions of higher learning.

No Action

APPENDIX B

RECORDED KENNEDY VOTES ON AID TO EDUCATION 1947–1960

Position of John F. Kennedy while in the United States House of Representatives and United States Senate on major aid-to-education legislation.

1950   To establish a National Science Foundation to promote basic research and scientific education. Approved March 1. Kennedy: For.

1950   To kill public library demonstration act providing $163 million in aid to states for promotion of library services. Rejected March 9. Kennedy: For.

1953   To provide that revenue from U.S. leasing of outer continental shelf be used for educational grants unless needed for a national defense emergency. Approved June 24. Kennedy: For.

1958   National Defense Education Act. Approved August 13. Kennedy: For.

1958   To authorize annual grants of $1 billion for two years for public school construction. Rejected August 13. Kennedy: For.

1959   To provide educational loans and grants for 1955–1963 military veterans. Approved July 21. Kennedy: For.

1959   To create a 150,000-member Youth Conservation Corps to combat delinquency, aid conservation. Approved August 13. Kennedy: For.

1960   To authorize appropriations for two years of $20 per child of school age—about $917 million per year. Approved February 4. Kennedy: For.

Congressional Quarterly Weekly Report 1960 (Washington, D.C.: Congressional Quarterly, 1960), p. 1280.

EDUCATIONAL LEGISLATION ENACTED DURING THE KENNEDY ADMINISTRATION 1961–1963 [1]

1961   PRACTICAL NURSE TRAINING

S. 278—Public Law 87-22
Approved April 24, 1961

Extended vocational education training programs for practical nurses.

COLLEGE HOUSING

S. 1922—Public Law 87-70
Approved June 30, 1961

Increased the loan authorization for college housing.

SCHOLARSHIPS

S. 539—Public Law 87-153
Approved August 17, 1961

Permitted legally classified American nationals to qualify and receive financial assistance under the Fulbright Act for advanced education abroad.

EDUCATIONAL AND CULTURAL EXCHANGE

H.R. 8666—Public Law 87-256
Approved September 21, 1961

[1] Laws enacted after November 22, 1963, were proposals recommended to Congress during the Kennedy Administration.

APPENDIX C

Consolidated international educational and cultural exchange programs administered and sponsored by the United States Government.

HOWARD UNIVERSITY

H.R. 6302—Public Law 87-262
Approved September 22, 1961

Established a teaching hospital for Howard University in Washington, D.C.

JUVENILE DELINQUENCY

S. 279—Public Law 87-274
Approved September 22, 1961

Provided Federal grants to combat juvenile delinquency (full text will be found on pp. 249–252).

TRAINING FOR TEACHERS OF DEAF

S. 336—Public Law 87-276
Approved September 22, 1961

Established a two-year program to assist in training additional teachers for deaf.

EDUCATION OF BLIND ACT AMENDMENT

H.R. 9030—Public Law 87-294
Approved September 22, 1961

Authorized wider distribution of books and special instruction materials for the blind.

IMPACT AID AND NDEA

S. 2393—Public Law 87-344
Approved October 3, 1961

Extended Impact Areas Aid (P.L. 815 and 874) and The National Defense Education Act of 1958 for two years.

WAR ORPHANS EDUCATION EXTENSION

H.R. 3587—Public Law 87-377
Approved October 4, 1961

Provided additional time within which certain children may complete a program of education under the War Orphans Educational Assistance Act of 1956.

NDEA

H.R. 9053—Public Law 87-400
Approved October 5, 1961

Amended Title II (Student Loans) of The National Defense Education Act of 1958.

1962   ## MANPOWER RETRAINING ACT

S. 1991—Public Law 87-415
Approved March 15, 1962

APPENDIX C

Authorized a manpower training program to help alleviate the long-term unemployment problem.

EDUCATIONAL TELEVISION

S. 205—Public Law 87-447
Approved May 1, 1962

Legislation designed to assist the construction of educational television broadcasting facilities (full text will be found on pp. 277–281).

WAR ORPHANS EDUCATIONAL ASSISTANCE ACT

H.R. 1811—Public Law 87-546
Approved July 25, 1962

Permitted eligible beneficiaries under the War Orphans Educational Assistance Act to attend foreign educational institutions under certain limited conditions.

ARMED FORCES—EDUCATIONAL OPPORTUNITIES

H.R. 7727—Public Law 87-555
Approved July 27, 1962

Permitted qualified members of the Armed Forces and the Public Health Service to accept, from nongovernmental sources, competitive fellowships, scholarships, or grants for educational purposes.

DEPOSITORY LIBRARIES

H.R. 8141—Public Law 87-579
Approved August 9, 1962

Increased total of depository libraries.

COLLEGE AID

H.R. 6984—Public Law 87-683
Approved September 5, 1962

Provided for a method of payment of indirect cost of research and development contracted by the Federal Government at universities, colleges, and other educational institutions.

CAPTIONED FILMS FOR THE DEAF

S. 2511—Public Law 87-715
Approved September 28, 1962

Raised ceiling of $250,000 to $1,250,000 for the established loan service of captioned films for the deaf in the Department of Health, Education, and Welfare and authorized the Secretary to provide for (a) research in the use of educational and training films for the deaf, (b) production and distribution of training films for the deaf, and (c) training persons in the use of films for the deaf.

VETERANS EDUCATIONAL RIGHTS

S. 2697—Public Law 87-815
Approved October 15, 1962

Extended the time for certain individuals to pursue and complete a program of education or training under the Korean training program for veterans and the war orphans' education assistance program.

WAR ORPHANS EDUCATION AID

H.R. 9737—Public Law 87-819
Approved October 15, 1962

APPENDIX C

Made thirty-two the maximum age (formerly twenty-three) when a war orphan must complete his education provided suspension was due to conditions beyond his control.

SCHOOL LUNCH

H.R. 11665—Public Law 87-823
Approved October 15, 1962

Amended The National School Lunch Act to revise the formula for apportioning cash assistance funds among the states to provide school lunches.

NATIONAL SCIENCE FOUNDATION AMENDMENTS

H.R. 8556—Public Law 87-835
Approved October 16, 1962

Eliminated the non-Communist disclaimer from the National Science Foundation Act and The National Defense Education Act of 1958.

1963   ## WAR ORPHANS

S. 330—Public Law 88-126
Approved September 23, 1963

Designated State agencies to work with the Veterans' Administration in approving educational courses for war orphans.

MEDICAL SCHOOL EDUCATION

H.R. 12—Public Law 88-129
Approved September 24, 1963

Authorized a program of matching grants for construction of teaching facilities to train physicians, dentists, nurses, and professional public health personnel as well as pharmacists, optometrists, and podiatrists. In addition, it authorized loans for students of medicine, dentistry, and osteopathy.

STUDENT TRAINEES—TRAVEL EXPENSES

S. 814—Public Law 88-146
Approved October 16, 1963

Authorized payment of travel and transportation expenses to student trainees when assigned on completion of college work to positions for which there is determined by the Civil Service Commission to be a manpower shortage.

EXCEPTIONAL CHILDREN—TEACHERS

S. 1576—Public Law 88-164
Approved October 31, 1963

Title III of the Mental Retardation Act authorized grants to public or other nonprofit institutions of higher learning to assist in providing professional or advanced training for personnel engaged or preparing to engage in employment as teachers of handicapped children, as supervisors of such teachers, or as speech correctionists or other specialists providing special services for education of such children, or engaged or preparing to engage in research in fields related to education of such children

HIGHER EDUCATION

H.R. 6143—Public Law 88-204
Approved December 16, 1963

Authorized a five-year program of Federal grants and loans for construction of classrooms, laboratories, and libraries (full text will be found on pp. 282–305).

VOCATIONAL EDUCATION–IMPACTED AREAS– NATIONAL DEFENSE EDUCATION ACT

H.R. 4955—Public Law 88-210
Approved December 18, 1963

Authorized new matching grants to the states to expand vocational education programs, extended the National Defense Education Act, and extended the impacted areas legislation to June 30, 1965.

MANPOWER RETRAINING ACT

H.R. 8720—Public Law 88-214
Approved December 19, 1963

Extended and expanded the training programs under the Manpower Development and Training Act of 1962.

ADULT INDIAN VOCATIONAL TRAINING

S. 1868—Public Law 88-230
Approved December 23, 1963

Increased appropriations for the Indian vocational training program.

SELECTED ACTS AFFECTING YOUTH AND
EDUCATION PASSED DURING THE KENNEDY
ADMINISTRATION

PUBLIC LAW 87-274
EIGHTY-SEVENTH CONGRESS, S. 279
SEPTEMBER 22, 1961

An act to provide Federal assistance for projects which will demonstrate or develop techniques and practices leading to a solution of the Nation's juvenile delinquency control problems.

Be it enacted by the Senate and House of Representatives of the United States of America in Congress assembled, That this Act may be cited as the "Juvenile Delinquency and Youth Offenses Control Act of 1961."

FINDINGS AND POLICIES

SEC. 2. (a) The Congress hereby finds and declares that juvenile delinquency and youth offenses diminish the strength and vitality of the people of our Nation; that such delinquency and offenses are increasing in both urban and rural communities; that such delinquency and offenses occur disproportionately among school dropouts, unemployed youth faced with limited opportunities and with employment barriers, and youth in deprived family situations; and that prevention and control of such delinquency and offenses require intensive and coordinated efforts on the part of private and governmental interests.

(b) The policy of the Federal Government is to assist in developing techniques for the prevention and control of juvenile delinquency and youth offenses, and to encourage the coordination of efforts among governmental and nongovernmental educational, employment, health, welfare, law enforcement, correctional, and other agencies concerned with such problems.

APPENDIX D

DEMONSTRATION AND EVALUATION PROJECTS

Sec. 3. (a) For the purpose of demonstrating improved methods for the prevention and control of juvenile delinquency or youth offenses (which, for the purposes of this Act, includes treatment of juvenile delinquents and youthful offenders), the Secretary of Health, Education, and Welfare (hereinafter in this Act referred to as the "Secretary") is authorized to make grants for projects for the evaluation, or demonstration of the effectiveness, of techniques and practices which in the Secretary's judgment hold promise of making a substantial contribution to the prevention or control of juvenile delinquency or youth offenses, including techniques and practices for the training of personnel and for developing or securing more effective cooperation among public and other nonprofit agencies, organizations, and institutions.

(b) Such grants may be made to any State, local, or other public or nonprofit agency, organization, or institution; and to the extent he deems it appropriate, the Secretary shall require the recipient of any grant to contribute money, facilities, or services for carrying out the project for which such grant was made.

(c) The Secretary is further authorized to enter into contracts for any such projects with public or other agencies, organizations, or institutions, and with individuals.

(d) The full amount (as determined by the Secretary) of any grant for a project made under this section shall be reserved from the appropriation for the fiscal year in which the grant is made; and payments on account of such grant in that and subsequent fiscal years may be made only from the amount so reserved.

(e) Payments under this section may be made in installments, and in advance or by way of reimbursement, as may be determined by the Secretary, and shall be made on such conditions as he finds necessary to carry out the purposes of this section.

TRAINING OF PERSONNEL

Sec. 4. (a) For the purpose of training personnel employed or preparing for employment in programs for the prevention or control of juvenile delinquency or youth offenses, the Secretary is authorized to make grants for programs for such purpose which in his judgment hold promise of making a substantial contribution to the prevention or control of juvenile delinquency or youth offenses. Such programs may include, among other things, the development of courses of study, and the establishment of short-term traineeships with such allowances for travel and subsistence expenses, as the Secretary may determine to be necessary.

(b) Such grants may be made to any Federal, State, local, or other public or nonprofit agency, organization, or institution; and to the extent he deems it appropriate, the Secretary shall require the recipient of any grant to contribute money, facilities, or services for carrying out the program for which such grant was made.

(c) The Secretary is further authorized to enter into contracts for any such programs with public or other agencies, organizations, or institutions, and with individuals.

(d) The full amount (as determined by the Secretary) of any grant for a program made under this section shall be reserved from the appropriation for the fiscal year in which the grant is made; and payments on account of such grant in that and subsequent fiscal years may be made only from the amount so reserved.

(e) Payments under this section may be made in installments and in advance or by way of reimbursement, as may be determined by the Secretary, and shall be made on such conditions as he finds necessary to carry out the purposes of this section.

TECHNICAL ASSISTANCE SERVICES

SEC. 5. (a) The Secretary is authorized to make studies with respect to matters relating to the prevention or control of juvenile delinquency or youth offenses, including the effectiveness of projects or programs carried out under this Act, to cooperate with and render technical assistance to State, local, or other public or private agencies, organizations, and institutions in such matters, and to provide short-term training and instruction in technical matters relating to the prevention or control of juvenile delinquency or youth offenses.

(b) The Secretary is authorized to collect, evaluate, publish, and disseminate information and materials relating to studies conducted under this Act, and other matters relating to prevention or control of juvenile delinquency or youth offenses, for the general public or for agencies and personnel engaged in programs concerning juvenile delinquency or youth offenses, as may be appropriate.

AUTHORIZATION OF APPROPRIATIONS

SEC. 6. There is hereby authorized to be appropriated to the Secretary for the fiscal year ending June 30, 1962, and each of the two succeeding fiscal years, the sum of $10,000,000 for carrying out this Act.

MISCELLANEOUS

SEC. 7. (a)(1) The Secretary is authorized to appoint such technical or other advisory committees to advise him in connection with prevention or control of juvenile delinquency or youth offenses as he deems necessary.

(2) Members of any such committee not otherwise in the employ of the United States, while attending meetings of their committee, shall be entitled to receive compensation at a rate to be fixed by the Secretary, but not exceeding $75 per diem, including travel time, and while away from their homes or regular places of business they may be allowed travel expenses, including per diem in lieu of subsistence, as authorized by law (5 U.S.C. 73b–2) for persons in the Government service employed intermittently. The provisions of section 1003 of the National Defense Education Act of 1958 shall apply to members of such committees.

(b) The Secretary shall consult with the President's Committee on Juvenile Delinquency and Youth Crime on matters of general policy and procedure arising in the administration of this Act, and shall consider the recommendations, if any, of such Committee on program applications submitted under section 3 or 4 and on proposed studies or other actions to be undertaken pursuant to section 5.

(c) As used in this Act, the term "State" includes the District of Columbia, the Commonwealth of Puerto Rico, the Virgin Islands, Guam, and American Samoa.

PUBLIC LAW 87-293
EIGHTY-SEVENTH CONGRESS, H.R. 7500
SEPTEMBER 22, 1961

An act to provide for a Peace Corps to help the people of interested countries and areas in meeting their needs for skilled manpower.

Be it enacted by the Senate and House of Representatives of the United States of America in Congress assembled,

TITLE I—THE PEACE CORPS

SHORT TITLE

SECTION 1. This Act may be cited as the "Peace Corps Act."

DECLARATION OF PURPOSE

SEC. 2. The Congress of the United States declares that it is the policy of the United States and the purpose of this Act to promote world peace and friendship through a Peace Corps, which shall make available to interested countries and areas men and women of the United States qualified for service abroad and willing to serve, under conditions of hardship if necessary, to help the peoples of such countries and areas in meeting their needs for trained manpower, and to help promote a better understanding of the American people on the part of the peoples served and a better understanding of other peoples on the part of the American people.

AUTHORIZATION

SEC. 3. (a) The President is authorized to carry out programs in furtherance of the purposes of this Act, on such terms and conditions as he may determine.

(b) There is hereby authorized to be appropriated to the President for the fiscal year 1962 not to exceed $40,000,000 to carry out the purposes of this Act.

DIRECTOR OF THE PEACE CORPS AND DELEGATION OF FUNCTIONS

SEC. 4. (a) The President may appoint, by and with the advice and consent of the Senate, a Director of the Peace Corps, whose compensation shall be fixed by the President at a rate not in excess of $20,000 per annum, and a Deputy Director of the Peace Corps, whose compensation shall be fixed by the President at a rate not in excess of $19,500 per annum.

(b) The President may exercise any functions vested in him by this Act through such agency or officer of the United States Government as he shall direct. The head of any such agency or any such officer may promulgate such rules and regulations as he may deem necessary or appropriate to carry out such functions, and may delegate to any of his subordinates authority to perform any of such functions.

(c)(1) Nothing contained in this Act shall be construed to infringe upon the powers or functions of the Secretary of State.

(2) The President shall prescribe appropriate procedures to assure coordination of Peace Corps activities with other activities of the United States Government in each country, under the leadership of the chief of the United States diplomatic mission.

(3) Under the direction of the President, the Secretary of State shall be responsible for the continuous supervision and general direction of the programs authorized by this Act, to the end that such programs are effectively integrated both at home and abroad and the foreign policy of the United States is best served thereby.

(d) Except with the approval of the Secretary of State, the Peace Corps shall not be assigned to perform services which could more usefully be performed by other available agencies of the United States Government in the country concerned.

PEACE CORPS VOLUNTEERS

SEC. 5. (a) The President may enroll in the Peace Corps for service abroad qualified citizens and nationals of the United States (referred to in this Act as "volunteers"). The terms and conditions of the enrollment, training, compensation, hours of work, benefits, leave, termination, and all other terms and conditions of the service of volunteers shall be exclusively those set forth in this Act and those consistent therewith which the President may prescribe; and, except as provided in this Act, volunteers shall not be deemed officers or employees or otherwise in the service or employment of, or holding office under, the United States for any purpose. In carrying out this subsection no political test shall be required or taken into consideration, nor shall there be any discrimination against any person on account of race, creed, or color.

(b) Volunteers shall be provided with such living, travel, and leave allowances, and such housing, transportation, supplies, equipment, subsistence, and clothing as the President may determine to be necessary for their maintenance and to insure their health and their capacity to serve effectively. Transportation and travel allowances may also be provided, in such circumstances as the President may determine, for applicants for enrollment to or from places of training and places of enrollment, and for former volunteers from places of termination to their homes in the United States.

(c) Volunteers shall be entitled to receive termination payments at a rate not to exceed $75 for each month of satisfactory service as determined by the President. The termination payment of each volunteer shall be payable at the termination of his service, or may be paid during the course of his service to the volunteer, to members of his family or to others, under such circumstances as the President may determine. In the event of the volunteer's death during the period of his service, the amount of any unpaid termination payment shall be paid in accordance with the provisions of section 61f of title 5 of the United States Code.

(d) Volunteers shall be deemed to be employees of the United States Government for the purposes of the Federal Employees' Compensation Act (39 Stat. 742), as amended: *Provided, however,* That entitlement to disability compensation payments under that Act shall commence on the day after the date of termination of service. For the purposes of that Act—

(1) volunteers shall be deemed to be receiving monthly pay at the lowest rate provided for grade 7 of the general schedule established by the Classification Act of 1949, as amended, and volunteer leaders (referred to in section 6 of this Act) shall be deemed to be receiving monthly pay at the lowest rate provided for grade 11 of such general schedule; and

(2) any injury suffered by a volunteer during any time when he is located abroad shall be deemed to have been sustained while in the performance of his duty and any disease contracted during such time

shall be deemed to have been proximately caused by his employment, unless such injury or disease is caused by willful misconduct of the volunteer or by the volunteer's intention to bring about the injury or death of himself or of another, or unless intoxication of the injured volunteer is the proximate cause of the injury or death.

(e) Volunteers shall receive such health care during their service, and such health examinations and immunization preparatory to their service, as the President may deem necessary or appropriate. Subject to such conditions as the President may prescribe, such health care, examinations, and immunization may be provided for volunteers in any facility of any agency of the United States Government, and in such cases the appropriation for maintaining and operating such facility shall be reimbursed from appropriations available under this Act.

(f)(1) Any period of satisfactory service of a volunteer under this Act shall be credited in connection with subsequent employment in the same manner as a like period of civilian employment by the United State Government—

(A) for the purposes of the Civil Service Retirement Act, as amended (5 U.S.C. 2251, et seq.), section 852(a)(1) of the Foreign Service Act of 1946, as amended (22 U.S.C. 1092(a)(1), and every other Act establishing a retirement system for civilian employees of any United States Government agency; and

(B) except as otherwise determined by the President, for the purposes of determining seniority, reduction in force, and layoff rights, leave entitlement, and other rights and privileges based upon length of service under the laws administered by the Civil Service Commission, the Foreign Service Act of 1946, and every other Act establishing or governing terms and conditions of service of civilian employees of the United States Government: *Provided,* That service of a volunteer shall not be credited toward completion of any probationary or trial period or completion of any service requirement for career appointment.

(2) For the purposes of paragraph (1)(A) of this subsection, volunteers and volunteer leaders shall be deemed to be receiving compensation during their service at the respective rates of termination payments payable under section 5(c) and 6(1) of this Act.

(g) The President may detail or assign volunteers or otherwise make them available to any entity referred to in paragraph (1) of section 10(a) on such terms and conditions as he may determine: *Provided, however,* That any volunteer so detailed or assigned shall continue to be entitled to the allowances, benefits and privileges of volunteers authorized under or pursuant to this Act.

(h) Volunteers shall be deemed employees of the United States Government for the purposes of the Federal Tort Claims Act and any other Federal tort liability statute, and for the purposes of section 1 of the Act of June 4, 1920 (41 Stat. 750), as amended (22 U.S.C. 214).

(i) The service of a volunteer may be terminated at any time at the pleasure of the President.

(j) Upon enrollment in the Peace Corps, every volunteer shall take the oath prescribed for persons appointed to any office of honor or profit by section 1757 of the Revised Statutes of the United States, as amended (5 U.S.C. 16), and shall swear (or affirm) that he does not advocate the overthrow of our constitutional form of government in the United States, and that he is not a member of an organization that advocates the overthrow of our constitutional form of government in the United States, knowing that such organization so advocates.

PEACE CORPS VOLUNTEER LEADERS

SEC. 6. The President may enroll in the Peace Corps qualified citizens or nationals of the United States whose services are required for supervisory or other special duties or responsibilities in connection with programs under this Act (referred to in this Act as "volunteer leaders"). The ratio of the total number of volunteer leaders to the total number of volunteers in service at any one time shall not exceed one to twenty-five. Except as otherwise provided in this Act, all of the provisions of this Act applicable to volunteers shall be applicable to volunteer leaders, and the term "volunteers" shall include "volunteer leaders": *Provided, however,* That—

(1) volunteer leaders shall be entitled to receive termination payments at a rate not to exceed $125 for each month of satisfactory service as determined by the President;

(2) spouses and minor children of volunteer leaders may receive

such living, travel, and leave allowances, and such housing, transportation, subsistence, and essential special items of clothing, as the President may determine, but the authority contained in this paragraph shall be exercised only under exceptional circumstances;

(3) spouses and minor children of volunteer leaders accompanying them may receive such health care as the President may determine and upon such terms as he may determine, including health care in any facility referred to in section 5(e) of this Act, subject to such conditions as the President may prescribe and subject to reimbursement of appropriations as provided in section 5(e); and

(4) spouses and minor children of volunteer leaders accompanying them may receive such orientation, language, and other training necessary to accomplish the purposes of this Act as the President may determine.

PEACE CORPS EMPLOYEES

SEC. 7. (a) The President may employ such persons, not to exceed 275 persons permanently employed in the United States at any one time in fiscal year 1962, as the President deems necessary to carry out the provisions and purposes of this Act. Except as otherwise provided in this Act, such persons (hereinafter sometimes referred to as "employees") shall be employed in accordance with and shall be subject to the laws applicable to personnel employed by the United States Government.

(b) Of the persons so employed in the United States in activities authorized by this Act, not to exceed thirty may be compensated without regard to the provisions of the Classification Act of 1949, as amended, of whom not to exceed twenty may be compensated at rates higher than those provided for grade fifteen of the general schedule established by the Classification Act of 1949, as amended, and of these not to exceed two may be compensated at a rate in excess of the highest rate provided for grades of such general schedule but not in excess of $19,000 per year. Such positions shall be in addition to those authorized by section 4(a) of this Act to be filled by Presidential appointment, and in addition to the number authorized by section 505 of the Classification Act of 1949, as amended.

(c) For the purpose of performing functions under this Act outside the United States, the President may—

(1) employ or assign persons, or authorize the employment or assignment of officers or employees of agencies of the United States Government, who shall receive compensation at any of the rates provided for persons appointed to the Foreign Service Reserve and Staff under the Foreign Service Act of 1946, as amended (22 U.S.C. 801 et seq.), together with allowances and benefits thereunder; and persons so employed or assigned shall be entitled, except to the extent that the President may specify otherwise in cases in which the period of the employment or assignment exceeds thirty months, to the same benefits as are provided by section 528 of that Act for persons appointed to the Foreign Service Reserve, and the provisions of section 1005 of that Act shall apply in the case of such persons, except that policymaking officials shall not be subject to that part of section 1005 which prohibits political tests;

(2) utilize such authority, including authority to appoint and assign persons for the duration of operations under this Act, contained in the Foreign Service Act of 1946, as amended, as the President deems necessary to carry out functions under this Act. Such provisions of the Foreign Service Act of 1946 as the President deems appropriate shall apply to persons appointed or assigned under this paragraph, including in all cases, the provisions of section 528 of that Act: *Provided, however,* That the President may by regulation make exceptions to the application of section 528 in cases in which the period of the appointment of assignment exceeds thirty months: *Provided further,* That Foreign Service Reserve officers appointed or assigned pursuant to this paragraph shall receive within-class salary increases in accordance with such regulations as the President may prescribe; and

(3) specify which of the allowances and differentials authorized by title II of the Overseas Differentials and Allowances Act (5 U.S.C. 3031 et seq.) may be granted to any person employed, appointed or assigned under this subsection (c) and may determine the rates thereof not to exceed those otherwise granted to employees under that Act.

(d) The President is authorized to prescribe by regulation standards or other criteria for maintaining adequate performance levels for persons appointed or assigned pursuant to subsection (c)(2) of this section and section 527(c)(2) of the Mutual Security Act of 1954, as amended, and may, notwithstanding any other law, separate persons who fail to meet such standards or other criteria, and also may grant such persons severance benefits of one month's salary for each year of service, but not to exceed one year's salary at the then current salary rate of such persons.

(e) In each country or area in which volunteers serve abroad, the President may appoint an employee or a volunteer as a Peace Corps representative to have direction of other employees of the Peace Corps abroad and to oversee the activities carried on under this Act in such country or area. Unless a representative is a volunteer, the compensation, allowances and benefits, and other terms and conditions of service of each such representative, shall be the same as those of a person appointed or assigned pursuant to paragraph (1) or (2) of subsection (c) of this section, except that any such representative may, notwithstanding any provision of law, be removed by the President in his discretion.

VOLUNTEER TRAINING

SEC. 8. (a) The President shall make provision for such training as he deems appropriate for each applicant for enrollment as a volunteer and each enrolled volunteer. All of the provisions of this Act applicable respectively to volunteers and volunteer leaders shall be applicable to applicants for enrollment as such during any period of training occurring prior to enrollment, and the respective terms "volunteers" and "volunteer leaders" shall include such applicants during any such period of training.

(b) The President may also make provision, on the basis of advances of funds or reimbursement to the United States, for training for citizens of the United States, other than those referred to in subsection (a) of this section, who have been selected for service abroad in programs not carried out under authority of this Act which are similar to those authorized by this Act. The provisions of section 9 of this Act shall apply, on a similar advance of funds or a reimbursement basis, with respect to persons while within the United States for training under authority of this subsection. Advances or reimbursements received under this subsection may be credited to the current applicable appropriation, fund, or account and shall be available for the purposes for which such appropriation, fund, or account is authorized to be used.

(c) Training hereinabove provided for shall include instruction in the philosophy, strategy, tactics, and menace of communism.

PARTICIPATION OF FOREIGN NATIONALS

SEC. 9. In order to provide for assistance by foreign nationals in the training of volunteers, and to permit effective implementation of Peace Corps projects with due regard for the desirability of cost-sharing arrangements, where appropriate, the President may make provision for transportation, housing, subsistence, or per diem in lieu thereof, and health care or health and accident insurance for foreign nationals engaged in activities authorized by this Act while they are away from their homes, without regard to the provisions of any other law: *Provided, however,* That per diem in lieu of subsistence furnished to such persons shall not be at rates higher than those prescribed by the Secretary of State pursuant to section 12 of Public Law 84-885 (70 Stat. 890). Such persons, and persons coming to the United States under contract pursuant to section 10(a)(4), may be admitted to the United States, if otherwise qualified, as nonimmigrants under section 101(a)(15) of the Immigration and Nationality Act (8 U.S.C. 1101(a)(15)) for such time and under such conditions as may be prescribed by regulations promulgated by the Secretary of State and the Attorney General. A person admitted under this section who fails to maintain the status under which he was admitted or who fails to depart from the United States at the expiration of the time for which he was admitted, or who engages in activities of a political nature detrimental to the interests of the United States, or in activities not consistent with the security of the United States, shall, upon the warrant of the Attorney General, be taken into custody and promptly deported pursuant to sections 241, 242, and 243 of the Immigration and Nationality Act. Deportation proceedings under this section shall be summary and the findings of the Attorney General as to matters of fact shall be conclusive.

GENERAL POWERS AND AUTHORITIES

SEC. 10. (a) In furtherance of the purposes of this Act, the President may—

(1) enter into, perform, and modify contracts and agreements and

otherwise cooperate with any agency of the United States Government or of any State or any subdivision thereof, other governments and departments and agencies thereof, and educational institutions, voluntary agencies, farm organizations, labor unions, and other organizations, individuals and firms;

(2) assign volunteers in special cases to temporary duty with international organizations and agencies when the Secretary of State determines that such assignment would serve the purposes of this Act: *Provided,* That not more than one hundred and twenty-five Peace Corps volunteers or volunteer leaders shall be assigned to international organizations as described in this section;

(3) accept in the name of the Peace Corps and employ in furtherance of the purposes of this Act (A) voluntary services notwithstanding the provisions of 31 U.S.C. 665(b), and (B) any money or property (real, personal or mixed, tangible or intangible) received by gift, devise, bequest, or otherwise; and

(4) contract with individuals for personal services abroad, and with aliens (abroad or within the United States) for personal services within the United States: *Provided,* That no such person shall be deemed an officer or employee or otherwise in the service or employment of the United States Government for any purpose.

(b) Notwithstanding any other provision of law, whenever the President determines that it will further the purposes of this Act, the President, under such regulations as he may prescribe, may settle and pay, in an amount not exceeding $10,000, any claim against the United States, for loss of or damage to real or personal property (including loss of occupancy or use thereof) belonging to, or for personal injury or death of, any person not a citizen or resident of the United States, where such claim arises abroad out of the act or omission of any Peace Corps employee or out of the act or omission of any volunteer, but only if such claim is presented in writing within one year after it accrues. Any amount paid in settlement of any claim under this subsection shall be accepted by the claimant in full satisfaction thereof and shall bar any further action or proceeding thereon.

(c) Subject to any future action of the Congress, a contract or agreement which entails commitments for the expenditure of funds available for the purposes of this Act, including commitments for the purpose of paying or providing for allowances and other benefits of volunteers authorized by sections 5 and 6 of this Act, may extend at any time for not more than thirty-six months.

(d) Whenever the President determines it to be in furtherance of the purposes of this Act, functions authorized by this Act may be performed without regard to such provisions of law (other than the Renegotiation Act of 1951, as amended) regulating the making, performance, amendment, or modification of contracts and the expenditure of Government funds as the President may specify.

(e) The President may allocate or transfer to any agency of the United States Government any funds available for carrying out the purposes of this Act including any advance received by the United States from any country or international organization under authority of this Act, but not to exceed 20 per centum in the aggregate of such funds may be allocated or transferred to agencies other than the Peace Corps. Such funds shall be available for obligation and expenditure for the purposes of this Act in accordance with authority granted in this Act or under authority governing the activities of the agencies of the United States Government to which such funds are allocated or transferred.

(f) Any officer of the United States Government carrying out functions under this Act may utilize the services and facilities of, or procure commodities from, any agency of the United States Government as the President shall direct, or with the consent of the head of such agency, and funds allocated pursuant to this subsection to any such agency may be established in separate appropriation accounts on the books of the Treasury.

(g) In the case of any commodity, service, or facility procured from any agency of the United States Government under this Act, reimbursement or payment shall be made to such agency from funds available under this Act. Such reimbursement or payment shall be at replacement cost, or, if required by law, at actual cost, or at any other price authorized by law and agreed to by the owning or disposing agency. The amount of any such reimbursement or payment shall be credited to current applicable appropriations, funds, or accounts from which there may be procured replacements of similar commodities, services, or facilities, except that where such appropriations, funds, or accounts are not reimbursable except by reason of this sub-section, and when the owning or disposing agency determines that such replacement is not necessary, any funds received in payment therefor shall be covered into the Treasury as miscellaneous receipts.

REPORTS

SEC. 11. The President shall transmit to the Congress, at least once in each fiscal year, a report on operations under this Act.

PEACE CORPS NATIONAL ADVISORY COUNCIL

SEC. 12. (a) The President may appoint to membership in a board to be known as the Peace Corps National Advisory Council twenty-five persons who are broadly representative of educational institutions, voluntary agencies, farm organizations, and labor unions, and other public and private organizations and groups as well as individuals interested in the programs and objectives of the Peace Corps, to advise and consult with the President with regard to policies and programs designed to further the purposes of this Act.

(b) Members of the Council shall serve at the pleasure of the President and meet at his call. They shall receive no compensation for their services, but members who are not officers or employees of the United States Government may each receive out of funds made available for the purposes of this Act a per diem allowance of $50 for each day, not to exceed twenty days in any fiscal year in the case of any such member, spent away from his home or regular place of business for the purpose of attendance at meetings or conferences and in necessary travel, and while so engaged may be paid actual travel expenses and per diem in lieu of subsistence and other expenses, at the applicable rate prescribed by the Standardized Government Travel Regulations, as amended from time to time.

EXPERTS AND CONSULTANTS

SEC. 13. (a) Experts and consultants or organizations thereof may, as authorized by section 15 of the Act of August 2, 1946, as amended (5 U.S.C. 55a), be employed by the Peace Corps for the performance of functions under this Act, and individuals so employed may be compensated at rates not in excess of $75 per diem, and while away from their homes or regular places of business, they may be paid actual travel expenses and per diem in lieu of subsistence and other expenses at the applicable rate prescribed in the Standardized Government Travel Regulations, as amended from time to time, while so employed: *Provided,* That contracts for such employment may be renewed annually.

(b) Service of an individual as a member of the Council authorized to be established by section 12 of this Act or as an expert or consultant under subsection (a) of this section shall not be considered as service or employment bringing such individual within the provisions of section 281, 283, or 284 of title 18 of the United States Code, or of section 190 of the Revised Statutes (5 U.S.C. 99), or of any other Federal law imposing restrictions, requirements, or penalties in relation to the employment of persons, the performance of service, or the payment or receipt of compensation in connection with any claim, proceeding, or matter involving the United States Government, except insofar as such provisions of law may prohibit any such individual from receiving compensation in respect of any particular matter in which such individual was directly involved in the performance of such service; nor shall such service be considered as employment or holding of office or position bringing such individual within the provisions of section 13 of the Civil Service Retirement Act, as amended (5 U.S.C. 2263), section 212 of the Act of June 30, 1932, as amended (5 U.S.C. 59a), section 872 of the Foreign Service Act of 1946, as amended, or any other law limiting the reemployment of retired officers or employees or governing the simultaneous receipt of compensation and retired pay or annuities.

DETAIL OF PERSONNEL TO FOREIGN GOVERNMENTS
AND INTERNATIONAL ORGANIZATIONS

SEC. 14. (a) In furtherance of the purposes of this Act, the head of any agency of the United States Government is authorized to detail, assign, or otherwise make available any officer or employee of his agency (1) to serve with, or as a member of, the international staff of any international organization, or (2) to any office or position to which no compensation is attached with any foreign government or agency thereof: *Provided,* That such acceptance of such office or position shall in no case involve the taking of an oath of allegiance to another government.

(b) Any such officer or employee, while so detailed or assigned, shall be considered, for the purpose of preserving his allowances, privileges, rights, seniority, and other benefits as such, an officer or employee of the United States Government and of the agency of the United States Government from which detailed or assigned, and he shall continue to receive compensation, allowances, and benefits from funds authorized by this Act. He may also receive, under such regulations as the President may prescribe, representation allowances similar to those allowed under section 901 of the Foreign Service Act of 1946 (22 U.S.C. 1131). The authorization of such allowances and other benefits, and the payment thereof out of any appropriations available therefor, shall be considered as meeting all of the requirements of section 1765 of the Revised Statutes (5 U.S.C. 70).

(c) Details or assignments may be made under this section—

(1) without reimbursement to the United States Government by the international organization or foreign government;

(2) upon agreement by the international organization or foreign government to reimburse the United States Government for compensation, travel expenses, and allowances, or any part thereof, payable to such officer or employee during the period of assignment or detail in accordance with subsection (b) of this section; and such reimbursement shall be credited to the appropriation, fund, or account utilized for paying such compensation, travel expenses, or allowances, or to the appropriation, fund, or account currently available for such purpose; or

(3) upon an advance of funds, property or services to the United States Government accepted with the approval of the President for specified uses in furtherance of the purposes of this Act; and funds so advanced may be established as a separate fund in the Treasury of the United States Government, to be available for the specified uses, and to be used for reimbursement of appropriations or direct expenditure subject to the provisions of this Act, any unexpended balance of such account to be returned to the foreign government or international organization.

UTILIZATION OF FUNDS

Sec. 15. (a) Funds made available for the purposes of this Act may be used for compensation, allowances and travel of employees, including Foreign Service personnel whose services are utilized primarily for the purposes of this Act, for printing and binding without regard to the provisions of any other law, and for expenditures outside the United States for the procurement of supplies and services and for other administrative and operating purposes (other than compensation of employees) without regard to such laws and regulations governing the obligation and expenditure of Government funds as may be necessary to accomplish the purposes of this Act.

(b) Funds made available for the purposes of this Act may be used to pay expenses in connection with travel abroad of employees and, to the extent otherwise authorized by this Act, of volunteers, including travel expenses of dependents (including expenses during necessary stopovers while engaged in such travel), and transportation of personal effects, household goods, and automobiles when any part of such travel or transportation begins in one fiscal year pursuant to travel orders issued in that fiscal year, notwithstanding the fact that such travel or transportation may not be completed during the same fiscal year, and cost of transporting to and from a place of storage, and the cost of storing automobiles of employees when it is in the public interest or more economical to authorize storage.

(c) Funds available under this Act may be used to pay costs of training employees employed or assigned pursuant to section 7(c)(2) of this Act (through interchange or otherwise) at any State or local unit of government, public or private nonprofit institution, trade, labor, agricultural, or scientific association or organization, or commercial firm; and the provisions of Public Law 84-918 (7 U.S.C. 1881 et seq.) may be used to carry out the foregoing authority notwithstanding that interchange of personnel may not be involved or that the training may not take place at the institutions specified in that Act. Such training shall not be considered employment or holding of office under section 2 of the Act of July 31, 1894, as amended (5 U.S.C. 62), and any payments or contributions in connection therewith may, as deemed appropriate by the head of the agency of the United States Government authorizing such training, be made by private or public sources and be accepted by any trainee, or may be accepted by and credited to the current applicable appropriation of such agency: *Provided, however,* That any such payments to an employee in the nature of compensation shall be in lieu, or in reduction, of compensation received from the United States Government.

(d) Funds available for the purposes of this Act shall be available for—

(1) rent of buildings and space in buildings in the United States, and for repair, alteration, and improvement of such leased properties;

(2) expenses of attendance at meetings concerned with the purposes of this Act, including (notwithstanding the provisions of section 9 of Public Law 60-328 (31 U.S.C. 673)) expenses in connection with meetings of persons whose employment is authorized by section 13(a) of this Act;

(3) rental and hire of aircraft;

(4) purchase and hire of passenger motor vehicles: *Provided,* That, except as may otherwise be provided in an appropriation or other Act, passenger motor vehicles for administrative purposes abroad may be purchased for replacement only, and such vehicles may be exchanged or sold and replaced by an equal number of such vehicles, and the cost, including exchange allowance, of each such replacement shall not exceed $2,500 in the case of an automobile for any Peace Corps country representative appointed under section 7(e): *Provided further,* That passenger motor vehicles may be purchased for use in the United States only as may be specifically provided in an appropriation or other Act;

(5) entertainment (not to exceed $5,000 in any fiscal year except as may otherwise be provided in an appropriation or other Act);

(6) exchange of funds without regard to section 3561 of the Revised Statutes (31 U.S.C. 543) and loss by exchange;

(7) expenditures (not to exceed $5,000 in any fiscal year except as may be otherwise provided in an appropriation or other Act) not otherwise authorized by law to meet unforeseen emergencies or contingencies arising in the Peace Corps: *Provided,* That a certificate of the amount only of each such expenditure and that such expendi-

ture was necessary to meet an unforeseen emergency or contingency, made by the Director of the Peace Corps or his designee, shall be deemed a sufficient voucher for the amount therein specified;

(8) insurance of official motor vehicles acquired for use abroad;

(9) rent or lease abroad for not to exceed five years of offices, health facilities, buildings, grounds, and living quarters, and payments therefor in advance; maintenance, furnishings, necessary repairs, improvements, and alterations to properties owned or rented by the United States Government or made available for its use abroad; and costs of fuel, water, and utilities for such properties;

(10) expenses of preparing and transporting to their former homes, or, with respect to foreign participants engaged in activities under this Act, to their former homes or places of burial, and of care and disposition of, the remains of persons or members of the families of persons who may die while such persons are away from their homes participating in activities under this Act;

(11) use in accordance with authorities of the Foreign Service Act of 1946, as amended (22 U.S.C. 801 et seq.), not otherwise provided for; and

(12) ice and drinking water for use abroad.

APPOINTMENT OF PERSONS SERVING UNDER PRIOR LAW

SEC. 16. (a) Under such terms and conditions as the President may prescribe, volunteer personnel who on the effective date of this Act have been engaged by contract by, or pursuant to agreement with, the Peace Corps agency established within the Department of State pursuant to Executive Order Number 10924, dated March 1, 1961, may be enrolled as volunteers or volunteer leaders under this Act. Such enrollment may be made effective, for any or all purposes, as of a date prior to the effective date of this Act but not earlier than the date of commencement of training of the person in question. All allowances and termination payments similar to those authorized by this Act received by any such person or by members of his family or payable with respect to any period between the effective date and the actual date of such enrollment shall be deemed for all purposes to have been received or to be payable under the appropriate provision of this Act.

(b) Any person who was appointed by and with the advice and

consent of the Senate to be Director of the Peace Corps prior to the enactment of this Act may be appointed by the President to be Director of the Peace Corps under section 4(a) of this Act without further action by the Senate.

USE OF FOREIGN CURRENCIES

SEC. 17. Whenever possible, expenditures incurred in carrying out functions under this Act shall be paid for in such currency of the country or area where the expense is incurred as may be available to the United States.

APPLICABILITY OF MUTUAL DEFENSE ASSISTANCE CONTROL ACT

SEC. 18. The Mutual Defense Assistance Control Act of 1951 (22 U.S.C. 1611 et seq.) shall apply with respect to functions carried out under this Act except in cases where the President shall determine that such application would be detrimental to the interests of the United States.

SEAL

SEC. 19. The President may adopt, alter, and use an official seal or emblem of the Peace Corps of such design as he shall determine, which shall be judicially noticed.

MORATORIUM ON STUDENT LOANS

SEC. 20. Section 205 of the National Defense Education Act of 1958 (20 U.S.C. 425) is amended by deleting the word "or" immediately preceding clause (ii) of section 205 (b)(2)(A) and by adding immediately after that clause the following: "or (iii) not in excess of three years during which the borrower is in service as a volunteer under the Peace Corps Act: *Provided,* That this clause shall apply to any loan outstanding on the effective date of the Peace Corps Act only with the consent of the then obligee institution,".

AMENDMENT TO CIVIL SERVICE RETIREMENT ACT

SEC. 21. Subsection (j) of section 3 of the Civil Service Retirement Act, as amended (5 U.S.C. 2253), is amended to read as follows:

"(j) Notwithstanding any other provision of this section or section

5(f) of the Peace Corps Act, any military service (other than military service covered by military leave with pay from a civilian position) performed by an individual after December 1956 and any period of service by an individual as a volunteer under the Peace Corps Act, shall be excluded in determining the aggregate period of service upon which an annuity payable under this chapter to such individual or to his widow or child is to be based, if such individual or widow or child is entitled (or would upon proper application be entitled) at the time of such determination, to monthly old-age or survivors benefits under section 202 of the Social Security Act, as amended (42 U.S.C. 402), based on such individual's wages and self-employment income. If in the case of the individual or widow such military service or service under the Peace Corps Act is not excluded under the preceding sentence, but upon attaining age sixty-two, he or she becomes entitled (or would upon proper application be entitled) to such benefits, the Commission shall redetermine the aggregate period of service upon which such annuity is based, effective as of the first day of the month in which he or she attains such age, so as to exclude such service. The Secretary of Health, Education, and Welfare shall, upon the request of the Commission, inform the Commission whether or not any such individual or widow or child is entitled at any specified time to such benefits."

SECURITY INVESTIGATIONS

SEC. 22. All persons employed or assigned to duties under this Act shall be investigated to insure that the employment or assignment is consistent with the national interest in accordance with standards and procedures established by the President. If an investigation made pursuant to this section develops any data reflecting that the person who is the subject of the investigation is of questionable loyalty or is a questionable security risk, the investigating agency shall refer the matter to the Federal Bureau of Investigation for the conduct of a full field investigation. The results of that full field investigation shall be furnished to the initial investigating agency, and to the agency by which the subject person is employed, for information and appropriate action. Volunteers shall be deemed employees of the United States Government for the purpose of this section.

APPENDIX D

SEC. 23. Notwithstanding the provisions of any other law or regulation, service in the Peace Corps as a volunteer shall not in any way exempt such volunteer from the performance of any obligations or duties under the provisions of the Universal Military Training and Service Act.

FOREIGN LANGUAGE PROFICIENCY

SEC. 24. No person shall be assigned to duty as a volunteer under this Act in any foreign country or area unless at the time of such assignment he possesses such reasonable proficiency as his assignment requires in speaking the language of the country or area to which he is assigned.

DEFINITIONS

SEC. 25. (a) The term "abroad" means any area outside the United States.

(b) The term "United States" means the several States and territories and the District of Columbia.

(c) The term "function" includes any duty, obligation, right, power, authority, responsibility, privilege, discretion, activity, and program.

(d) The term "health care" includes all appropriate examinations, preventive, curative and restorative health and medical care, and supplementary services when necessary.

(e) For the purposes of this or any other Act, the period of any individual's service as a volunteer under this Act shall include—

(i) except for the purposes of section 5(f) of this Act, any period of training under section 8(a) prior to enrollment as a volunteer under this Act; and

(ii) the period between enrollment as a volunteer and the termination of service as such volunteer by the President or by death or resignation.

(f) The term "United States Government agency" includes any department, board, wholly or partly owned corporation, or instru-

272

mentality, commission, or establishment of the United States Government.

(g) The word "transportation" in sections 5(b) and 6(2) includes transportation of not to exceed three hundred pounds per person of unaccompanied necessary personal and household effects.

CONSTRUCTION

SEC. 26. If any provision of this Act or the application of any provision to any circumstances or persons shall be held invalid, the validity of the remainder of this Act and the applicability of such provision to other circumstances or persons shall not be affected thereby.

EFFECTIVE DATE

SEC. 27. This Act shall take effect on the date of its enactment.

TITLE II—AMENDMENT OF INTERNAL REVENUE CODE AND SOCIAL SECURITY ACT

TAXATION OF ALLOWANCES

SEC. 201. (a) Section 912 of the Internal Revenue Code of 1954 (relating to exemption from gross income for certain allowances) is amended by adding at the end thereof the following new paragraph:

"(3) PEACE CORPS ALLOWANCES.—In the case of an individual who is a volunteer or volunteer leader within the meaning of the Peace Corps Act and members of his family, amounts received as allowances under section 5 or 6 of the Peace Corps Act other than amounts received as—

"(A) termination payments under section 5(c) or section 6(1) of such Act,

"(B) leave allowances,

"(C) if such individual is a volunteer leader training in the United States, allowances to members of his family, and

"(D) such portion of living allowances as the President may

determine under the Peace Corps Act as constituting basic compensation."

(b) Section 1303(b) of the Internal Revenue Code of 1954 (relating to definition of back pay) is amended by adding at the end thereof the following new paragraph:

"(4) Termination payments under section 5(c) or section 6(1) of the Peace Corps Act which are received or accrued by an individual during the taxable year on account of any period of service, as a volunteer or volunteer leader under the Peace Corps Act, occurring prior to the taxable year."

(c) Section 3401(a) of the Internal Revenue Code of 1954 (relating to the definition of wages for purposes of the collection of income tax at source on wages) is amended by striking out the period at the end of paragraph (12) and inserting in lieu thereof "; or", and by adding at the end thereof the following new paragraph:

"(13) pursuant to any provision of law other than section 5(c) or 6(1) of the Peace Corps Act, for service performed as a volunteer or volunteer leader within the meaning of such Act."

(d) The amendments made by subsections (a) and (b) of this section shall apply with respect to taxable years ending after March 1, 1961. The amendment made by subsection (c) shall apply with respect to remuneration paid after the date of the enactment of this Act.

SOCIAL SECURITY COVERAGE

SEC. 202. (a)(1) Section 3121(i) of the Internal Revenue Code of 1954 (relating to computation of wages for purposes of the Federal Insurance Contributions Act) is amended by adding at the end thereof the following new paragraph:

"(3) PEACE CORPS VOLUNTEER SERVICE.—For purposes of this chapter, in the case of an individual performing service, as a volunteer or volunteer leader within the meaning of the Peace Corps Act, to which the provisions of section 3121(p) are applicable, the term 'wages' shall, subject to the provisions of subsection (a)(1) of this section, include such individual's remuneration for such service only amounts paid pursuant to section 5(c) or 6(1) of the Peace Corps Act."

(2) Section 3121 of such Code is amended by adding at the end thereof the following new subsection:

"(p) PEACE CORPS VOLUNTEER SERVICE.—For purposes of this chapter, the term 'employment' shall, notwithstanding the provisions of subsection (b) of this section, include service performed by an individual as a volunteer or volunteer leader within the meaning of the Peace Corps Act."

(3) The first sentence of section 3122 of such Code (relating to Federal service) is amended by inserting after "section 3121(m)(1) are applicable," the following: "and including service, performed as a volunteer or volunteer leader within the meaning of the Peace Corps Act, to which the provisions of section 3121(p) are applicable."

(4) Section 6051(a) of such Code (relating to receipts for employees) is amended by adding at the end thereof the following new sentence: "In the case of compensation paid for service as a volunteer or volunteer leader within the meaning of the Peace Corps Act, the statement shall show, in lieu of the amount required to be shown by paragraph (5), the total amount of wages as defined in section 3121(a), computed in accordance with such section and section 3121 (i)(3)."

(b)(1) Section 210 of the Social Security Act (42 U.S.C. 410) is amended by adding at the end thereof the following new subsection:

"Peace Corps Volunteer Service

"(o) The term 'employment' shall, notwithstanding the provisions of subsection (a), include service performed by an individual as a volunteer or volunteer leader within the meaning of the Peace Corps Act."

(2) Section 209 of such Act (42 U.S.C. 409) is amended by adding at the end thereof the following new paragraph:

"For purposes of this title, in the case of an individual performing service, as a volunteer or volunteer leader within the meaning of the Peace Corps Act, to which the provisions of section 210(o) are applicable, (1) the term 'wages' shall, subject to the provisions of subsection (a) of this section, include as such individual's remuneration for such service only amounts certified as payable pursuant to section 5(c) or 6(1) of the Peace Corps Act, and (2) any such amount shall be deemed to have been paid to such individual at the time the service, with respect to which it is paid, is performed."

APPENDIX D

(3) The first sentence of section 205(p)(1) of such Act (42 U.S.C. 405(p)(1)) is amended by inserting after "are applicable," the following: "and including service, performed as a volunteer or volunteer leader within the meaning of the Peace Corps Act, to which the provisions of section 210(o) are applicable,".

(c) The amendments made by subsections (a) and (b) of this section shall apply with respect to service performed after the date of the enactment of this Act. In the case of any individual who is enrolled as a volunteer or volunteer leader under section 16(a) of this Act, such amendments shall apply with respect to service performed on or after the effective date of such enrollment.

PUBLIC LAW 87–447
87th CONGRESS, S. 205
MAY 1, 1962

An act to amend the Communications Act of 1934 to establish a program of Federal matching grants for the construction of television broadcasting facilities to be used for educational purposes.

Be it enacted by the Senate and House of Representatives of the United States of America in Congress assembled, That title III of the Communications Act of 1934 is amended by adding at the end thereof the following new part:

PART IV—GRANTS FOR EDUCATIONAL TELEVISION BROADCASTING FACILITIES

DECLARATION OF PURPOSE

Sec. 390. The purpose of this part is to assist (through matching grants) in the construction of educational television broadcasting facilities.

AUTHORIZATION OF APPROPRIATIONS

Sec. 391. There are authorized to be appropriated for the fiscal year ending June 30, 1963, and each of the four succeeding fiscal years such sums, not exceeding $32,000,000 in the aggregate, as may be necessary to carry out the purposes of section 390. Sums appropriated pursuant to this section shall remain available for payment of grants for projects for which applications, approved under section 392, have been submitted under such section prior to July 1, 1968.

GRANTS FOR CONSTRUCTION

Sec. 392. (a) For each project for the construction of educational television broadcasting facilities there shall be submitted to the Secretary an application for a grant containing such information with respect to such project as the Secretary may by regulation require, including the total cost of such project and the amount of the Federal grant requested for such project, and providing assurance satisfactory to the Secretary—

APPENDIX D

(1) that the applicant is (A) an agency or officer responsible for the supervision of public elementary or secondary education or public higher education within that State, or within a political subdivision thereof, (B) the State educational television agency, (C) a college or university deriving its support in whole or in part from tax revenues, or (D) a nonprofit foundation, corporation, or association which is organized primarily to engage in or encourage educational television broadcasting and is eligible to receive a license from the Federal Communications Commission for a noncommercial educational television broadcasting station pursuant to the rules and regulations of the Commission in effect on April 12, 1962;

(2) that the operation of such educational television broadcasting facilities will be under the control of the applicant or a person qualified under paragraph (1) to be such an applicant;

(3) that necessary funds to construct, operate, and maintain such educational television broadcasting facilities will be available when needed; and

(4) that such television broadcasting facilities will be used only for educational purposes.

(b) The total amount of grants under this part for the construction of educational television broadcasting facilities to be situated in any State shall not exceed $1,000,000.

(c) In order to assure proper coordination of construction of educational television broadcasting facilities within each State which has established a State educational television agency, each applicant for a grant under this section for a project for construction of such facilities in such State, other than such agency, shall notify such agency of each application for such a grant which is submitted by it to the Secretary, and the Secretary shall advise such agency with respect to the disposition of each such application.

(d) The Secretary shall base his determinations of whether to approve applications for grants under this section and the amount of such grants on criteria set forth in regulations and designed to achieve (1) prompt and effective use of all educational television channels remaining available, (2) equitable geographical distribution of educational television broadcasting facilities throughout the States, and (3) provision of educational television broadcasting facilities which will serve the greatest number of persons and serve them in as many areas as possible, and which are adaptable to the broadest educational uses.

(e) Upon approving any application under this section with respect to any project, the Secretary shall make a grant to the applicant in the amount determined by him, but not exceeding (1) 50 per centum of the amount which he determines to be the reasonable and necessary cost of such project, plus (2) 25 per centum of the amount which he determines to be the reasonable and necessary cost of any educational television broadcasting facilities owned by the applicant on the date on which it files such application; except that (A) the total amount of any grant made under this section with respect to any project may not exceed 75 per centum of the amount determined by the Secretary to be the reasonable and necessary cost of such project; and (B) not more than 15 per centum of any such grant may be used for the acquisition and installation of microwave equipment, boosters, translators, and repeaters which are to be used to connect two or more broadcasting stations. The Secretary shall pay such amount, in advance or by way of reimbursement, and in such installments consistent with construction progress, as he may determine.

(f) If, within ten years after completion of any project for construction of educational television broadcasting facilities with respect to which a grant has been made under this section—

(1) the applicant or other owner of such facilities ceases to be an agency, officer, institution, foundation, corporation, or association described in subsection (a)(1), or

(2) such facilities cease to be used for educational television purposes (unless the Secretary determines, in accordance with regulations, that there is good cause for releasing the applicant or other owner from the obligation so to do),

the United States shall be entitled to recover from the applicant or other owner of such facilities the amount bearing the same ratio to the then value (as determined by agreement of the parties or by action brought in the United States district court for the district in which such facilities are situated) of such facilities, as the amount of the Federal participation bore to the cost of construction of such facilities.

APPENDIX D

SEC. 393. (a) Each recipient of assistance under this part shall keep such records as may be reasonably necessary to enable the Secretary to carry out his functions under this part, including records which fully disclose the amount and the disposition by such recipient of the proceeds of such assistance, the total cost of the project or undertaking in connection with which such assistance is given or used, and the amount and nature of that portion of the cost of the project or undertaking supplied by other sources, and such other records as will facilitate an effective audit.

(b) The Secretary and the Comptroller General of the United States, or any of their duly authorized representatives, shall have access for the purpose of audit and examination to any books, documents, papers, and records of the recipient that are pertinent to assistance received under this part.

DEFINITIONS

SEC. 394. For the purposes of this part—

(1) The term "State" includes the District of Columbia and the Commonwealth of Puerto Rico.

(2) The term "construction", as applied to educational television broadcasting facilities, means the acquisition and installation of transmission apparatus (including towers, microwave equipment, boosters, translators, repeaters, mobile equipment, and video-recording equipment) necessary for television broadcasting, including apparatus which may incidentally be used for transmitting closed circuit television programs, but does not include the construction or repair of structures to house such apparatus.

(3) The term "Secretary" means the Secretary of Health, Education, and Welfare.

(4) The term "State educational television agency" means (A) a board or commission established by State law for the purpose of promoting educational television within a State, (B) a board or commission appointed by the Governor of a State for such purpose if such appointment is not inconsistent with State law, or (C) a State officer

or agency responsible for the supervision of public elementary or secondary education or public higher education within the State which has been designated by the Governor to assume responsibility for the promotion of educational television; and, in the case of the District of Columbia, the term "Governor" means the Board of Commissioners of the District of Columbia.

(5) The term "nonprofit" as applied to any foundation, corporation, or association, means a foundation, corporation, or association, no part of the net earnings of which inures, or may lawfully inure, to the benefit of any private shareholder or individual.

PROVISION OF ASSISTANCE BY FEDERAL COMMUNICATIONS COMMISSION

SEC. 395. The Federal Communications Commission is authorized to provide such assistance in carrying out the provisions of this part as may be requested by the Secretary. The Secretary shall provide for consultation and close cooperation with the Federal Communications Commission in the administration of his functions under this part which are of interest to or affect the functions of the Commission.

RULES AND REGULATIONS

SEC. 396. The Secretary is authorized to make such rules and regulations as may be necessary to carry out this part, including regulations relating to the order of priority in approving applications for projects under section 392 or to determining the amounts of grants for such projects.

FEDERAL INTERFERENCE OR CONTROL PROHIBITED

SEC. 397. Nothing contained in this part shall be deemed (1) to amend any other provision of, or requirement under this Act; or (2) to authorize any department, agency, officer, or employee of the United States to exercise any direction, supervision, or control over educational television broadcasting or over the curriculum, program of instruction, or personnel of any educational institution, school system, or educational broadcasting station or system.

APPENDIX D

PUBLIC LAW 88–204
88th CONGRESS, H.R. 6143
DECEMBER 16, 1963

An act to authorize assistance to public and other nonprofit institutions of higher education in financing the construction, rehabilitation, or improvement of needed academic and related facilities in undergraduate and graduate institutions.

Be it enacted by the Senate and House of Representatives of the United States of America in Congress assembled, That this Act may be cited as the "Higher Education Facilities Act of 1963."

FINDINGS AND DECLARATION OF POLICY

SEC. 2. The Congress hereby finds that the security and welfare of the United States require that this and future generations of American youth be assured ample opportunity for the fullest development of their intellectual capacities, and that this opportunity will be jeopardized unless the Nation's colleges and universities are encouraged and assisted in their efforts to accommodate rapidly growing numbers of youth who aspire to a higher education. The Congress further finds and declares that these needs are so great and these steps so urgent that it is incumbent upon the Nation to take positive and immediate action to meet these needs through assistance to institutions of higher education, including graduate and undergraduate institutions, junior and community colleges, and technical institutes, in providing certain academic facilities.

TITLE I—GRANTS FOR CONSTRUCTION OF UNDER-GRADUATE ACADEMIC FACILITIES

APPROPRIATIONS AUTHORIZED

SEC. 101. (a) The Commissioner of Education (hereinafter in this Act referred to as the "Commissioner") shall carry out during the fiscal year ending June 30, 1964, and each of the four succeeding fiscal years, a program of grants to institutions of higher education for the construction of academic facilities in accordance with this title.

(b) For the purpose of making grants under this title, there is hereby authorized to be appropriated the sum of $230,000,000 for the fiscal year ending June 30, 1964, and each of the two succeeding fiscal years; but for the fiscal year ending June 30, 1967, and the succeeding fiscal year, only such sums may be appropriated as the Congress may hereafter authorize by law. In addition to the sums authorized to be appropriated under the preceding sentence, there is hereby authorized to be appropriated for the fiscal year ending June 30, 1965, and the succeeding fiscal year, for making such grants the difference (if any) between the sums authorized to be appropriated under the preceding sentence for preceding fiscal years and the aggregate of the sums which were appropriated for such preceding years under such sentence.

(c) Sums appropriated pursuant to subsection (b) of this section shall remain available for reservation as provided in section 109 until the close of the fiscal year next succeeding the fiscal year for which they were appropriated.

ALLOTMENTS

SEC. 102. Of the funds appropriated pursuant to section 101 for any fiscal year, 22 per centum shall be allotted among the States in the manner prescribed by section 103 for use in providing academic facilities for public community colleges and public technical institutes. The remainder of the funds so appropriated shall be allotted among the States in the manner as prescribed in section 104 for use in providing academic facilities for institutions of higher education other than public community colleges and public technical institutes.

ALLOTMENTS TO STATES FOR PUBLIC COMMUNITY COLLEGES AND PUBLIC TECHNICAL INSTITUTES

SEC. 103. (a) The funds to be allotted for any fiscal year for use in providing academic facilities for public community colleges and public technical institutes shall be allotted among the States on the basis of the income per person and the number of high school graduates of the respective States. Such allotments shall be made as follows: The Commissioner shall allot to each State for each fiscal year an amount which bears the same ratio to the funds being allotted as the product of—

(1) the number of high school graduates of the State, and

(2) the State's allotment ratio (as determined under subsection (d))

bears to the sum of the corresponding products for all the States.

(b) The amount of each allotment to a State under this section shall be available, in accordance with the provisions of this title, for payment of the Federal share (as determined under sections 108(b)(3) and 401(d)) of the development cost of approved projects for the construction of academic facilities within such State for public community colleges and public technical institutes. Sums allotted to a State for the fiscal year ending June 30, 1964, shall remain available for reservation as provided in section 109 until the close of the next fiscal year, in addition to the sums allotted to such State for such next fiscal year.

(c) All amounts allotted under this section for the fiscal year ending June 30, 1965, and the succeeding fiscal year, which are not reserved as provided in section 109 by the close of the fiscal year for which they are allotted, shall be reallotted by the Commissioner, on the basis of such factors as he determines to be equitable and reasonable, among the States which, as determined by the Commissioner, are able to use without delay any amounts so reallotted for providing academic facilities for public community colleges or public technical institutes. Amounts reallotted under this subsection shall be available for reservation until the close of the fiscal year next succeeding the fiscal year for which they were originally allotted.

(d) For purposes of this section—

(1) The "allotment ratio" for any States shall be 1.00 less the product of (A) .50 and (B) the quotient obtained by dividing the income per person for the State by the income per person for all the States (not including Puerto Rico, the Virgin Islands, American Samoa, and Guam), except that (i) the allotment ratio shall in no case be less than .33⅓ or more than .66⅔, (ii) the allotment ratio for Puerto Rico, the Virgin Islands, American Samoa, and Guam shall be .66⅔, and (iii) the allotment ratio of any State shall be .50 for any fiscal year if the

Commissioner finds that the cost of school construction in such State exceeds twice the median of such costs in all the States as determined by him on the basis of an index of the average per pupil cost of constructing minimum school facilities in the States as determined for such fiscal year under section 15(6) of the Act of September 23, 1950, as amended (20 U.S.C. 645), or, in the Commissioner's discretion, on the basis of such index and such other statistics and data as the Commissioner shall deem adequate and appropriate; and

(2) The allotment ratios shall be promulgated by the Commissioner as soon as possible after enactment of this Act, and annually thereafter, on the basis of the average of the incomes per person of the States and of all the States for the three most recent consecutive calendar years for which satisfactory data are available from the Department of Commerce.

(3) The term "high school graduate" means a person who has received formal recognition (by diploma, certificate, or similar means) from an approved school for successful completion of four years of education beyond the first eight years of schoolwork, or for demonstration of equivalent achievement. For the purposes of this section the number of high school graduates shall be limited to the number who graduated in the most recent school year for which satisfactory data are available from the Department of Health, Education, and Welfare. The interpretation of the definition of "high school graduate" shall fall within the authority of the Commissioner.

ALLOTMENTS TO STATES FOR INSTITUTIONS OF HIGHER EDUCATION
OTHER THAN PUBLIC COMMUNITY COLLEGES AND
PUBLIC TECHNICAL INSTITUTES

SEC. 104. (a) Of the funds to be allotted for any fiscal year for use in providing academic facilities for institutions of higher education other than public community colleges and public technical institutes (1) one-half shall be allotted by the Commissioner among the States so that the allotment to each State under this clause will be an amount which bears the same ratio to such one-half as the number of students enrolled in institutions of higher education in such State bears to the total number of students enrolled in such institutions in all the States;

and (2) the remaining one-half shall be allotted by him among the States so that the allotment to each State under this clause will be an amount which bears the same ratio to such remainder as the number of students enrolled in grades nine to twelve (both inclusive) of schools in such States bears to the total number of students in such grades in schools in all the States. For the purposes of this subsection, (A) the number of students enrolled in institutions of higher education shall be deemed to be equal to the sum of (i) the number of full-time students and (ii) the full-time equivalent of the number of part-time students as determined by the Commissioner in accordance with regulations; and (B) determinations as to enrollment under either clause (1) or clause (2) of this subsection shall be made by the Commissioner on the basis of data for the most recent year for which satisfactory data with respect to such enrollment are available to him.

(b) The amount of each allotment to a State under this section shall be available, in accordance with the provisions of this title, for payment of the Federal share (as determined under sections 108(b)(3) and 401(d)) of the development cost of approved projects for the construction of academic facilities within such State for institutions of higher education other than public community colleges and public technical institutes. Sums allotted to a State for the fiscal year ending June 30, 1964, shall remain available for reservation as provided in section 109 until the close of the next fiscal year, in addition to the sums allotted to such State for such next fiscal year.

(c) All amounts allotted under this section for the fiscal year ending June 30, 1965, and the succeeding fiscal year, which are not reserved as provided in section 109 by the close of the fiscal year for which they are allotted, shall be reallotted by the Commissioner, on the basis of such factors as he determines to be equitable and reasonable, among the States which, as determined by the Commissioner, are able to use without delay any amounts so reallotted for providing academic facilities for institutions of higher education other than public community colleges and public technical institutes. Amounts reallotted under this subsection shall be available for reservation until the close of the fiscal year next succeeding the fiscal year for which they were originally allotted.

SEC. 105. (a) Any State desiring to participate in the grant program under this title shall designate for that purpose an existing State agency which is broadly representative of the public and of institutions of higher education (including junior colleges and technical institutes) in the State, or, if no such State agency exists, shall establish such a State agency, and submit to the Commissioner through the agency so designated or established (hereinafter in this title referred to as the "State commission"), a State plan for such participation. The Commissioner shall approve any such plan which—

(1) provides that it shall be administered by the State commission;

(2) sets forth, consistently with basic criteria prescribed by regulation pursuant to section 107, objective standards and methods (A) for determining the relative priorities of eligible projects for the construction of academic facilities submitted by institutions of higher education within the State, and (B) for determining the Federal share of the development cost of each such project other than a project for a public community college or public technical institute (unless such plan provides for a uniform Federal share for all such projects);

(3) provides that the funds allotted (or reallotted) for any year under section 103 will be available only for use for the construction of academic facilities for public community colleges and public technical institutes, and that funds allotted (or reallotted) for any year to the State under section 104 will be available only for use for the construction of academic facilities for institutions of higher education other than public community colleges and public technical institutes;

(4) provides (A) for assigning priorities solely on the basis of such criteria, standards, and methods to eligible projects submitted to the State commission and deemed by it to be otherwise approvable under the provisions of this title; and (B) for approving and recommending to the Commissioner, in the order of such priority, applications covering such eligible projects, and for certifying to the Commissioner the Federal share, determined by the State commission under the State plan, of the development cost of the project involved;

(5) provides for affording to every applicant, which has submitted

to the State commission a project, an opportunity for a fair hearing before the State commission as to the priority assigned to such project or as to any other determination of the State commission adversely affecting such applicant; and

(6) provides (A) for such fiscal control and fund accounting procedures as may be necessary to assure proper disbursement of and accounting for Federal funds paid to the State commission under this title, and (B) for the making of such reports, in such form and containing such information, as may be reasonably necessary to enable the Commissioner to perform his functions under this title.

(b) The Commissioner is authorized to expend not exceeding $3,000,000 during each of the first two fiscal years of the program under this title in such amounts as he may consider necessary for the proper and efficient administration of the State plans approved under this title, including expenses which he determines were necessary for the preparation of such plans.

ELIGIBILITY FOR GRANTS

SEC. 106. An institution of higher education shall be eligible for a grant for construction of an academic facility under this title (1) in the case of an institution of higher education other than a public community college or public technical institute, only if such construction is limited to structures, or portions thereof, especially designed for instruction or research in the natural or physical sciences, mathematics, modern foreign languages, or engineering, or for use as a library, and (2) only if such construction will, either alone or together with other construction to be undertaken within a reasonable time, (A) result in an urgently needed substantial expansion of the institution's student enrollment capacity, or (B) in the case of a new institution of higher education, result in creating urgently needed enrollment capacity.

BASIC CRITERIA FOR DETERMINING PRIORITIES AND FEDERAL SHARE

SEC. 107. (a) As soon as practicable after the enactment of this Act the Commissioner shall by regulation prescribe basic criteria to which the provisions of State plans setting forth standards and methods for determining relative priorities of eligible construction projects, and the application of such standards and methods to such projects under such plans, shall be subject. Such basic criteria (1) shall be such as will best tend to achieve the objectives of this title while leaving opportunity and flexibility for the development of State plan standards and methods that will best accommodate the varied needs of institutions in the several States, and (2) shall give special consideration to expansion of undergraduate enrollment capacity. Subject to the foregoing requirements, such regulations may establish additional and appropriate basic criteria, including provision for considering the degree to which applicant institutions are effectively utilizing existing facilities, provision for allowing State plans to group or provide for grouping, in a reasonable manner, facilities or institutions according to functional or educational type for priority purposes, and, in view of the national objectives of this Act, provision for considering the degree to which the institution serves students from two or more States or from outside the United States; and in no event shall an institution's readiness to admit such out-of-State students be considered as a priority factor adverse to such institution.

(b) The Commissioner shall further prescribe by regulation the basic criteria for determining the Federal share of the development cost of any eligible project under this title within a State other than a project for a public community college or public technical institute, to which criteria the applicable standards and methods set forth in the State plan for such State shall conform in the absence of a uniform statewide Federal share specified in or pursuant to such plan. In the case of a project for an institution of higher education other than a public community college or public technical institute, the Federal share shall in no event exceed $33\frac{1}{3}$ per centum of its development cost; and in the case of a project for a public community college or public technical institute, the Federal share shall be 40 per centum of its development cost.

(c) Section 4 of the Administrative Procedure Act shall apply to the prescription of regulations under this section, not withstanding the provisions of clause (2) thereof.

APPLICATIONS FOR GRANTS AND CONDITIONS FOR APPROVAL

SEC. 108. (a) Institutions of higher education which desire to obtain grants under this title shall submit applications therefor at such time or times and in such manner as may be prescribed by the Commissioner, and such applications shall contain such information as may be required by or pursuant to regulation for the purpose of enabling the Commissioner to make the determinations required to be made by him under this title.

(b) The Commissioner shall approve an application covering a project for construction of an academic facility and meeting the requirements prescribed pursuant to subsection (a) if—

(1) the project is an eligible project as determined under section 106;

(2) the project has been approved and recommended by the appropriate State commission;

(3) the State commission has certified to the Commissioner, in accordance with the State plan, the Federal share of the development cost of the project, and sufficient funds to pay such Federal share are available from the applicable allotment of the State (including any applicable reallotment to the State);

(4) the project has, pursuant to the State plan, been assigned a priority that is higher than that of all other projects within such State (chargeable to the same allotment) which meet all the requirements of this section (other than this clause) and for which Federal funds have not yet been reserved;

(5) the Commissioner determines that the construction will be undertaken in an economical manner and will not be of elaborate or extravagant design or materials; and

(6) the Commissioner determines that (in addition to the assurance required by section 403 and such assurance as to title to the site as he may deem necessary) the application contains or is supported by the satisfactory assurances—

(A) that Federal funds received by the applicant will be used solely for defraying the development cost of the project covered by such application.

(B) that sufficient funds will be available to meet the non-Federal portion of such cost and to provide for the effective use of the academic facility upon completion, and

(C) that the facility will be used as an academic facility during at least the period of the Federal interest therein (as defined in section 404).

(c) Amendments of applications shall, except as the Commissioner may otherwise provide by or pursuant to regulation, be subject to approval in the same manner as original applications.

AMOUNT OF GRANT—PAYMENT

SEC. 109. Upon his approval of any application for a grant under this title, the Commissioner shall reserve from the applicable allotment (including any applicable reallotment) available therefor, the amount of such grant, which (subject to the limits of such allotment or reallotment) shall be equal to the Federal share (ascertained by him under section 108(b)(3)) of the development cost of the project covered by such application. The Commissioner shall pay such reserved amount, in advance or by way of reimbursement, and in such installments consistent with construction progress, as he may determine. The Commissioner's reservation of any amount under this section may be amended by him, either upon approval of an amendment of the application covering such project or upon revision of the estimated development cost of a project with respect to which such reservation was made, and in the event of an upward revision of such estimated cost approved by him he may reserve the Federal share of the added cost only from the applicable allotment (or reallotment) available at the time of such approval.

ADMINISTRATION OF STATE PLANS

SEC. 110. (a) The Commissioner shall not finally disapprove any State plan submitted under this title, or any modification thereof, without first affording the State commission submitting the plan reasonable notice and opportunity for a hearing.

(b) Whenever the Commissioner, after a reasonable notice and opportunity for hearing to the State commission administering a State plan approved under this title, finds—

(1) that the State plan has been so changed that it no longer complies with the provisions of section 105(a), or

(2) that in the administration of the plan there is a failure to comply substantially with any such provision,
the Commissioner shall notify such State commission that the State will not be regarded as eligible to participate in the program under this title until he is satisfied that there is no longer any such failure to comply.

APPENDIX D

SEC. 111. (a) If any State is dissatisfied with the Commissioner's final action with respect to the approval of its State plan submitted under section 105(a) or with his final action under section 110(b), such State may appeal to the United States court of appeals for the circuit in which such State is located. The summons and notice of appeal may be served at any place in the United States. The Commissioner shall forthwith certify and file in the court the transcript of the proceedings and the record on which he based his action.

(b) The findings of fact by the Commissioner, if supported by substantial evidence, shall be conclusive; but the court, for good cause shown, may remand the case to the Commissioner to take further evidence, and the Commissioner may thereupon make new or modified findings of fact and may modify his previous action, and shall certify to the court the transcript and record of the further proceedings. Such new or modified findings of fact shall likewise be conclusive if supported by substantial evidence.

(c) The court shall have jurisdiction to affirm the action of the Commissioner or to set it aside, in whole or in part. The judgment of the court shall be subject to review by the Supreme Court of the United States upon certiorari or certification as provided in title 28, United States Code, section 1254.

TITLE II—GRANTS FOR CONSTRUCTION OF GRADUATE ACADEMIC FACILITIES

APPROPRIATIONS AUTHORIZED

SEC. 201. In order to increase the supply of highly qualified personnel critically needed by the community, industry, government, research, and teaching, the Commissioner shall, during the fiscal year ending June 30, 1964, and each of the four succeeding fiscal years, make construction grants to assist institutions of higher education to improve existing graduate schools and cooperative graduate centers, and to assist in the establishment of graduate schools and cooperative graduate centers of excellence. For the purpose of making grants under this title, there is hereby authorized to be appropriated the sum of $25,000,000 for the fiscal year ending June 30, 1964, and the sum of $60,000,000 each year for the fiscal year ending June 30, 1965, and the succeeding fiscal year; but for the fiscal year ending June 30, 1967, and the succeeding fiscal year, only such sums may be appropriated as the Congress may hereafter authorize by law. Sums so appropriated for the fiscal year ending June 30, 1964, shall remain available for grants under this title until the end of the next succeeding fiscal year.

GRANTS

SEC. 202. (a) Grants under this title may be made to institutions of higher education and to cooperative graduate center boards to assist them to meet the development costs for projects for construction of academic facilities for graduate schools and cooperative graduate centers. Such grants may be made only upon application therefor at such time or times, in such manner, and containing or accompanied by such information as the Commissioner finds necessary to determine eligibility for the grants and the amounts thereof.

(b) Grants under this title for construction of academic facilities may not exceed 33⅓ per centum of the development cost of any such construction project.

(c)(1) The Commissioner shall not approve any application for a grant under this title without the advice of the Advisory Committee established under section 203.

(2) In determining whether to approve applications for grants under this title, the order in which to approve such applications, and the amount of the grants, the Commissioner shall give consideration to the extent to which such projects will contribute to achieving the objectives of this title and also the extent to which they will aid in attaining a wider distribution throughout the United States of graduate schools and cooperative graduate centers.

(d) Notwithstanding the other provisions of this title the total of the payments from the appropriations for any fiscal year under this title made with respect to projects in any State may not exceed an amount equal to 12½ per centum of such appropriation.

ADVISORY COMMITTEE

SEC. 203. (a) There is hereby established in the Office of Education an Advisory Committee on Graduate Education, consisting of the

Commissioner, who shall be Chairman; one representative from the Office of Science and Technology in the Executive Office of the President; one from the National Science Foundation; and eight members appointed, without regard to the civil service laws, by the Commissioner with the approval of the Secretary of Health, Education, and Welfare. Such appointed members shall be selected from leading authorities in the field of education, at least three of whom shall be from the field of the humanities, with at least one of these three from a graduate school of education.

(b) The Advisory Committee shall advise the Commissioner (1) on the action to be taken with regard to each application for a grant under this title, and (2) in the preparation of general regulations and with respect to policy matters arising in the administration of this title, including the development of criteria for approval of applications thereunder. The Advisory Committee may appoint such special advisory and technical experts and consultants as may be useful in carrying out its functions.

(c) Members of the Advisory Committee and special advisory and technical experts and consultants appointed pursuant to subsection (b) shall, while serving on the business of the Advisory Committee, be entitled to receive compensation at rates fixed by the Secretary of Health, Education, and Welfare, but not exceeding $75 per day, including travel time; and, while so serving away from their homes or regular places of business, they may be allowed travel expenses, including per diem in lieu of subsistence, as authorized by section 5 of the Administrative Expenses Act of 1946 (5 U.S.C. 73b–2) for persons in the Government service employed intermittently.

TITLE III—LOANS FOR CONSTRUCTION OF ACADEMIC FACILITIES

LENDING AUTHORITY

SEC. 301. The Commissioner may, in accordance with the provisions of this title, make loans to institutions of higher education or to higher education building agencies for construction of academic facilities.

LOAN LIMIT FOR ANY STATE

SEC. 302. Not more than 12½ per centum of the funds provided for in this title in the form of loans shall be used for loans to institutions of higher education or higher education building agencies within any one State.

ELIGIBILITY CONDITIONS, AMOUNTS, AND TERMS OF LOANS

SEC. 303. (a) No loan pursuant to this title shall be made unless the Commissioner finds (1) that not less than one-fourth of the development cost of the facility will be financed from non-Federal sources, (2) that the applicant is unable to secure the amount of such loan from other sources upon terms and conditions equally as favorable as the terms and conditions applicable to loans under this title, and (3) that the construction will be undertaken in an economical manner and that it will not be of elaborate or extravagant design or materials.

(b) A loan pursuant to this title shall be secured in such manner, and shall be repaid within such period not exceeding fifty years, as may be determined by the Commissioner; and shall bear interest at a rate determined by the Commissioner which shall not be less than a per annum rate that is one-quarter of 1 percentage point above the average annual interest rate on all interest-bearing obligations of the United States forming a part of the public debt as computed at the end of the preceding fiscal year, adjusted to the nearest one-eighth of 1 per centum.

(c) The Commissioner shall, during the fiscal year ending June 30, 1964, and each of the four succeeding fiscal years, make loans to institutions of higher education for the construction of academic facilities in accordance with the provisions of this title. For the purpose of making loans under this title, there is hereby authorized to be appropriated the sum of $120,000,000 for the fiscal year ending June 30, 1964, and each of the two succeeding fiscal years; but for the fiscal year ending June 30, 1967, and the succeeding fiscal year, only such sums may be appropriated as the Congress may hereafter authorize by law. In addition to the sums authorized to be appropriated under the preceding sentence, there is hereby authorized to be appropriated for the fiscal year ending June 30, 1965, and the succeeding fiscal year, for making such loans the difference (if any) between the sums authorized to be appropriated under the preceding sentence for preceding fiscal years and the aggregate of the sums which were appropriated for such preceding years under such sentence.

GENERAL PROVISIONS FOR LOAN PROGRAM

SEC. 304. (a) Such financial transactions of the Commissioner as the making of loans and vouchers approved by the Commissioner in connection with such financial transactions, except with respect to administrative expenses, shall be final and conclusive on all officers of the Government.

(b) The Commissioner is authorized (1) to prescribe a schedule of fees which, in his judgment, would be adequate in the aggregate to cover necessary expenses of making inspections (including audits) and providing representatives at the site of projects in connection with loans under this title, and (2) to condition the making of such loans on agreement by the applicant to pay such fees. For the purpose of providing such services, the Commissioner may, as authorized by section 402(b), utilize any agency, and such agency may accept reimbursement or payment for such services from such applicant or from the Commissioner, and shall, if a Federal agency, credit such amounts to the appropriation or fund against which expenditures by such agency for such services have been charged.

(c) In the performance of, and with respect to, the functions, powers, and duties vested in him by this title, the Commissioner may—

(1) prescribe such rules and regulations as may be necessary to carry out the purposes of this title;

(2) sue and be sued in any court of record of a State having general jurisdiction or in any district court of the United States, and such district courts shall have jurisdiction of civil actions arising under this title without regard to the amount in controversy, and any action instituted under this subsection by or against the Commissioner shall survive notwithstanding any change in the person occupying the office of Commissioner or any vacancy in such office; but no attachment, injunction, garnishment, or other similar process, mesne or final, shall be issued against the Commissioner or property under his control, and nothing herein shall be construed to except litigation arising out

of activities under this title from the application of sections 507(b) and 2679 of title 28 of the United States Code and of section 367 of the Revised Statutes (5 U.S.C. 316);

(3) foreclose on any property or commence any action to protect or enforce any right conferred upon him by any law, contract, or other agreement, and bid for and purchase at any foreclosure or any other sale any property in connection with which he has made a loan pursuant to this title; and, in the event of any such acquisition (and notwithstanding any other provisions of law relating to the acquisition, handling, or disposal of real property by the United States), complete, administer, remodel and convert, dispose of, lease, and otherwise deal with, such property: *Provided,* That any such acquisition of real property shall not deprive any State or political subdivision thereof of its civil or criminal jurisdiction in and over such property or impair the civil rights under the State or local laws of the inhabitants on such property;

(4) sell or exchange at public or private sale, or lease, real or personal property, and sell or exchange any securities or obligations, upon such terms as he may fix;

(5) subject to the specific limitations in this title, consent to the modification, with respect to the rate of interest, time of payment of any installment of principal or interest, security, or any other term of any contract or agreement to which he is a party or which has been transferred to him pursuant to this section; and

(6) include in any contract or instrument made pursuant to this title such other covenants, conditions, or provisions (including provisions designed to assure against use of the facility, constructed with the aid of a loan under this title, for purposes described in section 401(a)(2)) as he may deem necessary to assure that the purposes of this title will be achieved.

TITLE IV—GENERAL PROVISIONS

DEFINITIONS

Sec. 401. As used in this Act—

(a)(1) Except as provided in subparagraph (2) of this paragraph, the term "academic facilities" means structures suitable for use as classrooms, laboratories, libraries, and related facilities necessary or appropriate for instruction of students, or for research, or for administration of the educational or research programs, of an institution of higher education, and maintenance, storage, or utility facilities essential to operation of the foregoing facilities.

(2) The term "academic facilities" shall not include (A) any facility intended primarily for events for which admission is to be charged to the general public, or (B) any gymnasium or other facility specially designed for athletic or recreational activities, other than for an academic course in physical education or where the Commissioner finds that the physical integration of such facilities with other academic facilities included under this Act is required to carry out the objectives of this Act, or (C) any facility used or to be used for sectarian instruction or as a place for religious worship, or (D) any facility which (although not a facility described in the preceding clause) is used or to be used primarily in connection with any part of the program of a school or department of divinity, or (E) any facility used or to be used by a "school of medicine", "school of dentistry", "school of osteopathy", "school of pharmacy", "school of optometry", "school of podiatry", "school of nursing", or "school of public health", as defined in section 724 of the Public Health Service Act. For the purposes of this subparagraph, the term "school or department of divinity" means an institution, or a department or branch of an institution, whose program is specifically for the education of students to prepare them to become ministers of religion or to enter upon some other religious vocation or to prepare them to teach theological subjects.

(b)(1) The term "construction" means (A) erection of new or expansion of existing structures, and the acquisition and installation of initial equipment therefor; or (B) acquisition of existing structures not owned by the institution involved; or (C) rehabilitation, alteration, conversion, or improvement (including the acquisition and installation of initial equipment, or modernization or replacement of built-in equipment) of existing structures; or (D) a combination of any two or more of the foregoing.

(2) The term "equipment" includes, in addition to machinery, utilities, and built-in equipment and any necessary enclosures or

structures to house them, all other items necessary for the functioning of a particular facility as an academic facility, including necessary furniture, except books, curricular and program materials, and items of current operating expense such as fuel, supplies, and the like; the term "initial equipment" means equipment acquired and installed in connection with construction as defined in paragraph (1)(A) or (B) of this subsection or, in cases referred to in paragraph (1)(C), equipment acquired and installed as part of the rehabilitation, alteration, conversion, or improvement of an existing structure which structure would otherwise not be adequate for use as an academic facility; and the terms "equipment", "initial equipment", and "built-in equipment" shall be more particularly defined by the Commissioner by regulation.

(c) The term "development cost", with respect to an academic facility, means the amount found by the Commissioner to be the cost, to the applicant for a grant or loan under this Act, of the construction involved and the cost of necessary acquisition of the land on which the facility is located and of necessary site improvements to permit its use for such facility, but excluding any cost incurred before, or under a contract entered into before, the enactment of this Act. There shall further be excluded from the development cost—

(1) in determining the amount of any grant under title I or II of this Act, an amount equal to the sum of (A) any Federal grant which the institution has obtained, or is assured of obtaining, under any law other than this Act, with respect to the construction that is to be financed with the aid of a grant under title I or II of this Act, and (B) the amount of any non-Federal funds required to be expended as a condition of such other Federal grant; and

(2) in determining the amount of any loan under title III of this Act, an amount equal to the amount of any Federal financial assistance which the institution has obtained, or is assured of obtaining, under any law other than this Act, with respect to the construction that is to be financed with the aid of a loan under title III of this Act.

(d) The term "Federal share" means, in the case of a project for an institution of higher education other than a public community college or public technical institute, a percentage (as determined under the applicable State plan) not in excess of 33⅓ per centum of its development cost; and such term means, in the case of a public community college or public technical institute, 40 per centum of its development cost.

(e) The term "higher education building agency" means (1) an agency, public authority, or other instrumentality of a State authorized to provide, or finance the construction of, academic facilities for institutions of higher education (whether or not also authorized to provide or finance other facilities for such or other educational institutions, or for their students or faculty), or (2) any corporation (no part of the net earnings of which inures or may lawfully inure to the benefit of any private shareholder or individual) (A) established by an institution of higher education for the sole purpose of providing academic facilities for the use of such institution, and (B) upon dissolution of which all title to any property purchased or built from the proceeds of any loan made under title III of this Act will pass to such institution.

(f) The term "institution of higher education" means an educational institution in any State which—

(1) admits as regular students only individuals having a certificate of graduation from a high school, or the recognized equivalent of such a certificate;

(2) is legally authorized within such State to provide a program of education beyond high school;

(3) provides an educational program for which it awards a bachelor's degree, or provides not less than a two-year program which is acceptable for full credit toward such a degree, or offers a two-year program in engineering, mathematics, or the physical or biological sciences which is designed to prepare the student to work as a technician and at a semiprofessional level in engineering, scientific, or other technological fields which require the understanding and application of basic engineering, scientific, or mathematical principles or knowledge;

(4) is a public or other nonprofit institution; and

(5) is accredited by a nationally recognized accrediting agency or association listed by the Commissioner pursuant to this paragraph or, if not so accredited, is an institution whose credits are accepted, on

transfer, by not less than three institutions which are so accredited, for credit on the same basis as if transferred from an institution so accredited: *Provided, however,* That in the case of an institution offering a two-year program in engineering, mathematics, or the physical or biological sciences which is designed to prepare the student to work as a technician and at a semiprofessional level in engineering, scientific, or technological fields which require the understanding and application of basic engineering, scientific, or mathematical principles or knowledge, if the Commissioner determines there is no nationally recognized accrediting agency or association qualified to accredit such institutions, he shall, under section 402(c), appoint an advisory committee, composed of persons specially qualified to evaluate training provided by such institutions, which shall prescribe the standards of content, scope, and quality which must be met in order to qualify such institutions for assistance under this Act and shall also determine whether particular institutions meet such standards: *Provided, however,* That the requirements of this clause (5) shall be deemed to be satisfied in the case of an institution applying for assistance under this Act, if the Commissioner determines that there is satisfactory assurance that upon completion of the project for which such assistance is requested, or upon completion of that project and others under construction or planned and to be commenced within a reasonable time, the institution will meet such requirements; and for the purposes of this paragraph the Commissioner shall publish a list of nationally recognized accrediting agencies or associations which he determines to be reliable authority as to the quality of education or training offered.

(g) The term "public community college and public technical institute" means an institution of higher education which is under public supervision and control and is organized and administered principally to provide a two-year program which is acceptable for full credit toward a bachelor's degree or a two-year program in engineering, mathematics, or the physical or biological sciences which is designed to prepare the student to work as a technician and at a semiprofessional level in engineering, scientific, or other technological fields which require the understanding and application of basic engineering, scientific, or mathematical principles or knowledge, and, if a branch of an institution of higher education offering four or more years of higher education, is located in a community different from that in which its parent institution is located.

(h) The term "cooperative graduate center" means an institution or program created by two or more institutions of higher education which will offer to the students of the participating institutions of higher education graduate work which could not be offered with the same proficiency and/or economy at the individual institution of higher education. The center may be located or the program carried out on the campus of any of the participating institutions or at a separate location.

(i) The term "cooperative graduate center board" means a duly constituted board established to construct and maintain the cooperative graduate center and coordinate academic programs. The board shall be composed of representatives of each of the higher education institutions participating in the center and of the community involved. At least one-third of the board's members shall be community representatives. The board shall elect by a majority vote a chairman from among its membership.

(j) The term "high school" does not include any grade beyond grade 12.

(k) The term "nonprofit educational institution" means an educational institution owned and operated by one or more corporations or associations no part of the net earnings of which inures, or may lawfully inure, to the benefit of any private shareholder or individual.

(l) The term "public educational institution" does not include a school or institution of any agency of the United States.

(m) The term "State" includes, in addition to the several States, the District of Columbia, the Commonwealth of Puerto Rico, the Virgin Islands, Guam, and American Samoa.

FEDERAL ADMINISTRATION

Sec. 402. (a) The Commissioner may delegate any of his functions under this Act, except the making of regulations, to any officer or employee of the Office of Education.

(b) In administering the provisions of this Act for which he is responsible, the Commissioner is authorized to utilize the services and facilities of any agency of the Federal Government and of any other public or nonprofit agency or institution in accordance with appropriate agreements, and to pay for such services either in advance or by way of reimbursement, as may be agreed upon.

(c) The Commissioner, with the approval of the Secretary of Health, Education, and Welfare, may appoint one or more advisory committees to advise and consult with the Commissioner with respect to the administration of any of his functions under title I or III of this Act. Members of any such committee, while attending conferences or meetings of the committee, shall be entitled to receive compensation at a rate to be fixed by the Secretary of Health, Education, and Welfare, but not to exceed $75 per diem, and while away from their homes or regular places of business they may be allowed travel expenses, including per diem in lieu of subsistence, as authorized by law (5 U.S.C. 73b–2) for persons in the Government service employed intermittently.

LABOR STANDARDS

SEC. 403 (a) The Commissioner shall not approve any application for a grant or loan under this Act except upon adequate assurance that all laborers and mechanics employed by contractors or subcontractors in the performance of work on construction assisted by such grant or loan will be paid wages at rates not less than those prevailing on similar construction in the locality as determined by the Secretary of Labor in accordance with the Davis-Bacon Act, as amended (40 U.S.C. 276a–276a–5), and will receive overtime compensation in accordance with and subject to the provisions of the Contract Work Hours Standards Act (Public Law 87–581); but, in the case of any nonprofit educational institution, the Commissioner may waive the application of this subsection in cases or classes of cases where laborers or mechanics, not otherwise employed at any time in the construction of the project, voluntarily donate their services for the purpose of lowering the costs of construction and the Commissioner determines that any amounts saved thereby are fully credited to the educational institution undertaking the construction.

(b) The Secretary of Labor shall have, with respect to the labor standards specified in subsection (a) of this section, the authority and functions set forth in Reorganization Plan Numbered 14 of 1950 (15 F.R. 3176; 64 Stat. 1267), and section 2 of the Act of June 13, 1934, as amended (40 U.S.C. 276c).

RECOVERY OF PAYMENTS

SEC. 404. (a) The Congress hereby finds and declares that, if a facility constructed with the aid of a grant or grants under title I or II of this Act is used as an academic facility for twenty years following completion of such construction, the public benefit accruing to the United States from such use will equal or exceed in value the amount of such grant or grants. The period of twenty years after completion of such construction shall therefore be deemed to be the period of Federal interest in such facility for the purposes of this Act.

(b) If, within twenty years after completion of construction of an academic facility which has been constructed in part with a grant or grants under title I or II of this Act—

(1) the applicant (or its successor in title or possession) ceases or fails to be a public or nonprofit institution, or

(2) the facility ceases to be used as an academic facility, or the facility is used as a facility excluded from the term "academic facility" by section 401(a)(2),

the United States shall be entitled to recover from such applicant (or successor) an amount which bears to the then value of the facility (or so much thereof as constituted an approved project or projects) the same ratio as the amount of such Federal grant or grants bore to the development cost of the facility financed with the aid of such grant or grants. Such value shall be determined by agreement of the parties or by action brought in the United States district court for the district in which such facility is situated.

METHOD OF PAYMENT

SEC. 405. Payments under this Act to any State or Federal agency, institution of higher education, or any other organization, pursuant to a grant or loan, may be made in installments, and in advance or by way of reimbursement, with necessary adjustments on account of overpayments or underpayments.

ADMINISTRATIVE APPROPRIATIONS AUTHORIZED

SEC. 406. There are hereby authorized to be appropriated for the fiscal year ending June 30, 1964, and for each fiscal year thereafter, such sums as may be necessary for the cost of administering the provisions of this Act.

FEDERAL CONTROL NOT AUTHORIZED

SEC. 407. No department, agency, officer, or employee of the United States shall, under authority of this Act, exercise any direction, supervision, or control over, or impose any requirements or conditions with respect to, the personnel, curriculum, methods of instruction, or administration of any educational institution.

DATE DUE

OCT 8 1977			
MAY 0 6 1981			
GAYLORD			PRINTED IN U.S.A